SECOND EDITION
Single-Case Design
for CLINICAL SOCIAL WORKERS

JENNIFER DI NOIA AND TONY TRIPODI

NASW PRESS
Washington, DC

Elvira Craig de Silva, DSW, ACSW, *President*
Elizabeth J. Clark, PhD, ACSW, MPH, *Executive Director*

Cheryl Y. Bradley, *Publisher*
Marcia D. Roman, *Managing Editor, Journals and Books*
Crystal McDonald, *Marketing Manager*
DeQuendre Bertrand, *Copy Editor*

Cover design by Metadog Design Group, Washington, DC
Interior design by Cynthia Stock, Electronic Quill, Silver Spring, MD
Printed by Books International, Dulles, VA

Library of Congress Cataloging-in-Publication Data

Single-case design for clinical social workers / Jennifer Di Noia and Tony Tripodi.
 p. cm.
 Includes bibliographical references and index.

 ISBN-13: 978-0-87101-381-1

1. Social case work—Research. 2. Psychiatric social work—Research. 3. Single subject research. I. DiNoia, Jennifer. II. Title.

HV43.D576 2007   2007028820

361.3'2—dc22

To
Paul and Sally Di Noia
and
Nicola and Christina Tripodi

Contents

Foreword

In 1959, Ayllon and Michael documented the rich clinical potential of a variety of single-case designs in understanding the dynamics of puzzling behavior of people admitted in a hospital mental health unit. Later in the 1960s, the groundbreaking work of applied behavior analysts (Allen & Harris, 1966; Allen, Hart, Buell, Harris, & Wolf, 1964) in a therapeutic nursery school program at the University of Washington illustrated the clinical diagnosis benefits of single-case design in isolating the antecedents and consequences of troublesome and self-injurious behavior among very young children.

Although it is generally acknowledged that the critical early work on single-case design was carried out by psychologists, it was Howe's (1974) review, following the early work of Edwin Thomas and other scholars of practice, that precipitated the introduction of this particular set of research tools to social work research, practice, and professional education. In fact, single-case designs became a key element in a movement chronicled by Reid (1994) called, "empirical-clinical practice," which had and continues to have a major influence on social work knowledge development.

To a certain extent, the acceptance of single-case design methodology has been stymied by its identification and association with behavioral methods and by the absence of agency-based systems to support and encourage information-driven practice. Happily, Jennifer Di Noia and Tony Tripodi's clear, straightforward, and practical volume arrives at an opportune moment, when evidence-based practice has become the standard for the profession. On the clinical practice level, much of the sharpness and polarization around behavioral/nonbehavioral practice has given way to a more eclectic orientation to practice. On the level of practice evaluation, there is a more sophisticated understanding of the multiple uses of research to inform practice. Thus, the context in which practitioners view single-case design envisions a host of potential uses from more accurate diagnosis to validation of specific treatment techniques to evaluation of treatment effectiveness. On the organizational level, the major movement toward managed health (and soon child welfare) creates a need for intervention that is outcome-oriented, information-based, and consumer-driven. These facts and the concomitant growth of agency-based client information systems argue for a second look at single-case design as an important methodology for communicating with clients and assuring quality of service processes and outcomes.

This densely packed yet tightly written volume explores the varieties of single-case designs, their different uses, and the arguments for and against different evaluation pathways. Suitable for both beginning and advanced practitioners, this book provides an excellent focal point for discussion in staff training and group supervisory sessions. Its lessons, if carefully adapted to meet the particular demands of differing agency contexts and community settings, will aid social work in reclaiming ownership of its own knowledge development function as opposed to accepting research that is all too often externally imposed. Ultimately, much of what Drs.

Di Noia and Tripodi write about will become incorporated into what is considered "best practices." For their view of quality, goal-oriented, information-driven practice, fully attuned to consumer feedback applied in a manner consistent with the core values of social work, we are in the authors' debt.

James K. Whittaker
University of Washington, Seattle

REFERENCES

Allen, K. E., & Harris, F. R. (1966). Elimination of a child's excessive scratching by training the mother in reinforcement techniques. *Behavior Research and Therapy, 4,* 79–84.

Allen, K. E., Hart, B., Buell, J. S., Harris, F. R., & Wolf, M. M. (1964). Effects of social reinforcement on isolate behavior of a nursery school child. *Child Development, 35,* 511–518.

Ayllon, T., & Michael, J. (1959). The psychiatric nurse as a behavioral engineer. *Journal of the Experimental Analysis of Behavior, 2,* 323–334.

Howe, M. W. (1974). Casework self-evaluation: A single-subject approach. *Social Service Review, 48,* 1–23.

Reid, W. J. (1994). The empirical practice movement. *Social Service Review, 68,* 165–184.

Preface and Acknowledgments

The purpose of this book is to provide for clinical social workers an introduction to the use of single-case design in clinical practice. The book shows how this methodology can serve as a frame of reference for making clinical decisions relevant to assessment, implementation, and evaluation of treatment and client follow-up through the use of statistical procedures and graphic analysis. The utility of single-case design is illustrated in a variety of clinical situations.

This book also was written for social work students and their supervisors in field practice so that the accreditation standards for evaluating a worker's practice, established by the Council on Social Work Education, can be adequately implemented.

We wish to acknowledge colleagues and students at Columbia University School of Social Work, University of Michigan, University of Pittsburgh, and Florida International University for their discussions of the topic of single-case design. Many thanks to students enrolled in the fall 2005 Clinical Case Evaluation course at Columbia University School of Social Work for reviewing drafts of the manuscript and providing responsive feedback.

Jennifer Di Noia, PhD
Columbia University, New York

Tony Tripodi, DSW
Ohio State University, Columbus

CHAPTER 1

Introduction

Building on work from June 1984, the Board of Directors of the National Association of Social Workers (NASW) in 2005 approved a dozen encompassing standards for practice among clinical social workers.

Standard 1. Ethics and Values
Clinical social workers shall adhere to the values and ethics of the social work profession, utilizing the NASW *Code of Ethic* as a guide to ethical decision making.

Standard 2. Specialized Practice Skills and Intervention
Clinical social workers shall demonstrate specialized knowledge and skills for effective clinical intervention with individuals, families, and groups.

Standard 3. Referrals
Clinical social workers shall be knowledgeable about community services and make appropriate referrals, as needed.

Standard 4. Accessibility to Clients
Clinical social workers shall be accessible to clients during nonemergency and emergency situations.

Standard 5. Privacy and Confidentiality
Clinical social workers shall maintain adequate safeguards for the private nature of the treatment relationship.

Standard 6. Supervision and Consultation
Clinical social workers shall maintain access to professional supervision and/or consultation.

Standard 7. Professional Environment and Procedures
Clinical social workers shall maintain professional offices and procedures.

Standard 8. Documentation
Documentation of services provided to or on behalf of the client shall be recorded in the client's file or record of services.

Standard 9. Independent Practice
Clinical social workers shall have the right to establish an independent practice.

Standard 10. Cultural Competence
Clinical social workers shall demonstrate culturally competent service delivery in accordance with the *NASW Standards for Cultural Competence in Social Work Practice.*

Standard 11. Professional Development
Clinical social workers shall assume personal responsibility for their continued professional development in accordance with the *NASW Standards for Continuing Professional Education* and state requirements.

Standard 12. Technology
Clinical social workers shall have access to computer technology and the Internet, as the need to communicate via e-mail and to seek information on the Web for purposes of education, networking, and resources is essential for efficient and productive clinical practice.

Implicit in these standards is the notion that clinical social workers should be accountable to their clients and conduct ethical practice—their goal being to improve the quality of services. Toward this end, the standards help establish professional expectations that can assist social workers in monitoring and evaluating clinical practice. In particular, an interpretation of standard 2 is that clinical social workers should have knowledge and skills from research to evaluate the effectiveness of their work (Minahan, 1987).

Approaches for using research to assist in the assessment and evaluation of clinical practice include interviews with clients, systematic observation, forms and questionnaires, content analysis of case records and taped recordings, surveys, rating scales, and the collection of information before treatment begins and after termination (Vonk, Tripodi, & Epstein, 2006). Because clinical social workers cannot use only one approach to evaluate the effectiveness of work with all clients, they must have a repertoire of available methodologies. One methodology clinical psychologists and social workers have used is single-case design (Barlow & Hersen, 1984; Bloom, Fischer, & Orme, 2006; Jayaratne & Levy, 1979; Kazdin, 1992). Every clinical social worker should be familiar with the basic notions and procedures of this methodology. Moreover, clinical social workers can use single-case designs to assess and evaluate as well as to provide input for clinical decisions (Hayes, 1992).

THE PURPOSE OF THIS BOOK

This book is an introduction to single-case design methodology for clinical social workers, students, and supervisors. The intent is to provide clinical social workers a perspective on the application of the methodology and the types and levels of knowledge it can generate to enable them to assess clinical problems and to evaluate practice. However, single-case design methodology cannot replace information obtained in clinical interviews and observations.

The three major objectives of this text are to:

1. present a basic model of single-case design methodology and selected variations of the model

2. show how the basic model can serve as a frame of reference for making clinical decisions with respect to assessing and evaluating the effectiveness of practice interventions
3. illustrate the utility of single-case design methodology in a variety of clinical settings.

The book refers to the term single-case design, rather than single-subject design or single-system design, for the following reasons:

- The term *case* refers to a single unit of analysis, that is, an individual, a couple, a family, or a group. These units coincide with the client units for clinical social workers.
- Although single-subject design was the preferred term when researchers first applied the methodology to social work in the 1970s (see for example, Jayaratne, 1977), single-case design is the preferred term in the current social work literature because it emphasizes application of the methodology to client units encountered in social work practice and because the word subject is synonymous with experimental research. Case is preferred by psychologists who developed the methodology in detail (see Hersen & Barlow, 1976). For purposes of this book, case and subject are synonymous.
- The term "subject" is misleading because it implies that the focus of investigation is the individual, when the methodology can be applied to other client units (that is, couples, families, and groups).
- Bloom and colleagues (2006) used single-system to refer to "one or more persons or groups being assisted by a helping professional to accomplish some goal" (p. 36), but their usage throughout the text appears to be synonymous with subject or case. Moreover, "system" implies an analysis of much more than a single unit, that is, an interrelationship among units. Single-case design methodology does not involve the study of interactions among units.

Authors, for example, Barlow and Hersen (1984), and Bloom and associates (2006), have adequately explained single-case designs in books from behavioral psychology and social work. However, although they have provided a comprehensive presentation of many complex designs, they have not distinguished between those few designs that are useful to clinical social workers and those that are impractical. Moreover, their examples generally pertain to behavioral psychology and often appear inapplicable to much of clinical practice. Furthermore, their presentations appear to be more complex than necessary. They do not adequately distinguish the levels of knowledge produced, leading readers to believe that causal knowledge is more obtainable than it is. In addition, the authors do not clearly show how to make inferences from single-case designs to inform the assessment and evaluative decisions of clinical social workers.

CLINICAL SOCIAL WORK

The following definition of clinical social work was accepted in January 1984 by the Board of Directors of NASW:

> Clinical social work shares with all social work practice the goal of enhancement and maintenance of psychosocial functioning of individuals, families, and small groups. Clinical social work practice is the professional application of social work theory and methods to the treatment and prevention of psychosocial dysfunction, disability, or impairment, including emotional and mental disorders. It is based on knowledge of one or more theories of human development within a psychosocial context.

The perspective of person-in-situation is central to clinical social work practice. Clinical social work includes interventions directed to interpersonal interactions, intrapsychic dynamics, and life-support and management issues. Clinical social work services consist of assessment; diagnosis; treatment, including psychotherapy and counseling; client-centered advocacy; consultation; and evaluation. The process of clinical social work is undertaken within the objectives of social work and the principles and values contained in the NASW *Code of Ethics* (Minahan, 1987).

This definition is broad and encompasses a variety of clinical services in public and private settings; a diversity of client populations with respect to such factors as income, race, social class, and so forth; a range of psychosocial problems; and use of different theories and assumptions about the relationship of the person to her or his situation. Clinical social workers may work in mental health agencies, hospitals, clinics, aftercare services; employee assistance programs (EAPs) for businesses, educational institutions, hospitals, factories, and the like; family therapy and family counseling agencies; criminal justice and juvenile institutional, probation, and parole facilities; child guidance clinics; and medical and public health facilities. Clinical social workers may engage in collaboration with other professionals such as psychiatrists, psychologists, and family counselors. Overall, clinical social workers function in a number of diverse human services agencies and organizations, as well as provide treatments or interventions (these terms are interchangeable) in private practice settings.

It therefore follows that clinical social workers deal with clients who represent different cultural and ethnic backgrounds and social classes. However, not all clinical social workers work with a vast range of clients. Some social workers in private practice may work exclusively with particular populations for example, male adolescents from middle-income families, focusing on problems of phobias, school adjustment, family relationships, and self-esteem. In contrast, clinical social workers employed in a mental heath clinic may work with a more diverse population. The eligibility requirements of the agency or setting in which social workers are employed tend to define client populations. Hence, clinical social workers in a Veterans Affairs (VA) neuropsychiatry hospital will work with veterans from the military who have psychiatric diagnoses and with their families. Social workers in a medical hospital may work primarily with cancer patients and their families, dealing with the realities and fears of cancer and its consequences. Clinical social workers in an EAP may focus on individual and small group interventions aimed at reducing stress in the workplace. Furthermore, clinical social workers in the child welfare system may focus on specific interventions, for example, family preservation services designed to prevent out-of-home placements, to increase the child management skills of parents, and to eliminate child abuse and neglect, and clinical social workers may work in teams with other mental health professionals to provide counseling when disasters occur, such as Hurricane Katrina in New Orleans, and in the aftermath of such devastating events as the Columbine High School tragedy and the September 11th terrorist attacks.

Collectively, clinical social workers use different theories about personality and the environment and about changes or the prevention of changes in knowledge, feelings, attitudes, behaviors, skills, and interpersonal interactions. Some clinical social workers are eclectic and use a range of techniques depending on the client, problem, and situation. They may use behavior modification techniques, cognitive interventions, and ego psychological perspectives within an ecological framework. Other clinicians may use one major approach stemming from a particular theoretical point of view. For example, they may specialize in the use of group techniques for teaching clients interpersonal skills or they may focus on the therapeutic transaction, providing a means for their clients to understand the dynamics of human relationships with the clinical social worker, their families, and other significant groups.

Tasks

Much of clinical social work practice progresses through interrelated phases. These phases or stages follow a problem-solving model that authors have incorporated into books about social work practice (Blythe & Tripodi, 1989; Hudson & Thyer, 1987; Vonk, Tripodi, & Epstein, 2006). The practice phases used by Vonk and colleagues—assessing the problem and formulating the treatment, treatment implementation and monitoring, and treatment evaluation—are used here because they are complementary to the basic single-case design model of baseline, intervention, and follow-up.

In the initial phase of practice with a client, the clinical social worker typically is involved in a number of tasks that are preliminary to the implementation of a treatment or intervention. The social worker gathers information about the client; the source of referral; the client's family, employment, and school history; and the nature and extent of the problems for which the client is referred, either by self or by others in voluntary or involuntary conditions such as mandatory treatment for child abusers or probationers. It is especially important for the clinical social worker to determine whether he or she can provide services appropriate to the client's problems. Hence, the social worker seeks information to make a judgment about what the problems are and whether he or she can engage the client in dealing with those problems. Many clients have issues related to finances, housing, and other basic needs, as well as with particular forms of illness, disease, and interpersonal communication and interactions. Hence, the clinical social worker must set priorities to the problems and deal first with those that are most immediately life-threatening or those that are most pressing because of environmental constraints through the courts and other community agents of control. During this phase, the clinical social worker uses his or her knowledge of theory, research about the effectiveness of interventions, and experience to formulate a treatment plan in cooperation with the client. The social worker devises a contractual arrangement, oral or written, to represent the mutual obligations of the clinical social worker and the client and operationalizes, to the extent possible, the treatment objectives and the means of achieving them. For example, treatment objectives for a client might include the reduction of anxiety and depression and an increase in positive interactions with his or her mother. The interactions may involve systematic desensitization for the client and counseling sessions with the client and his or her mother that include role plays about negative interactions and discussion about the ways in which both individuals might increase positive interactions.

Having decided which problems to deal with and determined an intervention plan, the clinical social worker, during the second practice phase, attempts to implement the treatment and to monitor compliance of the social worker and the client with the treatment contract. The social worker implements treatment procedures and makes observations about the degree to which the treatment is implemented as planned. Furthermore, the social worker makes judgments about the degree to which he or she should continue the treatment or intervention procedures if the social worker and client attain treatment objectives. The third practice phase involves the termination of treatment as well as follow-up to determine whether the effects of treatment, if obtained, are persistent. This is the evaluation phase in which the clinical social worker discontinues the intervention if the social worker and client attain the treatment objectives but plan to observe any changes that occur with the disruption of treatment. The clinical social worker may withdraw an intervention because he or she has accomplished an objective but still work with the client on another problem (Blythe & Tripodi, 1989). For example, systematic desensitization might reduce a client's anxiety. The clinical social worker may withdraw that intervention; however, he or she may continue to work with the client and the client's mother through counseling and role plays to increase positive interactions between the client and mother. On the other hand, the social worker may terminate social worker–client contacts if there are no additional problems. However, the social worker may continue services in long-term care facilities where the purpose of treatment is not to change feelings and behaviors but to maintain the client's state of feelings and attitudes about care.

Decisions

Clinical social workers make decisions-answers to questions pertaining to their major tasks-throughout the treatment phases. In the assessment and treatment formulation phase, the social worker answers questions such as the following:

- What is the client unit—an individual, couple, family, or group?
- What is the client unit's current status—living arrangements, occupation, or student status; identifying demographic variables; and social and psychological assets and deficits?
- How was the client referred to the social worker? Was the referral appropriate or should the client have been referred elsewhere?
- What are the client's problems and needs?
- Is the client sufficiently motivated to engage in the treatment process with the social worker?

- Can the social worker help the client resolve his or her problems, and does the clinical social worker have in his or her repertoire an intervention that will meet the client's needs?
- Can the social worker assist the client in prioritizing his or her problems or needs and can the social worker and the client agree on which problems to tackle?
- What are the treatment objectives for the designated problem? Do the clinical social worker and the client agree on those objectives?
- Can the social worker procure information about the nature and severity of the designated problems?
- Does it appear that the problem will continue and even become exacerbated without intervention? (Questions were adapted and modified from Vonk, Tripodi, & Epstein, 2006, p. 10.)

Decisions in the treatment implementation and monitoring phase focus on the delivery of the intervention, its appropriateness for the client, and whether progress occurs in realizing the treatment objectives. The social worker answers questions such as the following:

- Do the client, the clinical social worker, and others important for successful implementation understand what is expected in and between treatment sessions?
- Has the social worker implemented the intervention according to professional standards and the provisions of the treatment contract?
- Does the client appear to want to participate in the intervention plan? Is the intervention appropriate for the particular client? If not, should the social worker use another intervention?
- Are there any barriers to implementation? Can the social worker overcome these barriers?
- Should the social worker revise the initial assessment?
- If implementation of the intervention is inadequate, should the social worker modify the intervention or introduce a new intervention?

- Has there been progress in achieving the treatment objectives? If the social worker and the client have attained treatment objectives, should they terminate the treatment (or intervention)?
- If the social worker terminates the intervention, should he or she plan to follow up with the client to determine whether the attainment of treatment objectives persists? (Questions were adapted and modified from Vonk, Tripodi, & Epstein, 2006, pp. 87–88.)

The final phase of evaluation continues with questions about the achievement of treatment objectives, termination, and follow-up. The second and third phases are interrelated, but the third phase focuses more on the degree to which the intervention has been effective and continues to be effective. However, the clinical social worker also uses this phase to verify the initial assessment and possibly to uncover new problems that originally were not manifest. The social worker then makes decisions based on responses to questions such as the following:

- To what extent have the social worker and the client achieved the treatment objectives?
- If they have not achieved the treatment objectives, are there any discernible reasons why not? Was the treatment appropriate for the client?
- Was termination appropriate? Is there any evidence of client relapse?
- Has client progress persisted in follow-up with the withdrawal of the intervention?
- What level of knowledge did the intervention produce with respect to its relationship to the client's problems? Will this knowledge be useful in work with other clients?
- Did new problems emerge during the follow-up period?
- Should the social worker reinstitute the original intervention, a modified version of it, or introduce a new intervention for the client? (Questions were adapted and modified from Vonk, Tripodi, & Epstein, 2006, p. 151.)

SINGLE-CASE DESIGN METHODOLOGY

Single-case design methodology includes the specification and measurement of variables that indicate the client's problems; the systematic recording of the extent and severity of the problems before the social worker offers interventions; the systematic recording of the extent of the problems during and after the treatment or intervention; the use of designs, graphic procedures, pattern analysis, or statistical analysis; and a conception of levels of knowledge and necessary evidence to make inferences about the attainment of knowledge levels. In its simplest expression, the complete basic model involves three successive phases: (1) baseline, (2) intervention, and (3) follow-up. In each phase, the social worker takes repeated measurements of variables that indicate the client's problems or needs at specified intervals over time. The clinician then observes patterns of variation in the variables in each of the phases and between phases.

At baseline, there are measurements without an intervention, and analyses of those observations can assist in the assessment of a client's problems. The baseline phase provides a benchmark of where the client is without intervention; it can indicate the extent and severity of problems as well as the degree to which they may be spontaneously increasing or remitting to a nonproblem state. The intervention phase provides information about the extent of changes in the frequency of the problem as the social worker provides intervention for the client. During the intervention phase, the clinical social worker observes the degree to which he or she implements the planned intervention and whether the measurement patterns of the problem variables are similar to or different from those at baseline. This observation allows the clinical social worker to infer the effectiveness of intervention in relation to intervention goals and indicates whether a problem is stabilizing, increasing, or decreasing. The social worker can implement the intervention phase in most practice situations in which repeated measurements over time are possible (see chapter 5), including after-care treatment, residential treatment, psychotherapy in private practice, medical social work in hospital care facilities, probation and parole supervision, marital counseling, group therapeutic paradigms, and so forth. The social worker also can implement the intervention phase in short-term treatment, but it is impractical in one-shot crisis interviews, such as emergency intervention in natural disasters. In the follow-up phase, the clinical social worker continues to record the problem variables but terminates the intervention. This phase presumes that the clinical social worker has ethically withdrawn the intervention because both the client and clinical social worker have agreed to it or because the client has achieved therapeutic goals. Obtaining follow-up information requires planning and the use of extra resources by the social worker or the organization or agency in which the social worker is employed. This model of baseline, intervention, and follow-up is consistent with the phase model of direct practice, which incorporates a problem-solving approach, including assessment, planning interventions, implementing interventions, termination, and follow-up (Blythe & Tripodi, 1989).

The model presented in this book, a basic A-B-A design (Barlow & Hersen, 1984), is used because it is a logical extension of Cook and Campbell's (1979) interrupted time-series design applied to single cases, which may permit stronger inferences about the effectiveness of an intervention than the A-B design. The A refers to a phase without intervention, whereas B refers to intervention. Hence, the A-B-A design includes baseline, intervention, and return to baseline (the follow-up phase). The A-B design does not have a follow-up phase; hence, it does not permit analysis of what happens to the client after termination or withdrawal of the intervention. Because the clinical social worker can examine much information within the baseline, intervention, or follow-up phase for making decisions within the phases in addition to comparisons among phases, this book refers to those phases, rather than to the letters A and B.

This book intends to introduce readers to the A-B-A design model in detail; clinical examples in subsequent chapters illustrate procedures for analysis. However, the following example illustrates aspects of the model as well as potential problems in its application.

Example

Suppose a clinical social worker in private practice is working with Jim, a 15-year-old, who is depressed and who thinks critically of himself in relation to others each day. Jim has low self-esteem and does not engage in ordinary school activities with his classmates. As part of the diagnostic or assessment process, which also includes interviews with Jim's family and study of referral documents and protocols, the clinical social worker concentrates on the problems of depression and self-critical thoughts.

In discussions with Jim, the clinical social worker devises two variables: (1) frequency of self-critical thoughts and (2) degree of depression. Together, the worker and Jim devise a plan for measuring these variables. The plan must be realistic and feasible for Jim to carry out through baseline, intervention, and follow-up phases. Jim defines a self-critical thought as one in which he thinks about how incompetent he is compared with others. The clinical social worker asks Jim to tally the number of times he has self-critical thoughts each day and to record those numbers for one week. The social worker also devises a self-anchored rating scale of depression in consultation with Jim. The scale ranges from 0 to 10, where 0 = no depression, 2 = very little depression, 4 = some depression, 6 = moderate depression, 8 = a great deal of depression, and 10 = extreme depression. The social worker also asks Jim to rate his feelings of depression every day for one week. At the end of one week—in the second session with the clinical social worker—the social worker constructs graphs to show baseline patterns of self-critical thoughts and severity of depression (Figures 1 and 2).

Clearly, Jim perceives he is depressed. He indicates a great deal of depression (level 8 on the scale) or higher every day of the week except Tuesday, which he rated 7. Furthermore, the same pattern exists for the frequency of self-critical thoughts, which Jim rated 10 or higher every day except Tuesday. Thus, there apparently is a strong association between the number of self-critical thoughts and depression. However, it is unclear whether self-critical thoughts come before or after the depression. Jim, however, indicated in an interview that he tends to become depressed after he is self-critical. Within the social worker's overall treatment plan, which includes discussions of incidents at home and at

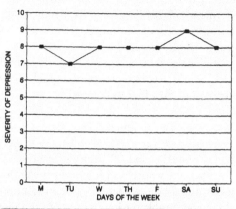

figure 1

Severity of Depression for One Week

NOTE: M = Monday, TU = Tuesday, W = Wednesday,
TH = Thursday, F = Friday, SA = Saturday, SU = Sunday.

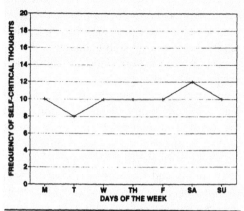

figure 2

Self-Critical Thoughts for One Week

NOTE: M = Monday, T = Tuesday, W = Wednesday,
TH = Thursday, F = Friday, SA = Saturday, SU = Sunday.

school as well as Jim's relationships with peers and family, the social worker decides to use an intervention designed to reduce Jim's self-critical thoughts and, in turn, possibly reduce his depression. The intervention is a cognitive intervention aimed at thought stopping and includes reframing the context of self-critical decisions. The social worker instructs Jim to change the comparisons from himself with others to only with himself whenever he has a self-critical thought and to think of successful performances he has had at school and in sports events. In addition, the social worker asks Jim to continue to record the frequency of self-critical remarks and perceived depression. After two weeks of intervention, the clinical social worker produces graphs to show the comparisons of intervention with baseline (Figures 3 and 4). Obviously, the frequency of self-critical thoughts (Figure 4) is reduced to 0 during Friday, Saturday, and Sunday—the last three days of the two-week intervention. However, the social worker notes that Jim's feelings of depression persist (Figure 3) and essentially are unchanged. The clinical

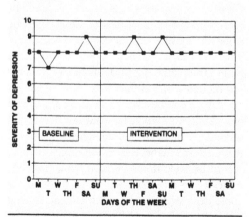

figure 3

Severity of Depression over Time, before and after Intervention

NOTE: M = Monday, T = Tuesday, W = Wednesday,
TH = Thursday, F = Friday, SA = Saturday, SU = Sunday.

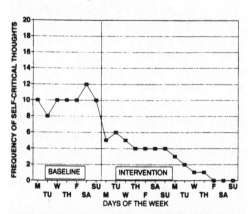

figure 4

Frequency of Self-Critical Thoughts over Time, before and during Intervention

NOTE: M = Monday, T = Tuesday, W = Wednesday,
TH = Thursday, F = Friday, SA = Saturday, SU = Sunday.

social worker learns that there is no simple relationship between depression and control of self-critical thoughts, contrary to what Jim believes. This observation implies that assessment of factors that might lead to depression should continue. Moreover, the social worker can eliminate the cognitive intervention directed toward Jim's self-critical thoughts in comparison with others. If Jim no longer invokes the intervention, he and the social worker can determine, by obtaining measurements of self-critical remarks on a daily basis during the follow-up period, whether there is a persistent change in the reduction of self-critical remarks.

As this example illustrates, single-case design methodology is merely a tool, but it can aid the social worker in making decisions pertinent to assessment and practice effectiveness. When the clinical social worker uses the full single-case design model and adds other design variations (see chapter 7), he or she can make inferences that approximate causal relationships between the intervention and designated outcomes or planned results. The emphasis in this book is on using the model and variations of it as a framework for making clinical decisions. However, the clinical social worker ultimately bases the decisions on his or her previous experiences, theory, and knowledge of interventions and on other information derived from clinical observations and interviews.

Levels of Knowledge

Single-case designs produce or approximate three levels of knowledge: (1) descriptive, (2) correlational, and (3) causal (Tripodi, 1983). Descriptive knowledge consists of simple facts. For example, Jim's ratings of perceived depression for each day of the week constitute descriptive knowledge about the severity of his depression. Correlational knowledge is the description of a relationship between variables. In comparing baseline to intervention on self-critical remarks for Jim, it is apparent that, at baseline without intervention there is a greater frequency of self-critical remarks, but during the administration of the intervention, there is a reduction in the number of self-critical remarks, hence, there is a correlation between the intervention and the number of self-critical remarks. The relation-

ship can be more aptly described as inverse or negative: As intervention is introduced, the frequency of self-critical remarks is reduced. If self-critical remarks increased as the intervention was introduced, the relationship would be considered direct or positive. The highest level of knowledge is causal, which includes correlational knowledge between an intervention and changes in a problem variable as well as evidence that no variables other than the intervention are responsible for the changes. Single-case designs cannot achieve causal knowledge with complete certainty; it can only be approximated. If the clinical social worker could withdraw the intervention for Jim and the result was a reversion to baseline when Jim had a relatively high number of self-critical remarks, the clinical social worker might obtain evidence for causality. This evidence would show that Jim would again eliminate self-critical remarks when the cognitive intervention is reintroduced.

What evidence does the clinical social worker need to obtain different levels of knowledge? The social worker can only have descriptive knowledge if there is evidence of reliability (consistency) and validity (accuracy) for the variables the social worker is measuring. These concepts are discussed in detail in chapter 3. Correlational knowledge exists when there are reliable and valid variables and when there is graphic or statistical evidence of a relationship among the variables. Procedures to determine the existence of correlational knowledge are discussed in chapter 5. Causal knowledge about an intervention depends on the following criteria:

1. The intervention precedes changes in problem variables. For example, the social worker introduces the cognitive intervention for Jim before he makes reductions in self-critical remarks.
2. There is a correlation or association between the intervention and the variables that indicate change. It is standard practice to conceive of the intervention as an independent variable and the change variables as dependent variables.
3. No other variables are responsible for observed changes in the dependent variable. These other variables are internal validity threats (Cook & Campbell, 1979) (see chapter 5).

RELATIONSHIP BETWEEN CLINICAL PRACTICE AND SINGLE-CASE DESIGN METHODOLOGY

Single-case design methodology is insufficiently comprehensive to provide the basic information for all practice decisions. Rather, single-case design provides information that clinical social workers can use to make key decisions in practice. Figure 5 shows the relationship between information obtained from single-case designs and decisions clinical social workers make in practice. The baseline occurs during the assessment and treatment formulation phase; intervention (treatment), during the treatment implementation and monitoring phase; and follow-up, during the treatment evaluation phase. However, the decisions designated for the practice phases do not include all of the decisions clinical social workers make. Instead, they show that there is a direct relationship between information obtained from single-case design methodology and critical practice decisions. For example, at baseline, the social worker can obtain information about the measurement of a problem and its nature, severity, and persistence over time without intervention. The clinical social worker makes inferences in single-case design methodology by comparing measurements between phases (see Figures 1 and 4). For example, the social worker compares measurements he or she made during intervention with measurements on the same variable at baseline. If there are significant changes from problem severity to the reduction or elimination of the problem, the social worker infers that there is a relationship between the reduction of the problem and the introduction of the treatment.

SINGLE-CASE DESIGN METHODOLOGY IN HISTORICAL CONTEXT

The introduction of single-case design methodology to social work practice occurred in the 1970s with the emergence of the empirical practice movement (Reid, 1994). Led by social

---

figure 5 *Relationship of Clinical Practice Decisions and Information Provided by Single-Subject Design Methodology*

	Phases		
Clinical Social Work Practice	Assessment and Treatment Formulation	Treatment Implementation and Monitoring	Treatment Evaluation: Termination and Follow-Up
Decisions	Is the designated problem severe and persistent and is treatment required?	Has the social worker implemented treatment and has the severity and nature of the client's problem changed?	Should the social worker withdraw treatment? Will the social worker and client successfully attain treatment objectives following withdrawal of the treatment?

	Phases		
Single-Subject Design Methodology	Baseline	Intervention (Treatment)	Follow-Up
Information	Specification of treatment objectives into measurable problems. Measurement of nature, severity, and persistence of problem without intervention.	Measurement of changes in nature and severity of problem over time. Inferences about the attainment of objectives. Observations of treatment implementation.	Measurement of maintenance of changes. Provision of descriptive, correlational, and approximations to causal knowledge. Observations of the emergence of new problems.

work practitioner/researchers and researchers based in academic settings, this movement sought to strengthen the scientific basis of practice by advancing the use of research methods in clinical practice, promoting the use of interventions with empirical evidence of effectiveness, and expanding the knowledge base for practice through the dissemination of studies carried out by social work practitioner/researchers. Single-case designs were among the research methods promoted by the movement. Their use, in addition to group research designs, was considered essential to developing a knowledge base of effective social work interventions.

The ideal of practice grounded in science was not new when the movement began. It was present at the dawn of the profession as reflected in the writings of early social work pioneers (Gellis & Reid, 2004). In its earliest years, social work faced great pressure to establish itself as a legitimate profession. The adoption of a scientific approach to service delivery was one way in which the profession sought to earn this legitimacy (Dore, 1990). Practice was scientific to the extent that caseworkers followed a scientific model in the delivery of services, an approach exemplified in the writings of Mary Richmond. In her landmark publication *Social Diagnosis*, Richmond (1917) delineated a casework paradigm of study–diagnosis–treatment. Study entailed the collection of social evidence, defined as "any and all facts as to personal and family history" (Richmond, 1917, p. 43), which was used to draw inferences about the case. The interpretation of these inferences led to a diagnosis, an indication of "the nature of the client's social difficulties" (Richmond, p. 43). The diagnosis informed the course of treatment, which was then tested with case data.

The psychoanalytic movement that dominated professional practice in the 1940s and 1950s also reinforced a scientific approach to practice (Gellis & Reid, 2004). The study–diagnosis–treatment paradigm delineated by Richmond was enriched by psychoanalytic theory, which provided insights for understanding the psychological and emotional aspects of cases and offered practitioners a range of treatment techniques. Whereas Richmond developed proce-

dures for collecting and weighing the facts in a case, her approach was not directly tied to theory. The psychoanalytic movement in social work provided clinicians with a way to organize case data based on psychoanalytic principles and develop interventions based on those principles. Psychoanalytic theory was the forerunner to practice innovations and theoretical approaches that would dominate professional practice in the decades to follow.

During the psychoanalytic movement, efforts to strengthen the scientific basis of practice encompassed the development of casework typologies for defining the scope of practice. Some were based on the dynamics of the procedures used and others on goals and method (Germain, 1974). The typologies were intended to structure service delivery in clearly defined steps and to organize client and worker tasks toward a diagnostically based sequence of objectives. Pioneering work by Florence Hollis exemplified one such approach. Her 1964 publication *Casework: A Psychosocial Therapy* delineated an extensive typology of treatment procedures for describing the casework process. Her classification system was not an empirical base on which casework rested, but instead a tool for describing the procedures that were used when changes in cases occurred (Woods & Hollis, 2000).

Concern for the evidence base of practice became a focus of the empirical practice movement that began two decades later. The movement emerged against the backdrop of the "effectiveness controversy" and growing emphasis on accountability in the human services (Reid, 1994). Studies of casework services found limited evidence of effectiveness (Fischer, 1973, 1976; Meyer, Borgatta, & Jones, 1965; Mullen & Dumpson, 1972; Wood, 1978), raising serious questions regarding whether practitioners actually helped those they served. At the same time, decreasing resources for social programs increased competition among the helping professions, underscoring the profession's need to legitimate its services as worthy of public support (Witkin, 1996).

Group experimental research studies documenting effective practice approaches were needed;

however, master's degree-level practitioners lacked the expertise and resources for conducting experimental research (Witkin, 1996). Moreover, results from group experimental research studies were not easily translated into prescriptions for practice. Single-case designs required less time and resources to implement than group designs (Reid, 1994). Single-case design methodology could be taught to master's degree-level practitioners. Their use of the methodology to evaluate their work was one way in which the profession could develop a knowledge base of effective interventions. Studies conducted by practitioner/researchers would be deeply grounded in practice, address what clinicians were most interested in—what was best for addressing a problem in a particular case—and generate knowledge for informing practice with similar cases.

In the early 1970s, content on single-case designs was introduced into research and practice courses in social work education programs (Reid, 1994). Proponents of the method advocated for the board of the Council of Social Work Education (CSWE) to require graduate and undergraduate social work programs to prepare students to evaluate their practice. In 1982, CSWE adopted a new accreditation policy calling for the integration of content on the systematic evaluation of one's practice (Fischer, 1993). By the end of the following decade, a survey of research offerings at graduate schools of social work revealed that one-third emphasized single-case designs and self-practice evaluation in their curricula (Reid, 1994).

Initial studies examining whether students trained in the use of practice evaluation methods subsequently applied them to their practice produced disappointing results. The use of these methods did not differ between students taught to use them and those who were not (Briar, 1992). These dismal findings have been attributed, in part, to methodological limitations of these early studies, notably, their small sample sizes (Briar, 1992). A 1983 study with a large sample of practitioners who participated in an integrated research-practice sequence as part of their graduate training yielded more promising results; 40 percent of practitioners reported

using one or more research designs (surveys, single-group pretest to posttest designs, and single-case designs) in their practice. Recent research examining social workers' use of each of four research methods (single-case designs, social surveys, qualitative methods, and quasi-experimental or experimental methods) revealed that more than half (56 percent) reported using at least one of the four methods (Marino, Green, & Young, 1998). Numerous studies have documented substantial use of components of the methodology such as specifying target problems and goals, describing goals in measurable terms, and monitoring client progress (Reid, 1994). Increased use of the methodology in practice is also evident in the growing number of published single-case design studies. A review of the practice research literature identified several hundred outcome studies that used single-case designs to evaluate social work interventions (Thyer & Thyer, 1992). A recent development supporting the dissemination of single-case design studies is the establishment of journals such as *Research on Social Work Practice* and the *Journal of Evidence-Based Social Work* devoted to publishing practice research studies.

The move to managed care in the human services and the concomitant emphasis on efficient and effective service delivery has fueled continuing interest in the use of practice evaluation methods in social work and related disciplines. Some managed care companies no longer provide reimbursement solely on the basis of the credentials of the service provider, instead requiring additional evidence of empirically documented outcomes (Thyer, 1996). Moreover, as a condition of continued funding, many federal and state agencies require documentation of the effectiveness of social work services. Indications that government authorities, insurers, and accreditation bodies will increasingly require evidence of treatment effectiveness implicates continued use of single-case design methodology to ensure that standards are met.

ADVANTAGES OF USING SINGLE-CASE DESIGN METHODOLOGY

Practice issues and decisions to help clients are the basic priorities in clinical social work.

Clinical social workers will use single-case design methodology if it follows natural occurrences of practice and if they can incorporate it as a tool within practice. The methodology does not fit all practice situations; however, there are a number of advantages to using single-case designs.

Single-case designs are one of several methodologies that can be used for practice research. Group research designs can also be used for this purpose (see for example, Grinnell, 2001). The chief advantage of using single-case versus group research designs for practice research is that they generate knowledge that is specific to the case. Although there are similarities between cases encountered in practice, each is unique. Single-case designs allow practitioners to monitor and evaluate their practice given the unique attributes of the case. This information is lost with group research designs. Findings from group research studies are reported in aggregate; thus, individual differences are washed out. Although there are methodological limitations on the use of single-case designs for practice research, they are currently the most rigorous approaches available for monitoring and evaluating social work practice with individual cases (Mattaini, 1996).

A second advantage to using single-case designs is that they provide information to aid clinicians and supervisors in practice decision making. Use of the basic design can generate three levels of knowledge within and between phases of the components baseline, intervention, and follow-up (Table 1). Social workers can obtain descriptive knowledge regarding the existence, magnitude, duration, and frequency of a problem within each of the three phases. They can obtain correlational knowledge of the intervention and problem existence, magnitude, duration, and frequency by comparing observations in the intervention phase with baseline or with follow-up observations. Clinical social workers can infer causal knowledge, which is only approximate, based on information on all components plus other information, such as interviewing, to help rule out alternative explanations for changes associated with the intervention. The resulting information can be used to assist them in making decisions about assessment, treatment implementation, and treatment evaluation (see Table 1). In addition, supervisors can learn which problems social workers are focusing on and whether social workers have made progress in reducing or maintaining those problems. Supervisors might then use this information as a stimulus for discussing a particular client: Why is the intervention working? Is it appropriate for this client? Is the information reliable? What is the client's response when he or she sees a graph showing progress?

A third advantage to using single-case design methodology is that it provides clinicians with tools for enhancing their practice. Clinical social work practice entails the related tasks of identifying and prioritizing problems for work, setting intervention goals, and monitoring progress toward those goals. Using features of the methodology such as defining problems in measurable terms and systematically monitoring their occurrence can add precision to these tasks. By selecting indicators of client variables, the number of times a client is late for work, for

table 1	Levels of Knowledge and Components of Single-Case Design
Level of Knowledge	Components of Single-Case Design
Descriptive	Obtained within any of the components: baseline, intervention, follow-up
Correlational	Obtained by comparing observations between intervention and either baseline or follow-up
Causal	Inferred by comparing observations among all three components and between additional design variations, such as the reinstitution of intervention, and by interviews

example, as an indicator of his or her poor work performance, the clinician can be assured that he or she and the client share a common understanding of this problem. By systematically monitoring this variable over time, for example, a one-week interval between client and worker contacts, the clinician can determine problem frequency. The resulting information can be used to establish treatment goals in measurable terms, for example, to decrease the frequency of tardiness from four times a week to none at all over a three-week interval. Continued monitoring of this target during intervention and follow-up provides the clinician with information for determining whether agreed-upon goals have been met. Use of these systematic procedures affords the clinician greater confidence in observed changes than passive observations can provide.

A fourth advantage to using single-case design methodology is that it provides information that is useful to clients. As active participants in the change process and the ultimate beneficiaries of social work intervention, clients are entitled to information regarding the extent to which services they are receiving are contributing to the accomplishment of agreed-upon clinical objectives. Clinicians have an array of tools at their disposal for measuring case variables and sharing the results of measurement with clients. Standardized instruments can be used for this purpose (see for example, Corcoran & Fischer, 2000a, 2000b). The Beck Depression Inventory (BDI) (Beck, Ward, Mendelson, Mock, & Erbaugh, 1961), for example, includes clinical cut-off points for determining whether the severity of reported depression is clinically significant. Using this instrument in the context of practice with a depressed client can help the client gain a greater understanding of the severity of his or her depression. Clinicians can also create self-anchored rating scales for use in addition to or in lieu of standardized measures. Doing so can be empowering for the client who is asked to describe, in his or her own terms, how a "5" on such a scale differs from a "1." The resultant measure reflects the client's subjective experience of depression and also provides a common language for the clinical social worker and client to discuss the client's depression. For example,

the clinical social worker can ask: Was it a five in that situation or event? How did that differ from how you were feeling before or after that happened?

The resulting information can be used to show clients their scores on repeated measures of case variables with simple graphs. Graphic patterns observed prior to intervention may indicate that the problem was not as severe as the client originally perceived it to be and uncover additional problems or issues that warrant deeper investigation. On the other hand, graphic patterns may confirm the presence of a severe and persistent problem that warrants intervention, validating the client's experience of the problem and setting a benchmark against which treatment goals can be established. Because the collection of repeated measures of case variables involves a considerable investment of time and effort on the part of the client, showing the client graphs of repeated measures can help reinforce the value of monitoring and show the client that his or her efforts have not been wasted.

A fifth advantage to using single-case design methodology is that it produces information for the profession. Clinical social workers can accumulate a log of similar cases in which a particular intervention has or has not been effective. For example, a social worker may use a method of providing information about operations to close friends and relatives of a patient who is undergoing surgery to reduce the anxiety of the patient and his or her family and friends. The social worker may find that 18 of 20 people showed a reduction in anxiety; hence, he or she justifiably retains that particular intervention in the clinical repertoire. In this way, clinical social workers also can systematize their experiences in using different interventions for their clients. Blythe and Briar (1985) have suggested that practitioners can use single-case designs to develop models of empirically based practice, that is prescriptions of what should be done and what is likely to be effective in specific practice situations. Clinical social workers can also generate knowledge for the profession regarding the effectiveness of various social work interventions by publishing single-case design studies reflecting their work with clients.

DISADVANTAGES OF USING SINGLE-CASE DESIGN METHODOLOGY

When used for practice research, single-case design methodology can only approximate causal knowledge. This is due to limitations on the extent to which internal validity threats (competing explanations for change) can be controlled (see chapter 5 for a discussion of internal validity threats and chapter 7 regarding procedures for minimizing these threats). We discuss one such threat here to orient the reader to the types of challenges that arise when single-case design methodology is used to approximate causal knowledge. The reader will recall that the methodology can be used to generate additional levels of knowledge that are useful for practice decision making.

Clients encountered in practice are often engaged in other helping networks for similar or related problems. When the client is receiving other interventions from additional sources, it is difficult for the social worker to determine whether observed changes are due to the intervention that he or she is providing or to other services the client is receiving. This introduces the internal validity threat of multiple treatment interference, the occurrence of other interventions that may account for changes observed in the problem of interest. In multidisciplinary settings, for example in a medical or psychiatric hospital, the client has contact with many professionals from which he or she may receive intervention. In a neuropsychiatry hospital, a patient may receive occupational therapy, group counseling, and individual counseling from a psychiatrist, or counseling from a clinical social worker. Interventions may overlap, precluding the study of one intervention. Social workers can deal with this problem by assessing the degree to which the evaluation methodology is appropriate (See chapter 5 for a discussion on the procedures for discerning the context of intervention). In assessing the problem, the social worker may find the following:

- No other discernible intervention conflicts with the one he or she is evaluating. That is, the intervention is unique, and the social worker can evaluate it using single-case design methodology.

- The intervention and one or more other interventions overlap so the social worker can only evaluate the joint effects of the interventions.
- The intervention and other interventions overlap, and the nature of the intervention the clinical social worker is providing is so ambiguous and diffuse that evaluation is unwarranted until the social worker can specify the intervention more precisely.

Another disadvantage to using single-case design methodology is that it does not fit all practice situations and clients. For example, social workers in EAPs that provide services on a time-limited basis may not be able to implement all of the phases of the design. The methodology may also be difficult to implement with clients who lack the ability to monitor their behavior, for example, those with cognitive impairments. It is likewise challenging to use the methodology with clients who can monitor their behavior but lack the motivation to do so, for example, in work with clients who are mandated to treatment but who lack readiness to examine their problem behaviors.

In settings that afford limited opportunities to implement all phases of the model, the clinical social worker can use available sources of data, for example, information provided by referral sources or other archival data to retrospectively reconstruct the baseline phase of the design and establish treatment goals. This will allow the client and worker to utilize available sessions to implement the intervention and monitor progress toward goals. In work with involuntary clients, the clinician can present the methodology from a strengths perspective, emphasizing that the choice to engage in the therapeutic process is the client's and discussing the ways in which monitoring can help the client gain a deeper understanding of the situations and events that brought him or her to treatment. The clinician may need to explore a voluntary client's lack of motivation to monitor their behaviors to determine their readiness to address the issue for which treatment was sought or possibly consider using other data collection strategies (for example, the use of available records or direct observation by others) to gather information on salient case variables.

A third disadvantage to using single-case design methodology is that it does not capture the whole view of the case. Although the social worker uses systematic procedures, such as the repeated measurement of variables at baseline, those measures do not represent the case in its entirety. Measurements are indices of the client's problems, selected for assessment and potential change through intervention. Any specification of a phenomenon, whether in practice (by prioritizing and focusing on specific features of a client in his or her situation) or in research (by systematically obtaining repeated measurements over time for a particular problem variable), reduces the phenomenon to a segment of its totality. However, the clinical social worker may still view the total situation of the client in his or her environment. The social worker can interpret in that context the specific findings of problem changes selected for intervention by the clinical social worker and the client.

A fourth disadvantage to using single-case designs is that many clinicians find it difficult, and perhaps impossible, to obtain baseline and follow-up measurements. In practice situations where it is unethical to withhold intervention, for example, in work with a client who is at imminent risk of harming himself or herself, the worker cannot delay intervention. Similarly, it is difficult to collect follow-up measurements with clients who prematurely terminate services. Maintaining a client's motivation to continue monitoring after clinical objectives have been met can also be challenging. The social worker may approximate baseline measurements through retrospection or by using available data from other sources when there is insufficient time to obtain measurements before intervention (see chapter 3 on measurement). In work with clients who are lost during the follow-up phase, the clinical social worker can initiate follow-up contacts to gain follow-up measurements through retrospection as in baseline (see chapter 6 on follow-up). To enhance client retention and motivation to continue collecting measurements of case variables through the follow-up phase, the social worker can stress the importance of follow-up data early on in the treatment process and acknowledge that motivation to continue monitoring may decrease when clinical objectives have been met.

The absence of baseline or follow-up data is problematic when the social worker uses single-case design methodology to approximate causal knowledge regarding whether changes observed in case variables resulted from intervention. For approximating this knowledge, reliable and valid time-series data gathered at baseline and follow-up are required. Although the worker cannot approximate causal knowledge in the absence of these data, he or she can obtain descriptive knowledge by studying trends in measurements within the intervention phase. Moreover, he or she can derive correlational knowledge from comparisons of baseline measurements and measurements taken during intervention (in the absence of follow-up data), and from comparisons between intervention measurements and measurements taken at follow-up (in the absence of baseline data).

GUIDELINES FOR EVALUATING SINGE-CASE DESIGN STUDIES

In the chapters that follow, we present the basic single-case design model of baseline, intervention, and follow-up, and discuss considerations that inform the implementation of this model in practice. Students learning the methodology can benefit from reading published single-case design studies even at this early stage in the learning process. Doing so can raise awareness of how the basic design and variations of it are implemented across a variety of practice settings and issues. However, because readers have not yet learned the methodology, they may not be aware of the types of information that should be included in such reports. Using the material presented in subsequent chapters of this book and drawing from similar guidelines developed for assessing the quality of group research design studies in social work (Thyer, 1991), we developed guidelines for evaluating published single-case design studies. Although they may seem overwhelming at first, information summarized in the guidelines will be fully discussed in subsequent chapters of the book. Students and practitioners can use the guidelines to become informed readers of such reports and for considering the types of information to include when reporting findings from single-case design studies carried out in their own practice.

The guidelines are organized according to broad headings used in reports of research, including introduction, method, results, and discussion. Under each heading, we summarize the types of information that should be presented. Appendix 1 summarizes the guidelines below as a series of questions for readers to consider when reviewing published single-case design studies.

Introduction

The study should introduce the clinical problem to be addressed. There should be a brief description of the case and the agreed upon targets for intervention. The intervention model or treatment techniques[1] for addressing these targets should be specified, and evidence of their effectiveness for addressing the target problem should be summarized. When available, data to support the efficacy of the intervention in work with similar cases should be summarized. If the study is exploratory (that is, it seeks to examine the utility of an approach that has not undergone efficacy testing), this should be explicitly stated and a rationale provided to support application of the intervention to the case in question. The introduction should conclude with a statement of intervention hypotheses. These should be tied to the level of knowledge sought (descriptive, correlational, and/or causal) and the design and procedures for generating this knowledge.

Method

Case. The description of the case and its unique features are a critical component of single-case design studies. Enough information should be provided so that another clinician working with the same problem can determine the extent of similarities and differences between the case presented and those encountered in his or her practice. The unit of analysis should be specified (whether an individual, couple, family, or group is the focus of intervention). This section should provide details regarding demographic characteristics of the case and features

of the case that are relevant to work with the problem described such as diagnostic information, prior occurrences of the problem and relevant treatment history, precipitating events that led to treatment, and prior or concurrent interventions the individual, couple, family or group is receiving. A brief description of the intervention setting should be provided. The scope of services (for example, job training and placement, supportive housing, mental health counseling) and the types, length, and duration of typical client contacts should be described. Factors that influence work with clients in the setting described should be discussed (for example, whether treatment is mandated or time limited).

Case Variables and Their Measurement. The target problem(s) to be addressed should be clearly stated. Conceptual definitions of identified targets for intervention and corresponding problem indicators for operationally defining each of these should be delineated. The report should include details regarding the measurement and data collection plan. For each problem indicator, a description of who will collect the data (the client, his or her significant other, a family member, or the clinician, for example), the time interval between measures (for example, on a per-episode basis immediately preceding or following problem occurrence, daily, episodically, or during preset intervals), and how measurements will be taken (for example, through direct observation, standardized instruments or self-anchored rating scales, the collection of behavioral byproducts, retrospective recall) should be provided. Plans for documenting repeated measures of problem indicators (for example, entering scores from a self-anchored scale in a log) should be described. Factors that influenced the design of the measurement plan should be addressed. Issues of relevance (the degree to which measured variables are tied to treatment goals), feasibility (the extent to which plans for measuring variables are realistic and can be carried out by the client and others engaged in the measurement process), reliability (the consistency of responses in measurement), validity (the extent to which measures adequately capture the meaning of the phenomenon under study), and non-reactivity (the extent to which the measurement

---

1. A treatment model is a well-specified and integrated approach for addressing a particular problem, whereas techniques refer to strategies that may be a subset thereof or intended for independent use.

process does not influence changes in behavior) should be addressed. Procedures for ensuring the reliability and validity of repeated measures collected during the study should be described.

Design. The report should describe the single-case design used (for example, baseline, intervention, follow-up, multiple baseline, graduated intensity, withdrawal-reversal). A rationale for the design choice should be provided. The level of knowledge sought (descriptive, correlational, and/or causal) and feasibility concerns relevant to implementing the design in practice should be addressed. The extent to which the design minimizes internal validity threats of history (variables or events such as natural disasters, changes in employment and occupational status, changes in family income and health outside of the intervention that occur between the first measurement of the variable at baseline and the last measurement during intervention), maturation (events that occur within the client due to changes in growth, psychological mechanisms, and illness), initial measurement effects (the influence of initial measurement on subsequent measurements of a problem variable), instrumentation (the possibility that the process of measurement is nonstandardized and observed changes are due to nonstandardization rather than to the intervention), statistical regression (the tendency for extreme scores to move toward the average, independent of intervention), multiple treatment interference (the occurrence of other interventions between baseline measurements and measurements taken during intervention), expectancy effects (changes in the problem variable that are due to client expectations about interventions and prognoses), interactions (the combined effects of history, maturation, initial measurement effects, instrumentation, statistical regression, multiple treatment interference, and expectancy effects), and other unknown factors should be discussed. Safeguards for minimizing these threats, such as the use of clinical interviews to identify other events that could affect changes in the problem variable, should be described. The duration of design phases and the factors that informed the timeframes selected, including the expected timeframe for documenting the presence, frequency, severity, or duration of the problem pri-

or to intervention, the amount of time required to achieve clinical intervention objectives, and the amount of time observed changes are expected to endure, should be addressed.

Intervention. A detailed description of the intervention model and/or techniques for addressing the problem(s) identified in the introduction should be provided in this section. For each problem, clinical intervention objectives should be specified and these objectives should be tied directly to the operational definitions of the problem (for example, a reduction in (target) from (value) to (value)). The length of time for achieving each objective and the length of time gains are expected to endure should be described. A tie to the relevant literature on which these timeframes are based should be presented. For each objective, the intervention model or techniques for accomplishing the objective should be adequately described. Details of the intervention should include the contents of intervention; the intervenors (that is, the person or persons responsible for delivering the intervention); and the location, frequency, and duration of intervention. Information should be provided regarding how the clinician ensured intervention fidelity (that is, that the intervention was implemented as intended) and that it was implemented reliably (that is, consistently), for example, through the use of checklists completed by the social worker, the client, or both.

Analysis. Information regarding the procedures for analyzing the time-series data should be provided. Specific phase comparisons should be delineated (for example, baseline and intervention; intervention and follow-up; and baseline and follow-up). Although a wide array of statistical procedures are available for evaluating time-series data, the focus of this discussion is on the two statistical methods addressed in this book: the C statistic (Tryon, 1982) and the binomial test for horizontal baseline (Blythe & Tripodi, 1989). If the C statistic was used, evidence that the requirement of collecting a minimum of eight measurements has been met should be presented, and the value of the statistic and its corresponding probability level should be reported. If the binomial test was used for phase comparisons, confirmation that horizontal stability was observed in the baseline phase of the study should be provided. Analyses should be appropriate to addressing study hypotheses and generating the levels of knowledge sought.

Results

Findings from statistical analyses should be summarized in the report. Findings should be discussed in terms of their statistical and clinical significance, and in terms of how they influenced the course of intervention. The narrative describing study results should be accompanied by graphs that depict repeated measurements of case variables. Graphs should summarize information described in the narrative; clearly delineate baseline, intervention, and follow-up phases; label each time series when data for multiple variables are concurrently displayed; and indicate values corresponding to the attainment of clinical objectives in intervention and follow-up phases. The reader should be able to ascertain progress or deterioration that occurred in the case through visual inspection of the graphs.

Discussion

This section should address whether study hypotheses were supported and describe alternative explanations (threats to internal validity) for study findings. The discussion should be limited to only those conclusions that can be made from the data. Implications of the research for clinical social work practice and practice-based research should be discussed. The authors should address whether study findings replicate findings from previous single-case design studies in similar agency settings and with similar cases. If the study reports findings from the application of a novel intervention approach that has not previously been evaluated, the reader should assess the replicability of the study from the standpoint of feasibility and the subsequent generation of knowledge for practice.

ORGANIZATION OF THE BOOK

- Chapter 2, on assessment and problem formulation, provides a framework for prioritizing issues for work, an essential precursor to operationally defining the identified issues for measurement. Ethical considerations and cultural sensitivity in assessment and problem formulation are discussed.
- Chapter 3, on measurement, presents criteria for selecting simple but useful measures of agreed upon targets for intervention. It describes problems that are typical for clients in mental health, industry, and other clinical settings and discusses the measurement of problems such as absenteeism, depression, anxiety, productivity, and stress.
- Chapter 4 defines baselines, the first phase of the single-case design model, and explicates their purposes for assessment and evaluation. In addition, the chapter details the process of constructing baselines, including the plotting and analysis of graphic patterns, statistical analysis, and the illustration of practice decisions.
- Intervention, the second phase of the basic model, is defined and discussed in chapter 5. We provide methods for specifying interventions. In addition, the chapter illustrates comparisons of patterns of measurement at the intervention phase to the baseline phase and considers different patterns of change or no change with respect to clinical social workers' decisions.
- Follow-up, the third phase of the model, is defined and discussed in chapter 6. The chapter illustrates the process of measurement during follow-up, shows how to derive patterns that are obtained by comparing follow-up to intervention and to baseline, and discusses those patterns with respect to practice decisions.
- Chapter 7 presents three variations of the basic single-case design model: (1) multiple baseline design with clients, situations, or problems; (2) graduated intensity design; and (3) natural withdrawal-reversal design. We present advantages and disadvantages of using these designs and discuss inferences that the social worker can make about the effectiveness of interventions.

TEACHING SUGGESTIONS

1. Locate a study in the social work literature that follows the basic single-case design model of baseline, intervention, and follow-up. Review the study with the class, limiting

the discussion to the following clinical aspects of the case:

- the case (individual, couple, family, or group) and the problem(s) for which intervention was sought;
- the intervention model and/or techniques for addressing the problem(s); and
- the phases of clinical practice exemplified by the design (for example, assessing the problem and formulating treatment, treatment implementation and monitoring, and treatment evaluation).

After reviewing these aspects of the case, break the students into small groups and distribute a copy of the study to each group. Assign each group one of the questions below. Initiate a discussion regarding methodological aspects of the study based on student responses to these items.

Discussion Questions

- Describe the single-case design phases of baseline, intervention, and follow-up as applied to this case. How long was each phase? Why were these timeframes selected?
- How were identified problems defined and measured? Who collected the data?
- How were data collected during the study used for treatment decision making?
- How were the data analyzed? Briefly describe study findings and indicate whether they were statistically significant. Were they clinically relevant? What levels of knowledge were generated in this study (descriptive, correlational, and/or causal)?

2. Initiate a class discussion about the history of single-case design methodology in clinical social work. Why is this history important? Is social work still struggling to define itself as a legitimate profession? How does single-case design methodology factor into this dialogue?

3. Break the class into two groups. Ask one group to summarize the advantages of using single-case design methodology in clinical social work practice. Have the other group summarize the disadvantages of using the methodology. Ask each group to provide examples from their practice that illustrate the advantages and disadvantages identified. Initiate a discussion about the strengths and limitations of using single-case design methodology based on the material presented by students.

STUDENT EXERCISES

1. Locate a single-case design study in the social work literature. The study you select will be used for this and subsequent exercises presented in this book. Using the guidelines described in the chapter and Appendix 1, describe and critically assess the introduction to the article and information provided regarding the case.

2. Describe a typical case encountered in your clinical practice setting. Could you use single-case design methodology to monitor and evaluate your work with this case? Why or why not?

CHAPTER 2

Assessment and Problem Formulation

Assessment is the first phase of the problem-solving practice model described in chapter 1. It coincides with the baseline phase of single-case design. During this practice phase, the clinical social worker explores the problem or problems for work and identifies those that will be the focus of intervention. For each identified problem, the clinical social worker collects information for clarifying the problem, assessing such factors as the conditions under which it occurs and other people involved, antecedents and consequences related to the problem, and the client's coping skills and resources for addressing it. The clinician uses the resulting information to define the problem and the variables related to it. The relevant variables are then operationalized for measurement. During the baseline phase of single-case design, the clinical social worker takes repeated measurements of the relevant variables to confirm the existence, frequency, severity, or duration of the problem; determine whether it is of sufficient magnitude to warrant intervention; and confirm the relationships between the problem and variables hypothesized to be influencing it. The process of assessment comprises the interrelated tasks of identifying and defining problems for work, operationalizing the identified problems for measurement, and collecting repeated measurements of those problems.

ASSESSMENT GOAL AND TASKS

The goal of assessment is to develop a tentative statement or statements about the problem or problems that will be the focus of intervention. The process of assessment involves progression through three interrelated phases that are defined based on the clinician's assessment tasks. In the first phase, the clinician observes, selects, and orders information or "raw data" about the case (Meyer, 1993). The clinical interview is the primary vehicle through which the clinical social worker obtains information for formulating his or her assessment, although he or she will also rely on information from collateral sources, including intake forms completed by the client; verbal reports provided by relatives, friends, teachers, employers and others; and other relevant records, such as reports from medical providers, courts, employers, and schools, to guide his or her assessment. In the second phase, the clinician interprets the interactions among the variables in the case, guided by his or her professional training, clinical judgment, and theories and evidence relevant to the presenting problem or problems for work. Information from collateral sources can be an invaluable aid in this process. When interpretation is called for, this information is useful for confirming what the client has said and determining the degree of consistency and logic in his or her unfolding story (Meyer, 1993). Based on his or her judgments, the clinician formulates one or more "working hypotheses," statements of the relations between the relevant variables. In the third phase, the clinical social worker shares his or her working hypotheses with the client for purposes of achieving consensus about the nature of the identified problem or problems and the relevant variables that will be the focus of the clinician's ongoing assessment. The clinical social worker then operationalizes the relevant variables for measurement, using procedures described in chapter 3. The clinician takes repeated measurements of the identified variables in the baseline phase of single-case design, as discussed in chapter 4. He or she uses the resulting information to examine the existence, frequency, severity, or duration of each identified problem; determine if it is of sufficient magnitude to warrant clinical intervention; and confirm the role of other influencing variables. For problems that are of sufficient magnitude to warrant intervention, the clinical social worker establishes treatment goals and uses information regarding variables that are sustaining, exacerbating, or diminishing the problem, and the client's coping skills and resources for addressing the problem to develop a treatment plan.

OBTAINING INFORMATION FOR ASSESSMENT

Assessment begins with the clinician's collection and ordering of information about the case. Although the types of information that he or she will attend to depends somewhat on his or her theoretical orientation, there are universal features that, using any perspective, are fundamental to his or her assessment (Meyer, 1993). Such information pertains to the client's social history, which he or she typically provides in an intake interview or by completing an intake form. Key areas of assessment include the following (Cormier & Cormier, 1991): identifying information (age, sex, ethnocultural affiliation, marital status, and occupation); general appearance and demeanor (his or her clothing, speech, body language, and the degree to which he or she appears to "belong" to his or her intimate group); history relating to the presenting problem(s) (the presenting complaint, when it began, how often it occurs, how much it interferes with the client's daily functioning, and the client's reason for seeking services, or if referred, his or her understanding of the reason for the referral); past psychiatric treatment and/or counseling (the type and length of treatment, setting(s) in which it was provided, the outcome(s) of the treatment and the client's current use of prescription drugs for emotional/psychological problems); education and job history (academic progress, relationships with teachers and peers, types and length of jobs held by the cli-

ent, relationships with coworkers, degree of job satisfaction); health and medical history (childhood diseases, prior significant illnesses, previous surgery, current health-related complaints or illnesses and treatments received, significant health problems or illnesses in the client's family of origin, current sleep patterns, appetite, use of prescription medications and recreational drugs, alcohol, and tobacco, dietary habits, and exercise patterns); social/developmental history (current living arrangement, occupation, economic situation, social/leisure time activities, religious affiliation, military background, and history of attaining developmental milestones); family/marital/sexual history (individuals in the client's family of origin, nature and quality of the client's current and past relationships with the identified individuals, history of psychiatric illness/hospitalization among members of client's family of origin; dating history, engagement/marital history and reason for termination of relationships, current relationship with spouse, prior and current sexual activity, previous or current concerns about sexual attitudes and/or behaviors, and for female clients, menstrual history, communication patterns (verbal and nonverbal behavior during sessions including use of eye contact, body movements, gestures, voice level, fluency, vocal errors, and use of personal space, and results of a mental status exam and diagnostic summary, if applicable).

After obtaining preliminary information about the client and his or her presenting concerns, the clinician explores and defines the parameters of these concerns more specifically. We recommend that the clinical social worker apply several principles adapted from Cormier and Cormier (1991, pp. 177–189):

- Explain the purpose of assessment. The clinical social worker explains the rationale for assessment and describes the types of questions that will be asked and their relationship to the goal of defining the problem or problems. The clinician then confirms that the process is understood by and acceptable to the client. At this early stage in the process, it is essential for the clinician to convey the message that the client is in control of his or her actions, including the types of information that he or she will provide, and that the clinician's task is to clarify the problems for work and the client's options for addressing them (Meyer, 1993).

- Identify the client unit. The clinician identifies the client unit, whether an individual, couple, family, or group is the focus of intervention. The person or persons who present for services define the boundaries of the case. In clinical social work practice with individuals, the person who presents for services and his or her unique attributes and circumstances will be the focus of intervention. Although other actors in the case may be engaged in treatment, the focus of the work is on the individual and the problems he or she is seeking to address through intervention.

The term "couple" and "family" are closely related terms. Hepworth and associates (1997) define family as "a system that has properties of its own and that is governed by a set of implicit "rules" specifying roles, power structure, forms of communication, and ways of negotiating and solving problems" (p. 277). Although the term family has traditionally referred to nuclear (parents and children) and extended (encompassing other relatives) forms, a variety of other arrangements constitute family. In recognition of these various forms, we use the definition of family provided by Meyer (1990) as cited in Hepworth and colleagues (1997, p. 276): "two or more people who are joined together by bonds of sharing and intimacy." The defining characteristic between "couple" and "family" is the number of persons involved; when two people present for family intervention, couple is the client unit; when more than two people are involved, family is the unit.

The term group refers to an assembly of individuals who are brought together to accomplish specific goals (Hepworth et al., 1997). Social work groups can be classified into two categories based on the types of goals they are designed to achieve: treatment groups and task groups. Treatment groups enhance the socioemotional needs and well-being of members, and task groups are assembled for purposes of completing a project or developing a product (Hepworth et al., 1997).

The identification of the client unit has both clinical and practical implications for assessment. Clinical practice approaches vary considerably based on whether the case is an individual, couple, family, or group. In social work practice with individuals, for example, emphasis is on building the individual's strengths and assets toward the amelioration of the problem or problems for which intervention is sought. Although this may involve intervention to enhance adaptations between the client and relevant interpersonal systems (family and friends) and institutional settings (school, work, health care), the clinician will draw upon intervention models, theories of human behavior, and empirically validated approaches to individual behavior change for intervening in the case. In contrast, systems approaches guide intervention with couples, families, and groups; the goal of intervention is to optimize the functioning of the couple, family, or group as a whole. The clinician's view of the case will be shaped by such systems concepts as internal and external system boundaries, power structures, decision-making and communication patterns, and member roles (Hepworth et al., 1997).

The way in which the client unit is defined determines the level at which the clinician gathers information for assessment. In clinical social work practice with individuals, information is gathered at the level of the individual, for example, through direct observation, the use of standardized instruments and assessment tools, clinical interviews and other data-gathering methods that provide information about the client's problem and the unique circumstances surrounding it. In work with couples, families, and groups, information gathered for purposes of assessment can be gathered by these same means; however, case issues and concerns are defined in relation to the couple, family, or group as a whole. A clinical social worker who is running a treatment group for individuals who suffer from panic disorder, for example, may collect information during assessment on participants' subjective levels of distress prior to intervention using a measure designed for this purpose. The social worker uses this information to calculate a score for the group, and uses this aggregate measure to establish group goals.

- Prioritize problems that will be the focus of assessment. The clinician identifies the range of problems that are of concern to the client, using open-ended questions to elicit information regarding issues that are troublesome for the individual, couple, family, or group. From these, the clinical social worker and client select the problem or problems that will be the focus of assessment. The clinical social worker prioritizes issues for work based on his or her consideration of several factors. First, he or she identifies problems for which he or she has an ethical or legal mandate to intervene, for example, suspected or known instances of child abuse, regardless of whether this is a client concern, and potentially serious or dangerous health or safety concerns that require urgent attention, for example, the client's expressed intention to harm himself or herself or others. The clinician maintains his or her focus on instances of the former and intervenes to ensure the safety of the client and that of others in instances of the latter before exploring additional client issues and concerns. Second, the clinician identifies the client's presenting request—his or her expressed reason for seeking services or his or her understanding of why he or she was referred (Meyer, 1993). Third, the clinical social worker identifies the problem or problems that the client considers to be the most important to address.

    Respect for client self-determination is a guiding principle in clinical social work practice and among the social worker's ethical responsibilities to clients (Reamer, 1999). The clinician considers the relative importance of the client's presenting request and the issue or issues that are considered to be the most important to him or her for determining those problems on which he or she and the client will focus. If, for example, the presenting request is also the problem of greatest importance to the client, the determination is straightforward. On the other hand, if the client was court-ordered to treatment and the problem for which the referral was made is of low importance to him or her, the clinician prioritizes the issue for which the client was remanded to treatment, communicating to the client his or her obligation to do so, and

encouraging the client to explore the issue or issues that led to the referral. Fourth, the clinician identifies issues of immediacy—problems or situations that require intervention before work on other issues can proceed (Blythe & Tripodi, 1989). For example, in work with a client who needs permanent housing and intervention to address parenting issues, the client's need for housing should take precedence. Fifth, the clinician prioritizes problems for which the requested intervention or service is provided by the agency in which he or she works and establishes linkages to providers capable of meeting the client's request for other services. Sixth, the clinician identifies problems for which he or she is capable of providing intervention (services that are within the boundaries of his or her education, training, licensure, certification, consultation received, supervised experience, and other relevant professional experience) (Reamer, 2004) and refers the client to other providers when the requested service is not within his or her areas of expertise.

- Determine components of the identified problems. For each of the identified problems, the clinical social worker assesses when and how the problem is manifest by exploring six problem components (described below). The way in which the problem is manifest can vary considerably across problems and clients. For example, depression can have many components relating to social behavior, cognitions, biochemistry, and affect (Corcoran & Fischer, 2000a). One client may present his or her symptoms in affective terms and another may do so in cognitive and/or somatic terms. The clinician explores each of the six dimensions below for determining the component or components that are indicative of the way in which the problem is manifest in the case.

    - *Affective.* Self-reported feelings about the problem, including the content (pleasant/unpleasant) and intensity of reported feelings and/or mood states, such as hopelessness, anxiety, hostility, and grief.
    - *Somatic.* Physical manifestations of the problem—factors such as fatigue, headaches, back pain, and sexual dysfunction. The clinician assesses the potential

influence of other physiological processes, for example, nutrition, exercise, hormone levels, and such lifestyle factors as smoking and substance use. When the magnitude of expressed reactions is considerable, the clinician should rule out the possibility that the client's somatizations are due to underling physical or psychological problems by referring the client to medical and/or psychiatric providers who are qualified to make that determination.

— *Behavioral.* Actions the client takes (overeating, withdrawing from others, crying) and does not take (failing to initiate requests on one's behalf or refusing unwanted requests) related to the problem, and situations or times when the problem is not present.

— *Cognitive.* Thoughts, beliefs, and internal dialogue, and the degree to which such cognitive processes are contributing to, exacerbating, or improving problematic situations. Assessment is directed toward exploring the presence of irrational beliefs ("shoulds" about oneself or others, "awfulizing" about things that don't turn out as expected, "perfectionistic standards" about oneself or others, and "externalization," the tendency to attribute responsibility for one's problems to outside persons or events) and rational beliefs (accurate appraisals of a situation) related to the problem and what the client does not say or think to himself or herself in relation to the problem.

— *Contextual.* Linkages of the problem to various situations, places, and events. Exploration attends to the following four contextual elements: (1) Cultural, ethnic, and racial affiliations, and any values associated with these affiliations, that influence the client's perception of the problem and of change; (2) situations or places in which the problem occurs and does not occur; (3) times when the problem occurs and does not occur; and (4) concurrent events that happen at or near the same time as the problem.

— *Relational.* Relationships with others and the extent to which they are involved in the problem. Key factors to consider are how those involved perceive the problem and what they might gain or lose from a change in the problem or the client, and the presence or absence of positive role models in the client's life who can exert a motivating influence on the client.

- Identify problem antecedents. The clinical social worker assesses contributing variables—internal or external events that precede and cue the problem and make it more or less likely to occur. Some antecedents occur immediately before the problem whereas others may have occurred a long time ago but continue to exert their influence (setting events). Like problem behaviors, the sources of antecedents are varied and may be affective, somatic, behavioral, cognitive, contextual, or relational. Key factors to consider in exploring antecedents are: (1) current conditions (covert and overt) that exist before the problem and make it more likely to occur; (2) current conditions (covert and overt) that exist before the problem and make it less likely to occur; and (3) previous conditions or setting events that continue to influence the problem.

- Identify problem consequences. The clinical social worker assesses influencing variables—internal or external events that occur after the problem and either maintain it, strengthen it, or decrease it in some way. Consequences are distinguished from problem outcomes based on their influencing effect. For example, an adolescent's delinquent behavior may result in his or her involvement with the courts or detention facilities (outcomes of the problem); these are distinguished from factors that may be sustaining his or her behavior, for example, positive attention from peers in response to his or her deviant acts. The clinician assesses whether the sources of consequences are affective, somatic, behavioral, cognitive, relational, or contextual.

- Identify secondary gains. The clinician explores whether secondary gains, a special type of consequence, are influencing the problem. The client may have a "vested interest" in maintaining the status quo of the problem due to secondary gains or payoffs the problem produces. Common payoffs include money, attention from significant others, immediate gratification of needs, avoidance of responsibility, security, and control. When there are secondary gains maintaining the problem, the client may resist intervention; the resistance is often a sign that payoffs the problem produces are being threatened.

- Explore previous solutions. The clinician assesses previous actions taken by the client to address the problem and determines whether they were effective in resolving it. Awareness of solutions attempted by the client reduces the potential for the clinician to recommend a strategy that the client has already tried. Moreover, this information is helpful for determining whether the attempted solution created new problems for the client or made his or her existing problem or problems worse.

- Identify coping skills, strengths, and resources.[1] The clinician explores internal and external resources available to the client for addressing the problem. Assessing client coping skills, strengths, and resources is important for three reasons. First, doing so conveys that despite problems the client may be having, he or she has strengths and resources that are available. Second, it recognizes the wholeness of the client by conveying that he or she is more than just his or her problem. Third, it allows the clinician to identify client coping strategies and resources that can be mobilized to address the current problem or problems for work. Key areas of exploration include the following:

  - *Behavioral assets and problem-solving skills,* the ability to engage in self-care, perform activities of daily living, complete age-appropriate tasks, act independently, express one's thoughts and feelings (verbally and nonverbally), and one's motivation to address problems.

  - *Cognitive coping skills,* the capacity for reality-based thinking, a positive perception of self, the ability to rationally appraise a situation, the ability to discriminate between rational and irrational thinking, selective attention and feedback from distraction, capacity for memory, capacity for insight and self-reflection, and the ability to engage in coping or calming "self-talk."

  - *Self-control management skills,* the ability to withstand frustration, assume responsibility for oneself, be self-directed, control problem behavior using self-reinforcing or self-punishing consequences, and the perception of oneself as in control of one's circumstances.

  - *Social cognition and regulation skills,* the capacity for perspective taking, the ability to understand social interactions, a sense of morality, the capacity for means–end thinking, and the ability to relate to others.

  - *Cultural assets and resources,* ethnic/racial/cultural identity, raised consciousness regarding discrimination and oppression, the ability to challenge discrimination and oppression, the use of culture-bound strategies to effectively address problems, and the availability of supportive indigenous helpers.

  - *Interpersonal resources,* supportive family members, friends, extended family members, and school, church, or work groups.

  - *Environmental resources,* access to housing, child support, welfare, health care, day care, educational and/or recreational facilities, employment training, and police protection.

- Explore the client's perception of the problem. For each identified problem, the clinician assesses the client's understanding of the issue. The clinician should explore aspects of the problem that the client stresses and those that he or she ignores. Moreover, the client's perception of the problem is an indicator of his or her "position," or strongly held beliefs and values about the nature of the problem. For example, the client may perceive himself or herself as commanding power over circumstances and events relevant to the problem when they are actually beyond his or her control, or assume the role of victim by attributing the problem to circumstances and events that are beyond his or her control. Exploring the client's perception of the problem is a critical task in assessment. By

---

1. Additional material for this assessment category was adapted from Ashford, LeCroy, & Lortie (1997) and Lee (2001).

conveying his or her interest in understanding the problem as seen by the client, the clinician joins with the client. Joining with the client is essential to the process of establishing a therapeutic relationship.

DEVELOPING A WORKING HYPOTHESIS

The clinical social worker uses information obtained in the aforementioned assessment categories for two different yet interrelated purposes: (1) to develop a "working hypothesis," a tentative statement about each problem and the variables related to it and (2) to identify client coping skills, assets, and resources for addressing the problem. The clinician uses his or her working hypothesis to inform the selection of variables for which data will be gathered during the baseline phase of single-case design. The clinician uses this information to confirm the existence, frequency, severity, or duration of the problem, determine whether it is of sufficient magnitude to warrant intervention, and confirm the role of other intervening variables (that is, variables that may sustain, exacerbate, or diminish the problem). Once the problems are known, the clinician draws upon his or her professional knowledge and training, clinical judgment, and theories and evidence relevant to addressing the problems to develop a treatment plan. The selection of intervention strategies is informed by his or her knowledge of the client's internal and external resources for addressing the problems.

A *hypothesis* is a statement about the relation between two or more variables (Kerlinger, 1985). Well-specified hypotheses describe two or more variables that are measurable and state how they are related. The clinician develops working hypotheses at two important stages of the helping process: (1) initial problem assessment and (2) formulation of the treatment plan. We refer to the former as assessment hypotheses and the latter as intervention hypotheses. The clinician then takes repeated measurements of the relevant variables and uses the resulting information to determine whether there is evidence to support the hypothesized relations.

The variable that is the target of change is referred to as the dependent or outcome variable; the variable or variables that sustain, exacerbate, or diminish the dependent variable are referred to as independent variables. Suppose, for example, that the clinician is working with a client to address his or her problematic drinking behavior. In the process of assessment, he or she learns that the client engages in binge drinking episodes when feeling overwhelmed by work-related stress. The clinician's assessment hypothesis is that the client's sense of being overwhelmed by work-related stress (independent variable) leads to his or her binge-drinking episodes (dependent variable). He or she operationalizes the relevant variables "feelings of being overwhelmed" and "binge-drinking episodes" for measurement and collects repeated measurements of these variables in the baseline phase of single-case design. If the posited relationship between these variables holds (that is, the clinician obtains correlational knowledge of the relationship between "feelings of being overwhelmed" and "binge-drinking episodes"), the clinician uses this information to develop his or her intervention hypothesis. The clinician may determine, based on his or her clinical judgment and theories and evidence from the stress and substance abuse literature, that the client can benefit from stress-reduction training to enhance his or her ability to use positive coping strategies to effectively manage his or her work-related stress. The clinician's intervention hypothesis is that stress-reduction training (independent variable) will lead to the client's increased use of effective stress management techniques (dependent variable). He or she operationalizes the relevant variables "stress-reduction training" and "use of effective stress-management techniques" for measurement and collects repeated measurements of these variables during the intervention phase of single-case design. Because he or she has already obtained correlational knowledge of the relationship between "feelings of being overwhelmed" and "binge drinking episodes," a reduction in the client's self-reported feelings of being overwhelmed should be accompanied by a reduction in binge drinking episodes. The clinician continues to take repeated measurements of the binge drinking episodes to determine the degree of observed change in this variable, information that he or she uses to inform subsequent treatment planning.

The process of generating an assessment hypothesis encompasses three steps. First, the clinician uses information regarding the relevant dimensions of the problem (whether these are affective, somatic, cognitive, behavioral, relational, or contextual) to define it. The reader will recall that well-specified hypotheses define the relevant variables in measurable terms. For satisfying this criterion, a key consideration is whether the variable is one of existence (Blythe & Tripodi, 1989), magnitude, duration, or frequency (Corcoran & Fischer, 2000a), characteristics that correspond to measurement scales. The existence of a variable refers to its presence or absence, for example, migraine headaches that the client does or does not experience. The magnitude of a variable refers to its intensity or degree, for example, feelings of anxiety that vary from mild to moderate to severe. The duration of a variable refers to how long it lasts, for example, the length, in minutes, of a child's temper tantrums. The frequency of a variable refers to how often it occurs, for example, the number of times the client interrupts others while speaking. As part of his or her assessment of the problem variable and of variables related to it, the clinician explores the way in which the client describes the relevant variables. He or she considers such factors as whether it is the presence or absence of a condition, feeling, or event that is of significance to the client, or whether the variable has to reach a certain degree of intensity before it is problematic, or if how long it lasts or how often it occurs are central to the client's concerns.

In the aforementioned example, the clinician and client agree that binge drinking is the problem. However, the clinician needs to move beyond this general description of the problem to one that is tied to its underlying component or components. The clinician's assessment of the problem reveals that it only occurs in response to work-related situations but not under other stressful conditions such as family-related stress. Thus, it comprises both behavioral (it involves an action on the part of the client) and contextual (it is related to stressful work-related situations) elements. The clinician uses this information to guide his or her definition of the problem by considering, for example, the action or actions that indicate manifestation of the problem and the conditions under which it occurs. The behavior is consumption of alcoholic beverages; an important factor to consider is the determination of binge drinking. The agreed-upon definition can be based on definitions provided in the scholarly literature or on what the clinician and client determine to be clinically significant, for example, consumption of four or more alcoholic beverages in one sitting. If the clinician and client determine that **any** occurrence of such episodes is problematic, then the problem is one of existence. On the other hand, if the clinical concern is the number of such episodes that occur over the course of a day, then the problem is one of frequency. Because the client's actions occur in relation to his or her feelings of being overwhelmed by work-related stress, the clinician factors this into his or her and the client's working definition of the problem. Suppose, for example that the agreed-upon definition of binge drinking is as follows: episodes during which the client consumes four or more alcoholic beverages in one sitting in response to work-related stress. This definition satisfies the first criterion of a well-specified hypothesis because the problem variable, binge drinking, has been stated in measurable terms. It is possible based on this definition to determine, for example, when binge drinking occurs and when it does not.

Second, the clinician defines the antecedents, consequences, and secondary gains that are sustaining, exacerbating, or diminishing the problem using his or her knowledge of their respective dimensions (affective, somatic, cognitive, behavioral, relational, or contextual). We will use the preceding example to illustrate the way in which this can be accomplished. Noted previously, the precipitating event that leads to the client's binge drinking is his or her feelings of being overwhelmed by stress (an affective antecedent). The clinician's assessment additionally reveals that the client's behavior is cued by "peer influences" or the presence of a group of his or her work peers who also drink and consider drinking to be a normative response to stress (a relational antecedent). The clinician explores the client's stress-related feelings and determines that they are both unpleasant and intense. The content of these feelings is focused on the client's concerns about meeting prescribed deadlines and completing work-related tasks on time. The clinician explores whether the client's concerns are reality-based to clarify his or her understanding of the problem. He or she learns that they are not; the client excels at his or her job and completes his or her work on time despite excessive worry over doing so. Had this not been the case, the focus of the clinician's assessment would shift to exploration of the client's options for restructuring his or her workload, talking with his or her supervisor regarding his or her performance-related concerns, and so forth.

The clinician determines that there is a threshold beyond which the client's self-reported feelings of being overwhelmed lead to his or her binge drinking. Thus, the problem variable is one of intensity. The clinician is already aware that the content of these feelings is focused on the client's concerns about meeting prescribed deadlines and completing work-related tasks on time. He or she also needs to determine, however, what distinguishes those feelings that are manageable from those that are not. For making this determination, the clinician asks the client to describe his or her feelings when they are at their worst—to the point at which his or her binge drinking is likely to occur. In addition, he or she asks the client to describe these feelings when they are at a minimum and when they are somewhere in between these two extremes. The clinician uses descriptors provided by the client to order his or her feelings of being overwhelmed by work-related stress along a continuum. For example, feelings that range from "mildly distracted, some concern over work-related issues," to "moderate concern, frequent feelings of worry," to "intense apprehension and anxiety over work-related issues." This definition lends itself to measurement because the clinician and client can distinguish feelings that are mildly overwhelming from those that are intensely overwhelming.

In a similar approach, the clinician explores the way in which the client's peer group is contributing to the problem, exploring such factors as what peers say or do to convey that drinking is a normative response to stress, as well as the client's beliefs regarding what peers may gain or lose from a change in his or her behavior. The clinician and client may determine that the presence of the client's peers increases the likelihood that a binge-drinking episode will occur, or alternatively, that the client's episodes are influenced by the frequency with which group members disregard his or her desire to stop drinking, for example, by ordering the client another drink after he or she has refused to have one. For example, the clinician and client may define peer influence as the number of times one or more members of the client's work-related peer group, defined as Bob, Ted, Kathy, and Jane, purchase an alcoholic beverage for the client after he or she has refused to have another drink.

Third, the clinician develops a statement or statements that describe the relationships between the defined variables. To guide the development of hypotheses, the clinician considers the direction of the hypothesized relationship between the variables of interest. The direction can be positive or negative. A positive relationship is one in which an increase in the presence, frequency, severity, or duration of one variable leads to an increase in the presence, frequency, severity, or duration of another variable. A negative or inverse relationship is one in which an increase in the presence, frequency, severity, or duration of one variable leads to a decrease in the presence, frequency, severity, or duration of another variable. In addition to his or her working hypothesis, it is clinically useful for the clinician to develop a statement about the problem and the criteria for determining whether its presence, frequency, severity, or magnitude is of sufficient magnitude to warrant clinical intervention. For example, the clinician and client may determine that a clinically significant drinking pattern is indicated by the presence of one or more binge drinking episodes over a five-day work week. Based on the preceding case example, an illustrative problem statement and the clinician's working hypotheses regarding the case are presented below.

(1) Problem statement: The identified problem is the client's binge drinking. Binge drinking is defined as episodes during which the client consumes four or more alcoholic beverages in one sitting in response to work-related stress. A clinically significant drinking pattern is indicated by the presence of one or more binge-drinking episodes over a five-day work week.

(2) As the client's self-reported feelings of being overwhelmed by work-related stress increase, binge drinking is more likely to occur. The client's feelings of being overwhelmed are defined as feelings that range from "mildly distracted, some concern over work-related issues," to "moderate concern, frequent feelings of worry," to "intense apprehension and anxiety over work-related issues."

(3) As peer influences increase, binge drinking is more likely to occur. Peer influences are defined as the number of times one or more members of the client's work-related peer group, defined as Bob, Ted, Kathy, and Jane purchase an alcoholic beverage for the client after he or she has refused to have another drink.

PREPARING FOR BASELINE DATA COLLECTION

The reader will recall that the clinician's assessment is not complete until he or she obtains data for confirming the existence, frequency, severity, or duration of the identified problem or problems and determines those that are of sufficient magnitude to warrant intervention. He or she additionally gathers data for confirming the posited relationships between variables related to the problem. Thus, his or her task at this stage of the assessment process is to share his or her hypotheses with the client and achieve consensus regarding the relevant variables for which repeated measurements will be taken.

When there is a lack of consensus, the clinician should explore the reasons for the disagreement between his or her and the client's understanding of the relevant problem variables, considering the potential role of two factors: (1) incomplete assessment information and (2) the presence of factors impinging on the problem.

For determining if the first of these two factors is at work, the clinician should explore if there are previously untapped sources of information for further clarification of the problem, for example, documents from such providers as the referring agency (if the client was referred), schools, employers, legal, medical, or psychiatric providers and so forth, and verbal reports from other relevant actors in the case. He or she obtains additional information from one or more of these sources and uses the resulting information to refine the working definition of the problem. To determine if the second factor is at work, the clinical social worker should consider factors previously identified as relevant to maintaining, exacerbating, or diminishing the identified problem, for example, the client's tendency to externalize, or attribute his or her problem to factors that are beyond his or her control, his or her perception of problematic behavior as nonproblematic, the presence of sustaining conditions such as positive attention from a sibling for disobeying parents, and so forth. When such factors are at work, the clinician should select for measurement those variables deemed by the client as relevant to the problem. Doing so serves two important functions in assessment: (1) it empowers the client by allowing the definition of the problem to be determined by him or her, and (2) it provides the clinician and client with additional information for further clarifying the problem.

Suppose that the clinician is working with an adolescent who attributes his or her frequent detentions to being "singled out" by one of his or her teachers at school rather than the result of his or her acting out behavior in the classroom. The clinician and client agree that the client's frequent detentions are the problem. However, there is disagreement regarding the source of the problem. The clinician and client agree to measure three variables: (1) the number of times the teacher disciplines the client; (2) the number of times the teacher disciplines other students in the class; and (3) what the client and other students in the class say or do prior to being disciplined by the teacher. Baseline measurements of these variables can provide the clinician and client with additional information for clarifying the source of the problem. For example, the resulting information may reveal that other students are disciplined for the same actions as the client, information that can be used to help the client see that problematic behaviors result in discipline, regardless of who enacts them.

CULTURAL SENSITIVITY IN ASSESSMENT

Meyer (1993), citing Nurius and Gibson (1990), emphasizes the requirement for clinical social workers to control biases in assessment that derive from cultural, political, ethnic, class, generational, psychological, and gender determinants that can distort our view of the client and his or her unique characteristics and circumstances:

> "[Beliefs, values, theories] generate certain expectations that are used to filter relevant from irrelevant information, and to read or assign meaning held in events and behavior. . . These cognitive building blocks thereby play an enormously influential role. They not only produce selective attention to cues and events consistent with expectations, but also fuel active searches for expected input from the social environment and discount or overlook information or possibilities inconsistent with expectations and proclivities" (Meyer, 1993, p. 52).

Among the clinical social worker's ethical responsibilities to clients as articulated in the NASW *Code of Ethics* is his or her obligation to "seek to understand the nature of social diversity and oppression with respect to race, ethnicity, national origin, color, sex, sexual orientation, age, marital status, political belief, religion, and mental or physical disability" (NASW, 2000). In this and subsequent chapters of this book, we define culturally sensitive practice as practice that is sensitive to the aforementioned factors and to differences among individuals and cultural groups.

Authors (for example, Hepworth et al., 1997; Meyer, 1993) have suggested strategies the clinical social worker can use to minimize biasing influences on the helping process. These include achieving knowledge of the client's culture of origin while maintaining a focus on his or her unique characteristics and circumstances, maintaining ongoing awareness of one's own biases, using objective measures to facilitate cross-cultural assessment, and enacting behaviors that demonstrate one's respect for and desire to understand clients whose culture of origin differs from one's own.

The clinical social worker achieves knowledge of the client's culture of origin by familiarizing himself or herself with scholarly texts (see, for example, McGoldrick, Giordano, & Garcia-Preto, 2005) and journal articles addressing cultural factors related to various aspects of the helping process, attending professional trainings and conferences on cross-cultural assessment and intervention, and through consultation with well-informed and cooperative members of the client's culture of origin (Hepworth et al., 1997). Authors (for example Balgopal, 2000; Cox & Ephross, 1998), have identified factors that are associated with ethnicity and hence, group attitudes, beliefs, and behaviors. We summarize below the relevant factors to explore in assessing the contextual component of problem behaviors. Noted previously, the clinician uses this information to explore the client's cultural, ethnic, and racial affiliations, and any values associated with these affiliations that influence the client's perception of the problem and of change.

- Cultural norms. Cultural norms refer to attitudes, beliefs, and behaviors shared by members of the client's ethnocultural group that that may influence the client's definition of the problem and the means to its resolution. The assessment of cultural values and assumptions requires consideration of such factors as:
  - *Activity* (the importance of goals, the person or persons responsible for decision-making and problem-solving processes)
  - *Definition of social relations* (role definitions, how individuals relate to those who are different, sex role definitions, and the meaning of friendship)
  - *Motivation* (the achievement motivation of the culture and whether cooperation or competition is emphasized)

- *Perception of the world* (predominant worldview and views on human nature, the nature of truth, the definition of time, and the nature of property)
- *Perception of the self and the individual* (how the self is defined, how a person's identity is determined, the importance of intra-ethnic group variations such as differences in generation and degree of heritage consistency, and their influence on an individual's ethnic orientation; the nature of the individual, and the kinds of people who are valued and respected)
- *Time* (whether the orientation is based on the past, present, or future)
- *Human relations* (the value placed on individuality, collateral relationships, or linear relationships)
- *Human activity* (the value placed on doing, being, or becoming);
- *Human nature* (whether individuals are viewed at birth as basically bad, good, neutral, or mixed)
- *Supernatural* (whether the relationship with the supernatural is one of control, subordination, or harmony).

Behaviors viewed as indicators of cultural identification include such factors as:
- *Ethnic foods* (their frequency of consumption and ethnic eating occasions, preparations, and ceremonies)
- *Language* (language(s) spoken at home and taught to children)
- *Religious affiliations* (congregations with the same cultural background, role of institution in life, ethnicity of clergy)
- *Marriage* (within cultural group, sanctions against deviance)
- *Family forms* (relationships, roles, kinship ties)
- *Community* (defined boundaries, interactions, and supports)
- *Education* (schools, patterns, and extra ethnic after-school classes)
- *Social roles* (traditional norms and expectations)
- *Help-seeking behavior* (individuals, groups, and/or institutions through which help is sought and the circumstances under which it is sought; culturally normative solutions to problems).

• Degree of acculturation. The clinician assesses the degree to which the client has been socialized into the majority culture, considering such factors as the number of generations that have passed since the client's emigration from their native land and their degree of bicultural socialization, the extent to which they have internalized the patterns of the dominant culture. The degree of acculturation varies among members of the same family and generation (Hepworth et al., 1997); thus, the clinician should consider the client's degree of bicultural socialization apart from that of his or her family members with similar and different emigration histories. Assessment of the client's degree of bicultural socialization should be geared toward an understanding of resources and supports that result from the client's ties to his or her cultural roots as well as avenues for promoting the client's adaptation to mainstream culture. Considerations in assessing the client's degree of bicultural socialization include the following six factors identified by Hepworth and colleagues (1997, p. 260) citing De Anda (1984):
- Degree of commonality between the two cultures with respect to norms, values, beliefs, perceptions and the like
- Availability of cultural translators, mediators, and models
- Amount and type (positive or negative) of corrective feedback provided by each culture regarding attempts to produce normative behaviors
- Conceptual style and problem-solving approach of the minority individual and their mesh with the prevalent or valued styles of the majority culture
- Degree of bilingualism
- Degree of dissimilarity in physical appearance from the majority culture with respect to factors such as skin color, facial features, and so forth.
• English language fluency. The clinical social worker uses the clinical interview to assess the client's command of English and the degree to which this is influencing the problem or problems for which intervention is sought. The assessment of the client's English-language proficiency includes such fac-

tors as his or her ability to read, write, and speak English; the language the client prefers to speak; that spoken most often in his or her home; and the language the client first learned to speak (Deyo, Diehl, Hazuda, & Stern, 1985). The clinician should proceed at a slower pace when the client has limited English-language proficiency and enlist the support of an interpreter, when available, to facilitate his or her communication with the client in the clinical interview.

• Availability of cultural resources. The clinician assesses cultural or indigenous resources available to assist the client who, due to a variety of factors, may not know what to do or where to turn when help is needed. In addition, assessing the availability of formal helping networks (that is, agencies that assist members of the client's cultural group in similar circumstances, for example, refugee resettlement programs), the clinician determines the availability of indigenous resources for providing services, including advocacy; linkages to social (family, friends, extended family, and social support or self-help groups), institutional (child care, welfare, and health benefits), and educational (language proficiency and job training) supports (Ashford, LeCroy, & Lortie, 1997); and technical assistance (for example, writing letters, completing forms, and establishing eligibility for services) (Hepworth, Rooney, & Larsen, 1997). The availability and quality of identified supports should be part of the clinician's assessment. Moreover, he or she should assess barriers to needed supports and explore avenues for addressing those barriers.

Obtaining knowledge of the client's culture of origin is necessary in cross-cultural practice; however, it is insufficient for ensuring culturally sensitive practice with individuals whose culture of origin differs from that of the clinician. Cultural sensitivity is enhanced when the clinician uses this information to become sensitive to the client's worldview, including his or her definition of the problem and the means to its resolution, distinguishing between attitudes, beliefs, and behaviors that are culturally mediated and those that are a product of individual personality (Hepworth et al., 1997). The behavior of

members of certain cultural groups is strongly influenced by their attitudes toward asking for help and by the types of help needed (Hepworth et al.); thus, the clinical social worker should use knowledge of such attitudes to anticipate behaviors that are seemingly "atypical" and avoid characterizing them as problematic. Equally important is the clinician's awareness of negative experiences that certain racial and ethnic minority groups have had with the dominant culture and of their potential influence on client reactions to assessment interview topics. Failure to consider such influences and respond empathically to the client can be an impediment to the relationship-building process.

The clinical social worker maintains awareness of his or her own biases by engaging in a self-reflective process. The required action is to "think about one's thinking" (Meyer, 1993). The clinical social worker maintains awareness of such factors as his or her own cultural heritage, gender, class, ethnic or racial identity, sexual orientation, disability, language, and age cohort (Hansen, 2002) and "stands back" from his or her personal values to critically assess their potential influence on his or her view of the case. Although the clinician can never achieve complete objectivity, he or she can endeavor to maintain awareness of his or her own characteristic biases and strive to keep them in check. Collegial and supervisory consultation can be invaluable in this endeavor. According to Meyer (1993), such activities require "reminding, trained thinking, and introspective habits to reflect upon and restrain one's characteristic biases" (p. 53).

The clinical social worker can also use standardized assessment inventories, when available, to mitigate stereotypical thinking. Standardized measures place limits on practitioner ambiguity and judgment by providing normative data from members of a cultural group that was previously scored on the measure against which the client's score can be compared. Numerous standardized instruments have been developed for assessing, among culturally diverse populations, such variables as acculturation (Stephenson, 2000), ethnic identity (Melis, Lipson, & Paul, 1992), English-language proficiency (Gonzalez, 1990), and mental health service use (Zane, Hatanka, Park, & Akutsu, 1994). A limitation on the use of standardized instruments is their availability. For assessing culture-bound syndromes commonly encountered in clinical social work practice, standardized measures are few. When such measures are unavailable, the clinician and client can develop self-anchored rating scales and rating scales to measure culture-bound client variables of interest. We discuss procedures for developing these tools in chapter 3. Because such measures assess problem variables in terms defined by the client, their use enhances culturally sensitive assessment and safeguards against potential biases that can result when assessments are based on the clinician's passive observations of the client.

The clinical social worker conveys his or her desire to understand clients whose culture of origin differs from that of his or her own using strategies that engender respect and trust. These include addressing the client in terms preferred by him or her, describing the process of assessment and the rationale for questions to be asked, disclosing one's lack of awareness or understanding of the client's culture and assuming the role of learner, and directly asking questions about the client's past experiences with practitioners whose culture of origin differed from theirs (Hepworth et al., 1997). Practitioner credibility is enhanced when the clinical social worker conceptualizes problems in a manner that is consistent with the client's belief systems, sets expectations for change that are compatible with the client's cultural values, and establishes treatment goals that are consonant with the client's perceptions of desired outcomes (Sue & Zane, 1987). "Gift giving" or enabling the client to experience a direct benefit from the helping relationship is also essential for enhancing worker credibility. According to Sue and Zane, this strategy can reduce the potential for clients engaged in cross-cultural practice to drop out from treatment, demonstrate the achieved credibility of the clinician and the treatment, and counter the clients' potential skepticism regarding western forms of treatment. One important benefit is normalization, defined as, "a process by which clients come to realize that their thoughts, feelings, or experiences are common and that many

individuals encounter similar experiences" (Sue & Zane, p. 42). Other immediate benefits the clinician can provide include hope and faith, skills acquisition, a coping perspective, and goal setting.

The clinician's ability to communicate and establish rapport with the client is also contingent upon his or her awareness of culture-bound interpretations of verbal and nonverbal cues, personal space, use of eye contact, and relationship patterns. Behaviors and relationship patterns can have different meanings for clients socialized in other cultures. Factors to consider in cross-cultural assessment include the following (adapted from Cox & Ephross, 1998):

- Physical use of self (for example, shaking hands, a gesture that has different meanings for clients socialized in other cultures; use of touch, a gesture that can violate taboos if the persons involved are adults of opposite sex, different ages, and/or the touch does not go in the direction of older-to-younger)
- Direct eye contact (for example, looking someone directly in their eyes may be viewed as intrusive, in particular, when the looker is younger than the person who is looked at)
- Clinician avoidance of direct questions about himself or herself, an action that may be perceived by the client as rejection rather than professional discipline
- Use of specific words or topics (for example, characterizing the client as a "parent," a term that can have negative or positive meanings for the client; failure to correctly pronounce the client's name or the name of his or her ethnocultural group)
- Discussion of sexual behavior (for example, asking the client direct questions regarding his or her sexual activities when this may be viewed as highly intrusive or dangerous)
- Sensitivity to topics that are appropriate and inappropriate to discuss at different stages of the relationship, and to timing and pace (allowing the client to raise issues that are of importance to him or her and to discuss them at a pace that is natural for him or her). Agency constraints on the time allotted for clinical interviews may limit the worker's ability to proceed at the client's preferred

pace. When time is limited, the clinical social worker should communicate this to the client to avoid the potential for the client to feel misunderstood or rushed.

- Punctuality (for example, attending to differences in the importance placed on being on time for appointments, a value that may not be shared by members of cultural groups who place a higher degree of importance on the relationship itself).

ETHICAL ISSUES IN ASSESSMENT

Social workers encounter a variety of ethical issues in their practice relating to the client populations they serve, treatment approaches for addressing client problems, practice settings, the design of their program of services, and staffing patterns (Reamer, 2004). It is essential for the clinical social worker to be aware of ethical issues relevant to his or her practice and ensure that he or she employs strategies for protecting clients and minimizing ethics-related risks. The profession's *Code of Ethics* provides guidance on a range of issues relevant to contemporary social work practice. Clinical social workers should familiarize themselves with the specific content areas addressed by the *Code*, and as suggested by Reamer (2004, p.36), pay particular attention to the following concrete ethics-related risks embodied in the code: privacy and confidentiality (section 1.07), informed consent (section 1.03), competence (sections 1.04 and 2.10), access to client records (sections 1.08 and 3.04), conflicts of interest (sections 1.06, 1.09, and 1.10), fraud (4.04), interruption and termination of services (sections 1.15 and 1.16), supervision and consultation (sections 2.05 and 3.01), referral (section 2.06), practitioner impairment (sections 2.09 and 4.05), and evaluation and research (section 5.02). Although these risks pertain to all phases of practice, we summarize below ethics-related risks relevant to the clinician's collection and use of information obtained in assessment, referral of clients to other service providers, and use of practice-monitoring and evaluation techniques, and provide guidelines the clinical social worker can use to minimize these risks. For additional information on ethics-related issues in social work practice and policies, practices,

and procedures for minimizing these risks, the reader is referred to Reamer (1999; 2004).

COLLECTION AND USE OF ASSESSMENT INFORMATION

Ethical standards pertaining to the collection and use of information obtained in assessment are delineated in standards pertaining to the clinician's ethical responsibilities to his or her clients. These are: competence (section 1.04), cultural competence and social diversity (section 1.05), privacy and confidentiality (section 1.07), informed consent (section 1.03) and access to client records (section 1.08).

Competence

Earlier in the chapter, we discussed the clinical social worker's assessment task of identifying and prioritizing issues for work. As part of this process, he or she identifies client problems and concerns for which he or she is able to provide services and those for which he or she lacks the requisite expertise to do so. These interrelated tasks are consonant with clinical social workers' ethical obligation to represent themselves "as competent only within the boundaries of their, education, training, licensure, certification, consultation received, supervised experience, or other relevant professional experience" (NASW, 2000).

This standard applies to services the clinical social worker provides, that is, counseling, case management, or advocacy, and so forth; the problem focus, for example, substance abuse, domestic violence, or depression; and the clinician's use of specific assessment tools or techniques, that is, his or her completion of an intake assessment interview. The clinician gathers information in assessment for determining if the requested service is one that he or she is capable of providing and, if it is, whether he or she possesses substantive expertise for assessing the problem further. In initial discussions with the client, the clinician may determine that he or she is able to meet the client's request for counseling services. However, upon further exploration, the clinician may learn that the client's request for counseling is related to a concern over a potential gambling problem, a substantive area for which the clinician lacks expertise for further exploring this issue. When the clinician is able to provide the requested service and the problem is one for which he or she possesses the requisite substantive expertise, he or she proceeds with assessment, using techniques that he or she is competent to provide. For example, a clinician in a family services agency may construct a genogram as part of an assessment of the family histories of marital partners seeking counseling, or a clinician in a mental health setting may use a screening questionnaire for determining the severity of a client's self-reported feelings of depression.

The use of standardized instruments or the development of tools for measuring client variables of interest during assessment requires special considerations. The clinician should have a rationale for the selection or development of the tools to be used (Knapp, 2006). He or she uses available information on standardized measures for determining their appropriateness for meeting the needs of the individuals being assessed. Scholarly publications and test manuals describing psychometric and other useful data, instructions for completing measures, and scoring protocols are an invaluable aid in this process. In work with clients from diverse ethnocultural populations, the clinician should carefully examine normative data against which the client's scores will be interpreted. Misinterpretations can occur when measures are used with groups for which such data have not been obtained (Knapp, 2006). Moreover, the clinician should consider the language-appropriateness of measures considered for use with clients whose primary language is not English. Generally, tests should be administered in the language the client prefers; the clinician should use tests that have been translated into or constructed in the client's primary language; and the clinician should discuss, in advance, the nature of the instrument and the types of questions that will be asked. When measures are developed for assessing client variables of interest, the clinical social worker should follow established standards for constructing such tools. In chapter 3, we present guidelines the clinician can use when developing measures for practice. In addition, we discuss factors the clinical social worker should

consider when selecting standardized instruments for use with diverse client populations.

For ensuring that he or she is engaged in competent practice, the clinical social worker should provide services in substantive areas or use assessment techniques for which he or she has had appropriate training and supervision. As articulated in the *Code* (NASW, 2000), he or she should endeavor to obtain training in areas that are new to him or her and use them only after sufficient training in theses areas has been received by individuals qualified to provide them. When generally recognized standards do not exist for an emerging area of practice, the clinical social worker should exercise careful judgment and take responsible steps to obtain training, consultation and supervision to ensure the competence of their work and protect clients from harm.

A related competence domain pertains to cultural competence and social diversity. The clinician has an ethical obligation to understand culture and its function in human behavior and society and to recognize the strengths that exist in all cultures (NASW, 2000). For ensuring engagement in culturally sensitive practice, the clinician uses the aforementioned processes of achieving knowledge of the client's culture of origin, maintaining a focus on his or her unique characteristics and circumstances, maintaining ongoing awareness of his or her own biases and their potential influence on the assessment process, using objective measures to facilitate cross-cultural assessment, and enacting behaviors that demonstrate respect for and desire to understand clients whose culture of origin differs from his or her own. The clinical social worker should obtain ongoing education and training to facilitate understanding of clients' cultures and the provision of services that are sensitive to these cultures and to differences among individuals and cultural groups.

Confidentiality

Confidentiality issues pertain to the collection, use, and disclosure of information obtained in the course of the clinician's professional relationship with clients. Confidentiality refers to the clinician's agreement not to disclose information obtained in the course of his or her professional relationship with the client to others. The clinician should establish policies and procedures to protect the confidentiality and privacy of this information, and maintain awareness of the circumstances under which such disclosures may be warranted and the procedures for making them.

The clinical social worker protects the confidentiality of information that is shared by clients using a number of safeguards. He or she collects information that is essential to assessment and constantly distinguishes between private information that is essential and that which is gratuitous; asks participants in couple, family, or group practice to respect the confidentiality of information that is shared in contacts where multiple persons are present and informs the client that he or she cannot guarantee that participants will protect the confidentiality of this information; establishes policies regarding the storage of client records and procedures for limiting others' access to these records; and avoids discussing confidential client information in public places such as hallways, waiting rooms, and elevators (Reamer, 2004).

The clinical social worker is obligated to protect the confidentiality and privacy of client information except for compelling professional reasons (NASW, 2000). There are practice situations in which the client's right to confidentiality is secondary to the clinician's obligation to protect clients from self-harm and from harm to third parties (Reamer, 2004). Disclosures are permissible to prevent serious, foreseeable, and imminent harm to a client or others. In such situations, the clinician should disclose the least amount of information that is required for achieving this goal.

There are also practice situations in which the sharing of confidential information is part of the clinician's coordinated assessment, for example, when he or she consults with colleagues for consultation or supervision, coordinates services with other providers, and interacts with third-party payers, utilization review panels, staff of EAPs, and so forth. In these circumstances, the clinical social worker should have clear policies regarding the types of information that are permissible to disclose, the communication channels through which such disclosures are permissible (for example, by telephone, computer, fax machine, e-mail, and the Internet), and procedures for obtaining the client's informed written consent for the release of confidential information, including any exceptions to these procedures.

There are also practice situations in which the clinician may be required to disclose confidential information, such as to comply with mandatory reporting laws or a court order. When these disclosures are warranted, the disclosure should be limited to the extent possible. The clinical social worker may be asked to disclose confidential information in the context of criminal or court proceedings, for example, malpractice cases, divorce or custody proceedings, paternity cases, and so forth. The clinical social worker is obligated to protect the client's confidentiality in such instances to the extent permitted by law and should follow established guidelines for responding to subpoenas (see, for example, Reamer, 2004).

To ensure the confidentiality and privacy of information obtained during assessment, the clinician should institute a number of safeguards. Early in the assessment process, he or she should explain the importance of confidentiality to the client, convey his or her understanding of relevant laws, ethical regulations, and policies pertaining to confidentiality, describe procedures that he or she will use to protect the clients' confidentiality (for example, with regard to the collection and storage of written and electronic information and the limiting of others' access to these records), and discuss the circumstances under which he or she is obligated to disclose confidential information (Reamer, 2004).

Informed Consent

Informed consent may be required during assessment when the clinician seeks to obtain or share confidential information with others for informing his or her understanding of the case, for purposes of program admission (for example, voluntary admission to a psychiatric inpatient or substance abuse treatment facility) or the receipt of services, and for such activities as using facsimile communication, videotaping or audiotaping the client or others, or permitting observation of services by others (Reamer, 2004). Informed consent refers to the client's agreement to receive services or allow the disclosure of confidential information deemed relevant to assessment and intervention. Key elements that that should be incorporated into consent procedures include the following:

- Coercion and undue influence must not have played a role in the client's decision to consent.
- Clients must be mentally capable of providing consent and able to understand the language and terms used during the consent process.
- Clients must consent to specific procedures or actions, not to broadly worded or blanket consent forms.
- The forms of consent must be valid (although some states require written authorization, most require both written and oral consent). All information is written on the form before the client signs it; no information is added after the client has signed the form.
- Client's written consent is renewed periodically, as needed.
- Clients must have the right to refuse or withdraw consent.
- Client's decisions must be based on adequate information: details of the nature and purpose of a service or disclosure of information; advantages and disadvantages of an intervention; substantial or possible risks to clients, if any; potential effects on clients' families, jobs, social activities, and other important aspects of their lives; alternatives to the proposed intervention or disclosure; and anticipated costs for clients. All of this information must be presented to clients in understandable language and in a manner that encourages them to ask questions. Consent forms also should be dated and include an expiration date. Social workers should be especially sensitive to clients' cultural and ethnic differences related to the meaning of such concepts as "self-determination" and "consent." When necessary, forms should be translated into the client's primary language and competent interpreters obtained. (Reamer, 2004)

Many state statutes and laws authorize clinical social workers to act without the client's consent in certain circumstances. Such instances include emergencies in which the client lacks the capacity to make an informed decision due to an injury or illness, alcohol or drug use, or any other disability, or in situations requiring immediate treatment to preserve the client's life or health or to protect the client or community from harm (Reamer, 2004). The clinical social worker should maintain awareness of the relevant laws governing such disclosures and ensure that the client is made aware of such policies.

When consent is sought, the clinician should explain the reason for which it is being obtained. He or she should review the consent document orally with the client to ensure that he or she fully understands it and respond to questions or concerns articulated by the client. When written consent is sought, the clinician should allow the client to independently review the consent form prior to signing it.

Client Records

The clinical social worker has an ethical responsibility to his or her clients to maintain accurate and up-to-date records, provide clients with access to those records, and protect the confidentiality of others in records that are shared. Key components that should be documented include a complete social history; assessment and treatment plan; informed consent procedures and signed consent forms for release of information and treatment; notes on contacts with third parties such as, insurers, family members, other professionals, consultants, and referrals; the clinician's reasoning regarding decisions relevant to assessment and intervention planning; information summarizing critical incidents such as suicide attempts, child abuse and family crises; instructions, recommendations, and advice provided to the client, including referrals to seek consultation from specialists; a description of all client contacts, including notification of failed or canceled appointments; summaries of previous psychological, psychiatric, or medical evaluations relevant to assessment and intervention; information regarding fees, charges, and payment; reasons for termination and final assessment; and copies of all relevant documents, for example, correspondence, fee arrangements, legal records and any additional documentation required by the practice setting in which the clinician is employed (Reamer, 2004).

In addition to ensuring that his or her records are accurate and up-to-date, the clinician has an ethical responsibility to the social work profession not to participate in activities that are fraudulent or deceptive (NASW, 2000). Such actions include falsifying or intentionally omitting information from case records. Examples include the submission of embellished insurance claim forms or vouchers for clients, signing official documents with the name of one's supervisor or other agency representative, arranging for physicians to sign off on claim forms for treatments that they did not directly provide, documenting services that were not provided or billing third-party payers for such services, exaggerating clinical diagnoses to obtain third-party payment, falsifying statistics on service use, or completing consent forms after clients have signed them (Reamer, 2004).

The clinician should make reasonable efforts to meet the client's request for access to their records. When the clinician is concerned that client access to their records could cause serious misunderstanding or harm, he or she should provide interpretive assistance and consultation regarding information contained in the records (Reamer, 1999). Such requests and the clinician's rationale for withholding some or all of the record should be documented in the client's file. The clinical social worker should also take steps to protect confidential information regarding other parties identified or discussed in such records, for example, by describing the types of information or records available to the client without disclosing specific details contained therein, and communicating to the client that such information is available but cannot be shared.

Client Referral
As part of his or her assessment, the clinical social worker identifies problems or concerns for which he or she is unable to provide services and establishes linkages with other providers who are capable of addressing the client's needs. Referrals may be required when specialized knowledge or expertise is required to fully serve clients, such as when the clinician seeks to ensure that manifest problems are not due to an underlying psychiatric or medical condition. Referrals may also be required when a requested service is beyond the scope of services provided by the clinician or the agency setting in which he or she works, such as a request for conjoint marital therapy by a couple who presents for services at an agency that provides case management services. Referrals may also be necessary when the clinician believes that he or she is not making reasonable progress with clients and additional services are required (NASW, 2000). According to the *Code* (2000), the clinical social worker should take appropriate steps to facilitate an orderly transfer of responsibility and disclose, with the client's consent, all pertinent case information to the new service provider.

According to Reamer (2004), the clinical social worker should follow certain guidelines when making referrals to other professionals. First, he or she should discuss reasons for the referral to ensure that the parties agree that it is in the client's best interests. The clinician should be prepared to respond to client concerns regarding the need for and appropriateness of a referral. Second, several possible sources should be identified and discussed with the client. Doing so provides the client with choices and avoids the potential for the client to perceive that he or she is being directed to a particular provider. Third, the clinician should identify and discuss with the client the nature and extent of case information that will be shared with the new provider, and obtain his or her written consent to release this information. As part of this process, he or she should discuss the potential risks and benefits associated with the disclosure. Fourth, the clinical social worker should follow up with the client after the referral has been made to ensure that contact was established. Although he or she cannot guarantee that the client will engage the new provider, a follow-up contact with the client conveys the clinician's earnest attempt to ensure that the client's needs were met.

Practice Evaluation and Research
Social work's *Code of Ethics* contains a number of guidelines pertaining to clinicians' involvement

in evaluation and research (see section 5.02). For purposes of discussing ethical considerations relevant to this section, we distinguish practice evaluation from research. Practice evaluation refers to the clinician's ongoing assessment, monitoring, and evaluation of his or her work with a case. The clinical social worker has a repertoire of tools available for monitoring and evaluating his or her practice, including direct observation of the client's progress, clinical interviews, questionnaires, and so forth. Single-case design methodology is one approach the clinical social worker can use for carrying out these interrelated activities. Practice research refers to a set of activities in which individuals are engaged as research participants in carefully designed studies undertaken to address a variety of issues that are of interest to the profession. Research activities are governed by such ethical considerations as the protection of research participants from harm, the requirement to obtain informed consent from individuals as a condition of study participation, and prescriptions and proscriptions regarding the collection and use of data obtained from study participants and the evaluation and reporting of research findings. Because we consider single-case design methodology to be an approach to practice monitoring and evaluation, we focus the discussion on the clinician's use of the methodology for meeting his or her ethical obligations relevant to these activities. These include his or her obligations to, "monitor and evaluate policies, the implementation of programs, and practice interventions. . . promote and facilitate evaluation and research to contribute to the development of knowledge. . . and keep current with emerging knowledge relevant to social work and fully use evaluation and research evidence" (NASW, 2000).

Single-case design is one of several methodologies the clinical social worker can use to monitor and evaluate programs and practice interventions. Practice monitoring occurs through his or her selection and operationalization of problems for work and the collection of repeated measurements of the identified variables during baseline, intervention, and follow-up phases of the model. He or she then uses these data for purposes of evaluation, by comparing data across phases of the model and using data from additional sources, such as clinical interviews, to rule out alternate explanations for positive changes associated with the intervention. The methodology can be applied to the evaluation of social work programs and practice interventions. The clinician can evaluate the former using aggregate measures of client variables of interest (for example, by averaging scores across clients enrolled in a program or service) and determine the effectiveness of practice interventions delivered at the level of the individual, couple, family, or group.

The application of single-case design methodology also enables the clinician to contribute to professional knowledge building. Clinical social workers can use information obtained from their application of the methodology to their practice to inform themselves, clients and their families, and the social workers' supervisors. Single-case design methodology facilitates clinical decision making. In each phase of the model, the clinician analyzes repeated measurements of problem variables for informing his or her subsequent work in the case. He or she constructs graphs of these measurements and uses them to keep clients and others appraised of clinical progress relative to agreed-upon treatment goals. The clinical social worker can use this information for engaging in discussions about the case with his or her clinical supervisor. With the client's informed consent and following established guidelines for reporting the results of evaluation research, the clinical social worker can publish the results of his or her work on the case. Similarly, he or she can use this information for teaching or training purposes.

Regardless of whether the clinician uses single-case design methodology for practice monitoring and evaluation, he or she has an obligation to critically examine and keep current with emerging professional knowledge and to fully use evaluation and research in his or her practice. He or she uses relevant theories and evidence to inform his or her assessment approach and the salient characteristics of the case to which he or she attends. Similarly, the selection of interventions for addressing the problems identified through assessment is informed by professional understanding of interventions that are effective in addressing the identified problems. As part of this process, the clinical social worker identifies relevant research for addressing the problem, using books, journals, research and clinical databases, and published practice guidelines (see for example, Howard & Jensen, 1999; Rosen & Proctor, 2003), then critically appraises this evidence in terms of its validity, clinical significance, and usefulness (Thyer, 2004).

Ethical decision making is an ongoing process. The clinical social worker should be familiar with decision-making protocols for systematically addressing ethical dilemmas encountered in practice. According to Reamer (2004, p. 35), one such protocol involves the following seven steps developed from Congress (1998), Joseph (1985), Lowenberg and Dolgoff (1996), and Reamer (1999):

1. Identify the ethical issues, including the social work values and duties that conflict.
2. Identify the individuals, groups, and organizations that are likely to be affected by the ethical decision.
3. Tentatively identify all possible courses of action and the participants involved in each, along with possible benefits and risks of each.
4. Thoroughly examine the reasons in favor of and opposed to each possible course of action, considering relevant ethical theories, principles, and guidelines; codes of ethics and legal principles; social work practice theory and principles; and personal values (including religious, cultural, and ethnic values and political ideology).
5. Consult with colleagues and appropriate experts such as agency staff, supervisors, agency administrators, attorneys, ethics scholars, and ethics committees.
6. Make the decision and document the decision-making process.
7. Monitor, evaluate, and document the decision.

TEACHING SUGGESTIONS

1. Using a hypothetical case example, illustrate the application of the guidelines presented in the chapter for identifying and prioritizing issues for work and collecting information relevant to assessment.
2. With the class, develop a working hypothesis or hypotheses using the identified problem or problems from the preceding example. Have students develop hypotheses for each identified problem.
3. Discuss the importance of achieving consensus with the client regarding the relevant variables for which repeated measurements will be taken in baseline. Ask students to identify potential impediments to the process using examples from their practice, and provide illustrative examples of clinician responses to client issues and concerns.
4. Break the class into three groups. Using an example from their practice, have students in each group select a case that involves practice with an individual, couple, family or group whose culture of origin differs from that of their own. Ask students to develop a case summary for presentation to the class that includes an overview of relevant literature pertaining to the client's culture of origin and practice guidelines for informing their assessment of the case.
5. Using material presented in the chapter, engage the class in a discussion of ethical considerations relevant to the assessment phase of practice. Have students identify issues encountered in their practice and review the steps for systematically addressing the identified dilemmas.

STUDENT EXERCISES

1. Using a case from your practice, identify a target/problem issue that has been the focus of your ongoing assessment of the case. Using material presented in the chapter, assess the degree to which you have obtained sufficient information for defining the identified problem in concrete, measurable terms. Describe additional information that may be needed for achieving this goal.
2. Using a case from your practice that involves work with a client whose culture of origin differs from that of your own, identify characteristic biases that might influence your work with this client. Develop a plan for

maintaining ongoing awareness of these bi-ases that identifies individuals and/or groups in your practice setting (that is, supervisors, colleagues, indigenous paraprofessionals) who can be enlisted to provide consultation and support in your work with this case.

3. Identify an ethical dilemma or dilemmas that have salience for your practice setting, the services you provide, and/or the client population(s) that you serve. Outline the dilemma or dilemmas and research relevant ethical theory, professional literature, stat-utes, regulations, codes of ethics and policies pertaining to the identified issues. Summa-rize the relevant literature. Develop practice guidelines for addressing the identified issues and review these with representatives in your agency who are responsible for handling ethics-related policies and practices. After making any required modifications, use the guidelines as a tool for ensuring that your practice protects clients from harm and min-imizes ethics-related risks that may arise in your practice.

4. Using the published single-case design study selected for purposes of completing Exercise 1 in chapter 1, identify the hypothesis or hy-potheses the study will test.

ASSESSMENT AND PROBLEM FORMULATION

CHAPTER 3

Measurement

Fundamental to single-case design is the measurement of practice problems during baseline, intervention, or follow-up. Through measurement, clinical social workers transform problem indicators into variables that have properties of measurement scales (Blythe & Tripodi, 1989; Corcoran & Fischer, 1987; Hudson & Thyer, 1987). Clinical social workers are well aware of the many important variables pertaining to direct practice. These variables often are tied to treatment goals, for example, reduction of anxiety, increase in positive relationships with children, elimination of child-abusing behavior, compliance with medical regimens to foster positive health, reduction of substance abuse, and increase in attendance at school.

The clinical social worker begins the transformation process of measurement by locating an indicator or indicators of the problem. Suppose the client has a problem with substance abuse. Potential indicators are the number of substances (alcohol or drugs) the client has taken during a fixed time period, identification of drug use in urine analysis, reported use of drugs, and so on. The practitioner then operationally defines the indicators so that anyone following the same procedures will reliably specify each indicator on any one of four measurement scales: (1) nominal, (2) ordinal, (3) interval, or (4) ratio. The operational definition ("recipe") might include the following: The client should indicate his or her weekly severity of drug use on a seven-point scale in which 0 = no drug use, 1 = use of drugs one day a week; 4 = use of drugs four days per week, 7 = use of drugs seven days per week, and so forth. The clinical social worker transforms

the problem of substance abuse into a variable of severity of drug use, which he or she measures on a seven-point ordinal scale. Before intervention, a client may show high severity (7). After intervention, using this same operational definition, the clinical social worker and the client hope to attain the severity of 0 and register it as the measurement for the client.

MEASUREMENT SCALES

Measurement scales, then, are the end products of operational definitions (Table 2). The simplest measurement scale is the nominal scale—the researcher classifies objects into two or more categories that are mutually exclusive and exhaustive. For example, the categories "abused child" and "did not abuse child" are mutually exclusive because assignment of the client to one category precludes assignment to the other. The scale is exhaustive if the practitioner assigns all of the objects (in this case, people) to either of the two categories. Many variables in clinical social work are nominal, particularly variables related to decisions (for example, place in foster care/do not place in foster care); diagnostic classification; characteristics of clients, such as gender, sexual orientation, or religious preference; and presence or absence of specified symptoms. Nominal scales perhaps are qualitative rather than quantitative because the practitioner need not assign numbers to the categories—A and B are just as useful as 1 and 2. However, the practitioner can use nominal scales quantitatively, for example, with the percentage or population of clients classified as schizophrenic in the *Diagnostic and Statistical Manual of Mental Disorders,*

table 2 *Measurement Scales*

Type of Scale	Properties of Scale	Examples of Variables
Nominal	Mutually exclusive categories	Abused child/Did not abuse child
	Exhaustive categories	Status of child: Remove from home; keep in home
Ordinal	Mutually exclusive categories	Degree of self-reported depression
	Exhaustive categories	Degree of comfort in discussing interpersonal conflicts
	Order among categories	
Interval	Mutually exclusive categories	Number of days in attendance at work for the past month
	Exhaustive categories	
	Order among categories	Number of work tasks completed within designated period
	Distance between adjacent categories	
Ratio	Mutually exclusive categories	Number of positive interactions with spouse
	Exhaustive categories	
	Order among categories	Amount of money earned in part-time job
	Distance between adjacent categories	
	A true zero point	

SOURCE: Blythe, B. J., & Tripodi, T. (1989). *Measurement in direct practice* (p. 30). Newbury Park, CA: Sage Publications. Adapted by permission.

Fourth Edition, Text Revision (DSM-IV-TR) (American Psychiatric Association, 2000); the proportion of client statements that are positive, neutral, or negative when discussing his or her spouse; and the proportion of interviews devoted to topics that represent interpersonal conflict.

Ordinal measurement scales contain the properties of nominal scales plus the property of order among categories. A 10-point rating scale to reflect a continuum of depression ranging from 0 = no depression to 10 = the greatest degree of depression possible is an ordinal scale. The numbers 0 through 10 are mutually exclusive and exhaustive, and the numbers between adjacent categories represent increased depression. Hence, a score of 10 reflects a greater degree of depression than 8, and so on. Although the practitioner may use numerals to represent categories in an ordinal scale, he or she should not treat them as having properties of numbers, because, for example, the practitioner does not know whether the degree of depression between 10 and 9 equals the differences between 9 and 8, 8 and 7, and so forth. Ordinal scales are useful in representing clients' perceptions of moods, feelings, and other subjective states, such as their degree of comfort in discussing interpersonal conflicts, their extent of fear in public speaking, their degree of anger toward significant others, their sense of betrayal by a spouse, and their degree of trust.

Interval scales have all the properties of nominal and ordinal scales plus the property of equidistance between adjacent categories. A clinical social worker in a corporate EAP may have the objective of reducing a client's substance abuse, thereby increasing the number of days the client attends work. The social worker may begin counting at an arbitrary date (hence, there is no true zero point as in ratio scales), represented by zero. Every day thereafter is a numerical category, with the difference between 9 and 8 days $(9 - 8 = 1)$ the same as the difference between 8 and 7 days $(8 - 7 = 1)$. The social worker uses interval and ratio scales for counting, for example, the number of work tasks or homework assignments completed to reflect productivity at work and performance at school. The clinical social worker also may use interval scales to represent the amount of time (such as number of days) a client exhibits an absence (or presence) of symptoms.

Ratio scales contain all of the properties of nominal, ordinal, and interval scales; in addition, they contain an absolute zero point. The number of positive interactions a client has with a significant person over designated periods (for example, in one week) or the amount of money a client gains or loses are examples of ratio scales.

The social worker can use all of the scales in single-case designs because he or she can obtain repeated measurements over time. These scales can represent a number of problems and needs involved in clinical practice.

TYPES OF VARIABLES

Blythe and Tripodi (1989) classified client variables into the following four types: (1) client characteristics; (2) moods, feelings, attitudes, beliefs, and values; (3) knowledge, ability, and achievement; and (4) observable behavior. Type 1 variables, which the clinical social worker typically obtains from social histories or intake information, reflect physical and mental health statuses and social characteristics. They refer to the presence or absence of symptoms, medical and psychiatric classifications, and social information. The social worker can use those variables that show change, for example, from the presence of symptoms to their absence, in single-case design. Nominal scales typically represent type 1 variables.

Either nominal or ordinal measurement scales can represent a type 2 variable, for example, a mood such as depression. Whereas a nominal scale would indicate whether depression (as defined by either the social worker or the client) is present or absent in a client, an ordinal scale would represent the degree (or severity) of depression on a specified scale. Practitioners often gear practice interventions toward changing clients' subjective states of moods, attitudes, beliefs, values, and feelings.

In contrast, practitioners gear many interventions toward changing the client's level of knowledge, ability, or achievement. Practitioners typically measure these type 3 variables, which are in the form of interval or ratio scales, as scores on objective tests (that is, the number of questions correctly answered). Whereas type 2 variables refer to subjective states that are neither correct nor incorrect, type 3 variables are objective—the number of correct responses indicates the degree of knowledge, ability, or achievement in selected areas. For example, a medical social worker whose attempts to impart knowledge to clients about breast cancer can measure client gains by referring to or developing an objective knowledge test that would provide a measure of how much the client has learned.

Observations of behavior are type 4 variables. The client, social worker, or significant others directly observe these variables, which typically are measured on interval or ratio scales. Hence, for instance, a spouse may observe the number of times her husband uses physical force to control their children, or she might observe the number of times her husband threatens her daily.

RELATIONSHIP OF VARIABLES TO ASSESSMENT AND EVALUATION

Repeated measurements of a variable at baseline can provide information about the extent of the problem. Moreover, baseline measurements can serve as a benchmark to evaluate how subsequent measurements during the intervention differ from those at baseline.

Information about problem variables can pertain to existence (Blythe & Tripodi, 1989), magnitude, duration, or frequency (Corcoran & Fischer, 2000a). These categories correspond to measurement scales (Table 3). The existence of a problem refers to its presence or absence. Hence, a psychiatric client may or may not report that he or she is experiencing hallucinations; a medical patient may or may not be ambulatory; and a parent may or may not be physically abusive to his or her child.

Problem severity or magnitude is an indicator of the extent of the problem. On a scale of perceived client stress ranging from 0 = no stress to 10 = the highest degree of stress possible, a magnitude of 9 indicates a problem, whereas a score of 1 does not. Furthermore, if the severity of the problem continues at a relatively high degree of stress on repeated measurements during baseline, it indicates a persistently high degree of problem severity, which warrants an intervention to alleviate the stress.

Another indicator of problems is their duration: How long has the problem been occurring? A high degree of anxiety for one day is less problematic than a high degree of anxiety every day for two months, which more likely is associated with difficulties in psychosocial functioning than is high anxiety for one day.

The frequency of problem occurrences within a designated period also indicates the nature of client problems. These frequency counts may be relatively trivial or they may be life threatening, for instance, the number of cigarettes smoked, the number of drugs taken, the number of times a patient follows a prescribed medical regimen, the number of times a couple argues, and the number of perceived conflicts in a relationship.

Practitioners can plot these indicators on graphs over time (subsequent chapters present more

table 3	Indicators of Problems

Indicator	Type of Measurement Scale	Example
Existence of problem	Nominal	Presence of clinical symptoms; absence of clinical symptoms
Magnitude of problem (severity)	Ordinal	A high degree of problem severity on a scale ranging from low severity to high severity
Duration of problem	Interval	The length of time that a problem persists from an arbitrarily designated point in time; for example, the persistence of clinical symptoms for two months
Frequency of problem	Ratio	The number of times the problem occurs within a specified time interval, for example, 20 occurrences within two weeks

detail on graphic analysis). In addition, each indicator provides different information. Suppose a clinical social worker has obtained repeated measurements of depression for a client on five successive days of the week. Figures 6 and 7 are graphs that depict the existence, magnitude, duration, and frequency of depression for the same client. For each graph, the vertical y-axis represents the indicator of depression and the horizontal x-axis represents days of the week (Monday through Friday).

As Figure 6a shows, the client was depressed on Monday, Tuesday, and Wednesday, but not on Thursday or Friday. The figure, however, does not show the magnitude or frequency of occurrences. Figure 6b shows a decreasing magnitude from 8 to 6 to 4 from Monday to Tuesday to Wednesday, respectively, followed by 0s

on Thursday and Friday. Figure 6b shows the perceived daily intensity of depression, whereas Figure 7b indicates the number of depressive occurrences during each day: increases from 4 to 6 on Monday and Tuesday, respectively, and then decreases to 4, 0, and 0 on Wednesday, Thursday, and Friday, respectively. Figure 7a shows a decrease in duration from three of five days to zero per five-day period.

These data are informative during the baseline, intervention, or follow-up phase of single-case design. Comparisons of patterns between intervention and between follow-up and baseline provide information clinical social workers can use to evaluate the extent to which there are or are not changes in indicators of depression. Methods for determining the extent of these changes are discussed in chapters 4, 5, and 6.

figure 6

Graphs of Depression for a Five Day Period: Existence (A) and Magnitude (B)

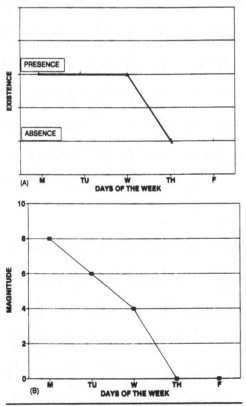

NOTE: M = Monday, TU = Tuesday, W = Wednesday, TH = Thursday, F = Friday.

figure 7

Graphs of Depression for a Five Day Period: Duration (A) and Frequency (B)

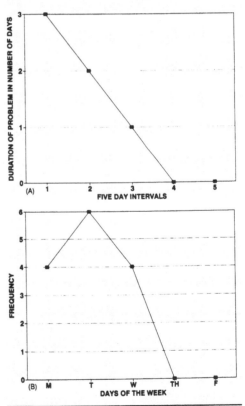

NOTE: M = Monday, T = Tuesday, W = Wednesday, TH = Thursday, F = Friday.

CHARACTERISTICS OF USEFUL VARIABLES

A useful variable is one that practitioners can measure over time and use in each of the three phases of the single-case design model. Practitioners can construct variables to uniquely represent a particular client or groups of clients. For particular clients, however, practitioners can only use the variables specific to those clients. For example, a practitioner may construct a self-anchored rating scale of depression for a male client who, when he feels depressed, shows symptoms of fatigue and apathy. On a self-anchored rating scale of depression, 0 may represent no feelings of apathy and fatigue and 10 the highest degree of depression possible (extremely intense feelings of apathy and fatigue). Another client may consider thoughts of suicide and unexplained tears as symptomatic of depression; that client's ratings of depression are unique to him or her and cannot be compared with other clients. In contrast, the practitioner might obtain "depression" by using an instrument with the intent to have standardized definitions and response systems represent a generalizable variable of depression. For example, the Costello-Comrey Depression Scale (Corcoran & Fischer, 2000b) consists of 14 items, each of which the client rates on a nine-point scale ranging from 1 = absolutely not or never to 9 = absolutely or always. The sum of the responses represents a variable ranging from possible scores of 14 to 126. Examples of items include "I feel that life is worthwhile;" "I feel that there is more disappointment in life than satisfaction;" "I am a happy person;" and "I feel blue and depressed."

Characteristics of useful variables will vary depending on whether the clinical social worker intends the variable to be unique or generalizable across clientele with similar problems. Variables that produce generalizable information (that is, information produced by available standardized instruments) can provide information about a client compared with others; however, the information may not be specifically geared toward the client's unique needs and problems. Therefore, the following discussion of characteristics of useful variables distinguishes the unique from the generalizable. The five characteristics of useful variables are (1) relevance, (2) reliability, (3) validity, (4) feasibility, and (5) nonreactivity.

Relevance

The variable must be relevant to the problem the practitioner is measuring and to the goals the social worker and the client have selected for treatment or intervention. The clinical social worker determines the relevance based on the contents of the variable and on his or her judgment. When the variable is unique to the client, relevance is at a maximum because the definition of the variable is within the client's frame of reference and both the social worker and the client can understand that definition. Hence, the contents of a rating scale of depression are relevant if the practitioner gears them toward the client's perceptions of depression and the goal of ameliorating that depression. In contrast, an instrument that attempts to measure depression and is standardized across a group of clients may or may not be relevant. The instrument is relevant if the items in the instrument are congruent with clinical usage of the term depression and if the items in the Costello-Comrey Depression Scale (Corcoran & Fischer, 2000b) refer to satisfaction with life and generalized feelings of depression, but not to symptoms of depression such as fatigue, difficulty sleeping, or withdrawal from interpersonal relationships. The contents are generally relevant depending on the social worker's conception of depression and depending on the fit of those contents with the particular client in treatment. Or, the contents are generally relevant if they appear to fit or be discrepant with items reflecting the client population's culture, economic status, or race.

Reliability

Reliability refers to the consistency of responses in measurement, given the same information on which to base judgments or responses. Corcoran and Fischer (1987) referred to three approaches for determining the reliability of an instrument: (1) internal consistency, (2) test–retest reliability, and (3) parallel forms. Correlation coefficients that range from zero to 1.00 assess the degree of reliability for these approaches; zero represents no reliability and correlations of .8 or higher indicate an adequate degree of reliability.

Internal consistency refers to the extent to which the responses of many respondents on one-half of an instrument are highly correlated with their responses to the other half. Two related procedures are coefficient alpha and split-half reliability. The practitioner determines coefficient alpha by randomly drawing one-half of the items from an instrument and then correlating the responses with responses from the other half. For example, responses to seven items randomly drawn from the Costello-Comrey Depression Scale (Corcoran & Fischer, 2000b) will correlate highly with responses to the other seven items if there is a high degree of internal consistency reflected in coefficient alpha. This type of reliability refers to the degree to which responses to the instrument are consistent at one point in time. It indicates whether the items in an instrument refer to the same variable, that is, whether the instrument is unidimensional. Split-half reliability is similar, but the social worker obtains the items systematically by comparing responses to odd versus even items. Internal consistency is not relevant when constructing an instrument for one client because there is no variation from other respondents.

Test–retest reliability is the extent to which the same people report similar responses to an instrument over repeated administrations. It reflects stability. For example, suppose the practitioner obtains the responses for a group of clients from an instrument designed to measure perceptions of anxiety. If the same group responds to the same instrument and if there are no changes in their situations at the two time periods, a high degree of correlation between the two sets of responses reflects test–retest reliability. Test–retest reliability is relevant for the selection of instruments for single-case designs because it is based on repeated measurements of variables over time. It is also pertinent for the individual client in that the practitioner may attain it when there is horizontal stability over time. Horizontal stability occurs when a line connecting points on a graph of repeated measurements over time is horizontal or parallel with the line representing 0 on the graph. For example, in Figure 8 self-ratings of depression stabilize at point 6 for the client who has had repeated measurements during baseline.

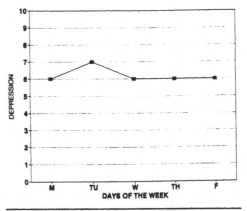

figure 8

Self-Ratings of Depression before Treatment

NOTE: M = Monday, TU = Tuesday, W = Wednesday, TH = Thursday, F = Friday.

Another approach for determining reliability is parallel forms. The practitioner correlates responses to one instrument with responses to another form of the same instrument (that is, the contents of the items are similar but not identical). This approach is relevant to the measurement of reliability across clients but is not germane to the measurement of a single client.

Interobserver reliability (Blythe & Tripodi, 1989) is the extent to which two or more observers independently agree in their observations. The practitioner assesses interobserver reliability by correlation or by percentage agreement, which is calculated as the percentage of the total number of agreements out of the total number of observations. Clinical social workers can use interobserver reliability for single-case designs or for research with many respondents, and with live observations, process recordings, taped recordings, or videotapes. Suppose a clinical social worker records an interview with a client to observe the number of times the client makes negative comments about his or her mother during a 15-minute segment of the tape. The social worker and the client can define "negative comments" and discuss when to record them. The social worker then rates each sentence as positive, negative, or neutral. The social worker and the client rate the sentences separately and then compare them for percentage agreement. For example, they may have identified 20 sentences about the client's mother (Table 4). The social worker calculates percentage agreements as follows:

Percentage agreement = 100 * (number of agreements/total number of possible agreements). The social worker and client agree on their ratings 18 out of 20 times (90 percent agreement). An acceptable degree of interobserver reliability is 70 percent to 80 percent agreement.

Validity

The two main types of validity considered in this book are content validity and empirical validity (Blythe & Tripodi, 1989). Content validity deals with the criteria of relevant contents of a conceptual sampling of representative contents in the measuring instrument. Content validity enables the social worker to judge whether the contents of the measuring instrument are measuring what they are supposed to mea-

sure. The social worker should base an instrument for measuring anxiety for one client on the client's definition of anxiety and his or her perception of whether he or she is anxious with respect to perceived relevant indicators. On the other hand, an instrument for assessing anxiety for many different clients should contain contents that are pertinent to all clients whom the social worker is measuring for anxiety. Zung's Self-Rating Anxiety Scale (Corcoran & Fischer, 2000b, p. 693) contains items that indicate bodily symptoms and perceptions of fear, anxiety, and nervousness, for example, "I feel more nervous and anxious than usual;" "I am bothered by headaches, neck and back pains;" and "I am bothered by dizzy spells."

Conceptual sampling of item representativeness refers to whether the items used to indicate anxiety represent the possible situations in which anxiety occurs and the different types of indicators that are manifest. Zung's measure of anxiety

table 4 *Rating of Negative Comments by Client and Social Worker*

Sentence	Client	Social Worker	Agreement
1	1	1	Yes
2	1	1	Yes
3	1	0	No
4	0	0	Yes
5	0	1	No
6	1	1	Yes
7	1	1	Yes
8	1	1	Yes
9	0	0	Yes
10	1	1	Yes
11	1	1	Yes
12	1	1	Yes
13	1	1	Yes
14	0	0	Yes
15	1	1	Yes
16	1	1	Yes
17	0	0	Yes
18	0	0	Yes
19	0	0	Yes
20	0	0	Yes

NOTE: 0 = positive or neutral; 1 = negative.

represents most physical indicators and does include items referring to generalized feelings of anxiety. However, it does not refer to behaviors such as crying for no apparent reason, nor does it refer to anxiety about specific domains of behavior, such as performance anxiety, anxiety related to anticipated loss of a loved one, or anxiety regarding the failure to exhibit culturally expected behavior. Hence, Zung's measure may not be useful for a client with anxiety related to specific events in his or her family and with cultural expectations that are, for example, based on religious holidays and family interactions.

Empirical validity is based on predictions with which the practitioner can use statistical methods. The practitioner uses empirical validity only when using instruments on the same variable for many clients. If the practitioner predicts the correlation of the score for the variable in question with an external criterion that is logically related, then the variable has empirical validity. There is no single criterion of empirical validity. There are as many criteria as there are predictions. Thus, when there is evidence of an expected prediction, the practitioner might use the term partial validation, or indicate there is evidence of validity. The three basic types of empirical validity are (1) concurrent validity, (2) predictive validity, and (3) construct validity (see Bloom, Fischer, & Orme, 2006; Blythe & Tripodi, 1989; Corcoran & Fischer, 2000a; Rubin & Babbie, 2001, for similar discussions and related concepts of validity).

With concurrent validity, the clinical social worker predicts that the variable measured by a particular instrument is correlated with the same variable measured by another instrument. For example, the practitioner should correlate clients' responses to Zung's measure of anxiety with their responses to another measure of anxiety such as the Clinical Anxiety Scale (Corcoran & Fischer, 1987, pp. 123–124), which contains items such as "I feel tense;" "I have spells of terror or panic;" and "My hands, arms, or legs shake or tremble." Concurrent validity could also be established when a diagnosed group of "anxious patients" score higher on Zung's measure of anxiety than a group diagnosed as nonanxious.

The social worker obtains predictive validity by demonstrating that a correlation exists between the variable measured and the future occurrence of a behavior. For example, a questionnaire on attitudes toward drug use might produce scores related to positive or negative attitudes about drug use. The practitioner might predict that those respondents with positive attitudes (for instance, "Cocaine increases reaction time" and "The use of marijuana gives me a wider perspective of life's events") will be more likely to report substance abuse in the future. If the prediction is borne out, there is evidence of predictive validity of the questionnaire.

Construct validity is a prediction based on theoretical expectations between the variable measured and other variables. For example, the practitioner can predict that individuals who indicate on self-ratings of depression they are depressed also will rate themselves as under stress and anxious. Hence, if the social worker correlates those responses to measures of depression, anxiety, and stress, there is evidence of construct validity.

Feasibility

Feasibility refers to the extent to which it is possible to use an instrument to obtain a measure of the variable in the context of clinical social work practice. The clinical social worker should gear the instrument to the language of the respondents and should ensure that the respondents can complete the instrument in a relatively short period. In addition, the clinician should have access to the information he or she will be using to measure the variable. Moreover, if the practitioner uses questionnaires or other paper-and-pencil formats, he or she should ensure that the respondents understand the contents of the measure and are able to respond appropriately.

Feasibility can be enhanced if the practitioner fully explains measurement procedures to the client. Furthermore, the clinical social worker who wishes to create instruments, such as questionnaires, forms, or self-rating scales, should develop them in consultation with clients, if possible. On the other hand, if using available instruments, the clinical social worker should explain why he or she is using them, what variables he or she is measuring, and how the social worker will use these variables to assess the degree to which the client is progressing in treatment.

Nonreactivity

Nonreactivity—the opposite of reactivity (Corcoran & Fischer, 2000a)—is a condition in which the process of measurement does not influence changes in behavior. The concern about reactivity is that the practitioner would be unable to attribute desirable changes to his or her intervention if the variable measured reacts to the measurement process. For example, if the social worker asked a client to monitor the number of times he or she had suicidal thoughts in a particular period—say one day—the number of times the client recorded suicidal thoughts daily might decrease over time owing to the influence of the measurement process. This state reactivity is not apparent if measurements over time at baseline are consistent, that is, there is test–retest reliability regarding the number of suicidal thoughts over time.

Contrary to Corcoran and Fischer's (2000a) apparent assumption, reactivity is only one possible explanation for change. Another explanation is that of spontaneous recovery, the reduction of a problem through natural occurrences, not as a result of any interventions. To distinguish a real change from reactivity, the practitioner would need to obtain repeated measurements for an extended period at baseline. Changes in reactivity presumably are shortlived, whereas consistency in the diminution of a problem may indicate spontaneous recovery. Hence, the lack of reactivity is related to the attainment of test–retest reliability in the variable the practitioner is measuring.

Cultural Relevance

Cultural relevance refers to the extent to which the measurement process (that is, the selection or development of measures, procedures for their administration and scoring, and the interpretation of scores) is congruent with the cultural characteristics of the individual, couple, family, or group for which information is sought (Padilla, 2001). Authors, including Kinzie et al., 1982; Land & Hudson, 1997; Lee, Jones, Menyama, & Zhang, 2002; and Warnecke et al. 1997, have identified the following factors that can diminish the cultural relevance of measurements:

- Instrument format, including the use of negative items, multiple choice questions, and mark-sense answer sheets. The use of Likert-response formats, for example, assumes understanding of an ordered continuum of responses that may be meaningless among some cultural groups. Some cultural groups are more likely to select extreme scores, provide answers outside of the range of responses, or prefer dichotomous response formats.

- Contents of measures, including the underrepresentation of cultural content, for example, lack of attunement to cultural values, beliefs, and normative behaviors; failure to differentiate concepts in culturally prescribed ways or to capture culture-bound syndromes, such as the Latino *susto* (symptoms of anxiety and depression following a fight involving possible soul loss) or *ataque de nervios* (a type of anxiety-panic condition); inadequate representation of coping mechanisms used in various cultures such as the importance of religion and spirituality to emotional well-being and the use of alternative healing or coping methods such as herbal remedies or the use of indigenous healers; the use of problem definitions that inadequately reflect culturally prescribed definitions of self and loci of emotion including measures that define depression as largely intrapsychic and ignore collaterally defined worldviews and ranges of emotion that differ markedly from individually defined experiences in dominant European American culture; the use of instruments that require English language proficiency with individuals who are not fluent in English; language inequivalence in words and expressions used in translated measures, for example, use of the term "depression" for which there is no semantic equivalent in some cultural groups or use of phrases such as "operating on an equal plane" for which there may not be a concordant cross-cultural counterpart.

- Availability of measures, including the limited number of instruments designed for specific cultural groups, the absence, in available instruments, of normative data on the performance of ethnic and racial groups that differ in important background characteristics such as gender, age, place of birth, degree of acculturation, and language proficiency that are essential for determining if the measured individual or group is similar to the population for which normative data are available.
- Lack of attention to characteristics of the measurement process, including cultural norms such as display rules for emotion that influence what is said and to whom and the types of information deemed appropriate for disclosure, for example, the use of active, self-declarative statements to measure depression in an Asian client who has a more reserved, and private style; client characteristics such as gender, age, primary language spoken, reading ability, immigration status, and degree of acculturation, for example, requesting written information from a client with undocumented citizenship status when such a request may arouse fear and suspicion in the client; client preferences for measurement procedures to be used (for example, face-to-face interviews, self-administered questionnaires, behavioral observations), for example, administering a questionnaire for measuring anxiety to a client who considers it inappropraite to record certain affective states in writing; failure to match clinician and client characteristics on such factors as gender, ethnicity, and primary language spoken, a procedure that has been shown to increase willingness to discuss emotionally sensitive topics and to report socially undesirable behvaiors such as alcohol consumption; and lack of attention to situational factors, such as the location of an interview or questionnaire administration session, a factor associated with the selective reporting of information deemed to be situationally relevant.

When the clinician seeks information that he or she intends to generalize across clients (for example, information provided by available standardized instruments) several strategies can be used to enhance the cultural relevance of measurements. If the client's culture of origin differs from that of the clinician's, the clinician can consult with well-informed members of the client's culture of origin when selecting a measure. The clinician should check normative data for the instrument to ensure that they are based on the scores of a group whose culture of origin is similar to that of the client's and that the client and group are similar on such characteristics as gender, age, degree of acculturation and language proficiency. The contents of the measure and response formats should be reviewed with the client in advance to ensure that items are relevant to the problem as understood by the client and response formats are meaningful to him or her. When the clinician intends to use a language-translated measure, he or she should determine if the measure was translated and back-translated by independent parties, a procedure for ensuring semantic equivalence between items in original and translated instruments (Mason, 2005). Equally important is an appraisal of whether the measure is a language-translated version of an earlier instrument or one that has also been modified for use with the population of interest; the former may fail to adequately capture the measured variable in ways that are culturally meaningful to the client. Measurement procedures, such as the location and frequency of measurements and steps for completing the instrument should be discussed with the client to ensure that they are understood by and acceptable to him or her and that he or she is aware of the types of data the measure will generate and the purposes for which these data will be used. When standardized instruments for measuring a client variable are unavailable or when existing measures fail to capture culture-bound concepts and coping mechanisms, the clinician can develop measures for assessing variables unique to the client for use in addition to or in lieu of available tools. Cultural relevance is at a maximum when items and response formats are developed in collaboration with the client, reflect his or her definition of the problem and the means to its resolution, and characteristics of the measurement process such as the person(s) involved, planned procedures, and the location of measurements are geared to the client's preferences and abilities and are fully understood by and acceptable to him or her.

TYPES OF MEASURES

Measurement tools discussed in this chapter include standardized instruments, self-anchored rating scales, rating scales, systematic observations, and questionnaires. Standardized instruments comprise structured statements or questions and response formats that do not vary over repeated administrations. There are uniform procedures for administering and scoring these tools, and data are typically available on their psychometric properties, including all or most of the following: the purpose and interpretation of the measure, reliability and validity, administration and scoring, and norms for comparing individual scores with the scores of groups who were previously scored on the instrument (Corcoran & Fischer, 2000a). An example of a standardized instrument is the ENRICH Marital Satisfaction Scale (EMS), a 15-item instrument designed to assess marital quality (Fowers & Olson, 1993). Respondents are presented with a series of statements (for example, "My partner and I understand each other perfectly") which they rate using 5-point Likert response options ranging from (1) strongly disagree to (5) strongly agree. The scale provides a score for each marriage partner and a combined couple score. Data are available on the construct and concurrent validity and the internal consistency and test–retest reliability of this tool, which was normed with a national sample of couples who were seeking marital counseling or enrichment (Fowers & Olson, 1993). If the couple the clinician is working with is representative of the couples for which normative data are available, obtained scores can be compared with reported scores to determine the relative degree of marital satisfaction the couple in treatment is experiencing. Standardized instruments are useful when the clinician wishes to generalize a variable across clients. In this case, a clinician can compare pretreatment EMS scores for several couples in their caseload and examine similarities and differences between these scores and normative data for couples who were previously scored on the measure.

Self-anchored rating scales are measures developed by the clinician and client for use by the client to assess the extent of a problem he or she is experiencing. Self-anchored rating scales measure an assessment dimension, for example, the extent to which a client is able to refuse a request to do something that he or she does not want to do, using an ordinal level scale that represents a continuum of responses, and client-defined examples that correspond to scale values. Sample responses on a five-point scale might include 1 = unable to refuse; 2 = say "yes" before considering request; 3 = difficulty refusing; 4 = consider request before responding but say "yes" anyway; and 5 = able to refuse; pause before responding to consider request and refuse if request is not something that I want to do. Self-anchored rating scales are individualized to the client. They are useful for gathering information unique to the client's problems, needs, and resources.

The clinician and client can develop a self-anchored rating scale, for example, when there are no existing measures for assessing a client variable of interest or when available measures fail to capture the variable in a way that is meaningful to the client. The variable depression, for example, has many dimensions relating to social behavior, cognitions, biochemistry, and affect (Corcoran & Fischer, 2000a). A clinician working with a client to address his or her depressive cognitions may find an existing measure for assessing such cognitions; however, upon review of the measure with the client, the clinician may learn that items in the measure are too general and do not reflect cognitions for which the client is seeking intervention to address. Together, the clinician and client can develop a self-anchored rating scale for assessing the relevant cognitions. The resulting tool will be unique to the client and allow the clinician and client to discuss the client's depression in terms defined by the client.

Self-anchored rating scales can also facilititate cross-cultural assessment and intervention. Suppose, for example, the clinician is working with a Native American client to address his or her concern over "spiritual loss," a culture-bound syndrome common in work with this population (Olson, 2003). The development of a self-anchored rating scale in collaboration with the client can communicate the clinician's genuine respect for and desire to understand this problem as understood by the client. Together, the clinician and client can devise a scale that is anchored at one end with client-defined descriptors of experiences or behaviors relevant to spiritual loss and circumstances, events, or coping strategies associated with its absence at the other end. The resulting measure provides a common language for the clinician and client to discuss the client's spiritual loss.

Rating scales are measures that are completed by someone other than the client to assess the severity of a problem that the client is experiencing. Several standardized rating scales are available for this purpose. When standardized measures are unavailable, the clinician and client can develop a rating scale to assess the severity of a variable of interest. Suppose, for example, a clinician is working with an adult male to improve his self-esteem. In discussions with the client, the clinician learns that others (for example, spouse, coworkers) have made him aware that he frequently makes self-deprecating statements. The clinician and client decide to focus on this behavior. They enlist the support of the client's wife to monitor the frequency of his self-deprecating remarks. A rating scale is devised that includes the question, "How often does your spouse make self-deprecating statements?" and includes Likert response options ranging from 1 = rarely, if ever to 5 = very frequently. The wife is instructed to observe her husband's behavior from the time he returns home from work until the end of the day for a one-week interval and to record, by circling the aproporiate response, the frequency of his self-deprecating remarks. The clinician and client can use the resulting information as a benchmark against which to establish a treatment goal of reducing the frequency of the client's self-deprecating remarks. Rating scales provide data that are unique to the client. They are useful when the client is unable to rate himself or herself, when an additional perspective on the problem is needed, or when the clinician wishes to rate an artificially created situation, such as a role play, to evaluate the client's performance on a behvaior of interest (Corcoran & Fischer, 2000a).

Systematic observations encompass the direct observation of a client's behavior and the systematic recording of those observations. Observations can be made by the client, the social worker, or another significant person in the client's life (for example, a relative, friend, or spouse). Behavaiors include those that are overt (observable by others), such as the amount of time a client spends with his or her spouse or children and those that are covert (observable by the client) such as the amount of time spent feeling anxious (Bloom, Fischer, & Orme, 2006). Direct observations of behvaior encompass measures of problem frequency or duration. Thus, a client can self-monitor such variables as the number of times he or she loses his or her temper, the duration of conversations between the client and his or her son during court-supervised visits, or in the case of a child, the number of times that homework assignments are turned in late, or the length of time spent watching television rather than completing homework assignments. Parents and teachers can record observations of a child's behavior, for example, the number of classroom disruptions or the duration of impulsive or inattentive behavior. Clients can self-monitor their own behaviors, for example, the number of times they interrupt while others are talking or the length of time spent worrying about finding a job. Systematic observations of a client's behavior capture the direct expression of the problem the client is experiencing and therefore tend to have a great deal of validity. Moreover, because behaviors can be specifically defined and counted, this form of measurement can add to the precision and reliability of assessments (Corcoran & Fischer, 2000a).

Questionnaires are sets of instructions, questions, and response systems that are used to obtain information from more than one client. The clinician can incorporate standardized instruments, standardized or clinician-developed rating scales, and checklists or other formats for recording systematic observations into a questionnaire for clients to assess, for example, their satisfaction with service delivery. Suppose, for example, that a clinician working in an inpatient psychiatric hospital setting wishes to obtain information from several clients on a measure of psychopathology and on the perceived helpfulness of services that he or she provided to clients during their course of treatment. The clinician devises a questionnaire that inludes the Symptom Questionnaire (SQ; Kellner, 1987), a standardized measure for assessing four major aspects of psychpathology (that is, depression, anxiety, somatization, and anger-hostility) and a rating scale for assessing the perceived helpfulness of art therapy sessions provided by the clinician. Clients complete the questionnaire as part of the discharge planning process. The clinician can use the resulting information to compare the degree of psychopathology observed in clients on each of the four dimensions assessed by the SQ and compare observed scores with normative data for this measure. In addition, the clinician can determine the extent to which clients found the services he or she provided helpful. The clinician can also average questionnaire data from several clients to derive an aggregate measure of a variable or variables of interest. For example, he or she could average ratings on the perceived helpfulness of art therapy sessions for a group of clients to obtain a measure of satisfaction for the group as a whole. Group scores for recently discharged patients could be compared, for example, with similar scores obtained from an art therapy group the clinician ran the preceding month. Questionnaires are useful for collecting information on several variables of interest, when information for making comparisons across clients is sought, or when the clinician wishes to obtain aggregate measures of a client variable at the level of the couple, family, or group.

In the sections that follow, we describe standardized instruments and procedures for developing self-anchored rating scales, rating scales, systematic observations, and questionnaires. Guidelines for selecting useful measures for practice are summarized in Table 5.

STANDARDIZED INSTRUMENTS

Standardized instruments are forms for gathering data and categorizing them into variables that are operationally defined, have acceptable degrees of reliability and validity, and may have norms or average scores for specified populations. Instruments may be paper-and-pencil

tests, questionnaires, interviewing schedules, observation forms, and so forth. To be feasible for use in clinical practice, instruments should be standardized, short, easy to administer and score, and focused on problems encountered in clinical practice. Such instruments, called rapid assessment instruments (RAIs), are readily available in *Measures for Clinical Practice: A Sourcebook* (Corcoran & Fischer, 2000a, 2000b). This reference includes RAIs that are categorized by populations (for example, adults, children, couples, and families) and by problem areas (for example, anxiety, family functioning, marital/couple relationship, self-efficacy, social support, and stress). Whereas RAIs are self-report measures that are completed by the client, standardized rating scales for completion by people other than the client are also available. These can be found in sourcebooks such as *Family Assessment Inventories for Research and Practice* (McCubbin & Thompson, 1987) and in journals on social problem areas such as gerontology, public health, and drug and alcohol addictions.

The clinical social worker should use standardized instruments if they are appropriate to and can facilitate his or her practice. For single-case design methodology incorporated into clinical social work practice, it is preferable that the social worker use RAIs because they do not require much time to administer and because the social worker can use them for repeated measurements.

The clinical social worker should appraise available instruments for their content, reliability, validity, and possible norms. For an illustration of how a clinical social worker could decide whether to use an RAI, refer to Hudson's Index of Self-Esteem (ISE) (Corcoran & Fischer, 1987) in Appendix 2. First, the clinical social worker should look at the ISE items. If the social worker is working with white middle-class adults, the contents of the questionnaire appear to be relevant because of the norms established for this questionnaire (Cocoran & Fischer, 1987). However, it is unclear whether the contents would be useful for African Americans, and they are not recommended for children. The reliability of the instrument is adequate because $\alpha = .93$ (an index of internal consistency) and stability

---

Scale and Description

Acculturation Rating Scale for Mexican Americans-II (ARSMA-II). This updated version of the original ARSMA is a 30-item instrument that yields a total score for measuring an individual's degree of acculturation and subscale scores for measuring the following dimensions of acculturation: (1) Anglo orientation, and (2) Mexican orientation. An optional experimental marginality scale is also available that yields a total score for assessing an individual's difficulty accepting one's own as well as other cultures and subscale scores for measuring the following dimensions of marginality: (1) Anglo marginality, (2) Mexican marginality, and (3) Mexican American marginality. Respondents rate the frequency of occurrence of behaviors described using Likert response options ranging from 1 = not at all to 5 = extremely often or almost always. The measure employs a bilingual format with English- and Spanish-language versions of items on each page. The ARSMA-II was validated with a sample of university students who represented five generation levels of Mexicans, Mexican Americans, and white non-Hispanics varying in socioeconomic status and proportionally representing both genders. Respondents' average level of educational attainments was between one and two years of college. Internal consistency and one-week test–retest reliability coefficients for scales included in the measure ranged from α = .68 to .91, and .72 to .96, respectively. Concurrent validity was examined with a separate sample of individuals (N = 171) who completed original and revised versions of the measure; the observed correlation between total scores on each measure was r = .89. Factor analysis of items in the ARSMA-II subscales identified three factors consistent with language, ethnic identity, and ethnic distance characteristics of acculturation identified in the literature. Scores on the measure discriminated between different generations of Mexicans and Mexican Americans. *Source:* Cuellar, I., Arnold, B., & Maldonado, R. (1995). Acculturation Rating Scale for Mexican Americans-II: A revision of the original ARSMA scale. *Hispanic Journal of Behavioral Sciences, 17,* 275–304.

Cultural Values Conflict Scale (CVCS). This 24-item scale yields a total score for measuring the degree to which South Asian women in the United States experience cultural value conflicts and subscale scores for measuring two dimensions of cultural value conflicts: (1) intimate relations, and (2) sex role expectations. Respondents rate their level of agreement with statements in the measure using five-point Likert response options ranging from 1 = strongly disagree to 5 = strongly agree. The measure was validated with a sample of English-speaking South Asian women (N = 319) aged 20 to 44 years (M = 27.2 years, SD = 5.54) who were primarily single (55 percent), well-educated (56 percent held bachelor's or master's degrees), and professionally employed (46 percent). Seventy percent of the sample was born outside of the United States (59 percent in India; 2 percent in Pakistan, Sri Lanka, and Bangladesh; and 5 percent in other countries); 147 of the respondents were first-generation women and the remaining 172 were second-generation women. Internal consistency reliability coefficients for the measure were α = .84 for the scale, α = .87 for the intimate relations subscale, and α = .85 for the sex role expectations subscale. The two-week test–retest reliability coefficient for the CVCS was r = .81. Factor analysis of scale items identified two factors reflective of cultural value conflict dimensions identified in the literature. Scores on the CVCS correlated with measures of anxiety and cultural adjustment difficulties, and distinguished between first- and second-generation South Asian women. *Source:* Inman, A. G., Ladany, N., Constantine, M. G., & Morano, C. K. (2001). Development and preliminary evaluation of the Cultural Values Conflict Scale for South Asian women. *Journal of Counseling Psychology, 48,* 17–27.

Ethnic, Culture, and Religion/Spirituality Scale (ECR). This 11-item scale yields a total score that measures resiliency among Native Americans and subscale scores for measuring three dimensions of resilience: (1) religious identification and community activities, (2) language, and (3) ethnic/cultural identity. Respondents rate items in the scale using Likert and dichotomous response formats. The measure was validated with a sample of Native American and non-Native American caregivers (N = 147) aged 16 to 60 years (M = 32.5 years) who were primarily female (94 percent) and high school graduates. Native American participants represented eight diverse tribal affiliations. Internal consistency reliability coefficients were α = .83 for the total sample and α = .76 for the Native American subsample. Factor analysis of scale items identified three factors corresponding to dimensions of Native Americans' resiliency identified in the literature. Scores on the ECR correlated with measures of cultural loss, self-esteem, and help from the church; cultural (primarily religious) identity as measured by the ECR correlated with child behavior problems. ECR scores were differentiated from measures of family functioning, child functioning, parenting, and depression. For Native Americans, ECR scores correlated with perceptions of the clan as helpful and were differentiated from measures of helpfulness of the church and self-esteem. *Source:* Long, C. R., & Nelson, K. (1999). Honoring diversity: The reliability, validity, and utility of a scale to measure Native American Resiliency. *Journal of Human Behavior in the Social Environment, 2,* 91–107.

(table continues)

Scale and Description

Multidimensional Inventory of Black Identity (MIBI). This 51-item scale yields a total score for measuring African American racial identity and subscale scores for measuring the following dimensions of African American racial identity: (1) centrality, (2) private regard, (3) assimilationist ideology, (4) humanist ideology, (5) oppressed minority ideology, and (6) nationalist ideology. Respondents rate the extent to which they endorse items in the scale using seven-point Likert response options ranging from 1 = strongly disagree to 7 = strongly agree. The MIBI was validated with a sample of African American college students (N = 474) who were predominantly female (68 percent) with median reported family incomes between $45,000 and $54,999. One hundred eighty-five were enrolled at a predominantly black university, and 289 were enrolled at a predominantly white university. Internal consistency reliability coefficients ranged from α = .60 to α = .79 for subscales in the measure. Factor analysis of scale items identified three factors corresponding to the centrality, regard, and ideology dimensions of African American racial identity described in the literature. MIBI scores correlated with measures of race-relevant activities. *Source:* Sellers, R. M., Rowley, S. A. J., Chavous, T. M., Shelton, J. N., & Smith, M. A. (1997). Multidimensional Inventory of Black Identity: A preliminary investigation of reliability and construct validity. *Journal of Personality & Social Psychology, 73*, 805–815.

Stephenson Multigroup Acculturation Scale (SMAS). This 32-item instrument yields a total score that measures acculturation among five dominant U.S. racial and ethnic groups (that is, African American, Asian American, European American, Hispanic American, and African descent) and subscale scores that measure the following dimensions of acculturation among these groups: (1) dominant society immersion, and (2) ethnic society immersion. Respondents rate the degree to which a series of statements is true for them using Likert response options ranging from false to true. The SMAS was validated with a sample of community residents and students (N = 436) aged 18 to 73 years (M = 29.98 years, SD = 13.3) who were predominantly female (70 percent) and married (62 percent) with a mean of 13 years of education (SD = 1.5). Respondents were 8 percent African American, 8 percent Asian American, 29 percent European American, 19 percent Hispanic American, and 36 percent African descent; 47 percent were first or immigrant generation, 19 percent were second generation, 13 percent were third generation, and 20 percent were fourth generation or more. Internal consistency reliability coefficients were α = .86 for the scale, α = .97 for the ethnic society immersion subscale, and α = .90 for the dominant society immersion subscale. Factor analysis of scale items identified two factors consistent with the theoretical conceptualization of acculturation described in the literature. Ethnic society immersion subscale scores were positively correlated with measures of ethnic orientation and negatively correlated with subscale measures of Anglo orientation. Dominant society immersion subscale scores correlated positively with measures of Anglo orientation. *Source:* Stephenson, M. (2000). Development and validation of the Stephenson Multigroup Acculturation Scale (SMAS). *Psychological Assessment, 12*, 77–88.

or test–retest reliability is .92. An adequate degree of reliability is .80 or higher (Corcoran & Fischer, 1987). Validity also is adequate because the contents of the instrument apparently are related to self-esteem, and the instrument is measuring what it is supposed to measure.

The section description (Corcoran & Fischer, 1987) indicates that the clinical social worker can use ISE scores to identify clinical problems (scores of 30 ± 5, that is, scores ranging from 25 to 35, are indicators of clinical problems). Hence, the social worker can compare a client's score with the norms to determine whether the client has a clinically significant problem.

Despite the availability of a sizable number of standardized instruments for assessing various problems encountered in clinical social work practice, many available tools have been normed with majority group members and therefore may not be suitable for use with clients from diverse cultures of origin. Approaches to addressing the limited availability of measures for specific cultural groups include the adaptation of existing instruments for use with such groups and the development of new measures based on cultural or group standards and language (Mason, 2005).

An example of an adapted instrument is the Chinese Depressive Symptom Scale (CDS; Lin,

Scale and Description

The Homesickness and Contentment Scale (HC). This 20-item scale yields subscale scores for measuring the emotional and psychological adjustment to a new culture among Asian populations. Respondents rate their endorsements of items on their degree of homesickness and contentment in the scale using five-point Likert response options ranging from 1 = very often to 5 = never. The HC was validated with 144 Chinese and 57 Korean undergraduate and graduate students and spouses between 24 and 46 years of age (M = 31 years, SD = 3.8). Internal consistency reliability coefficients were α = .79 for the scale, α = .86 for the homesickness subscale, and α = .93 for the contentment subscale. HC subscale scores were differentiated from measures of demographic variables and the program in which the participant was enrolled. Homesickness subscale scores were correlated with measures of the participants' length of stay in the United States, perception of coming to the United States, and adjustment in society. *Source:* Shin H., & Abell, N. (1999). The Homesickness and Contentment Scale: Developing a culturally sensitive measure of adjustment for Asians. *Research on Social Work Practice, 9,* 45–60.

African American Acculturation Scale (AAAS). This 74-item scale yields a total score for measuring African American acculturation and subscale scores for assessing the following dimensions of acculturation in this population: (1) traditional African American religious beliefs and practices, (2) traditional African American family structure and practices, (3) traditional African American socialization, (4) preparation and consumption of traditional foods, (5) preferences for African American things, (6) interracial attitudes, (7) superstitions, and (8) traditional African American health beliefs and practices. Respondents rate their level of agreement with statements in the measure using seven-point Likert response options ranging from 1 = I totally disagree, this is not true of me to 7 = I totally agree, this is absolutely true of me. The measure was validated with a sample of adults (N = 183) ranging in age from 15 to 72 years (M = 32.81 years) and who were predominantly female (72 percent) and single (47 percent). Of the total sample, 118 participants were African American, 37 were white, 13 were Latino, 10 were Asian American, and 5 were of mixed African American heritage. Alpha coefficients of reliability for the AAAS subscales ranged from α = .71 to α = .90; the split-half reliability coefficient for the measure was r = .93. AAAS scores were significantly higher among African American than non-African American respondents. Scale scores also differed between African American participants who lived in ethnic and racial minority neighborhoods and those who lived in white or integrated neighborhoods. AAAS scores were differentiated from measures of social class and education. *Source:* Landrine, H., & Klonoff, E. A. (1994). The African American Acculturation Scale: Development, reliability, and validity. *Journal of Black Psychology, 20,* 104–127.

1989). This 22-item Chinese-language measure is an adapted version of the Center for Epidemiologic Studies Depression Scale (CES-D) that includes six new items for assessing common idioms of psychiatric complaints (Corcoran & Fischer, 2000b). Respondents rate their endorsements of items in the scale using four-point response options ranging from 0 = never to 3 = always. Scores can range from 0 to 66, with higher scores indicating greater depressive symptomatology (Corcoran & Fischer, 2000b). The CDS was validated with a predominantly married (94 percent) sample of 1,000 adults living in Tianjin, China; the sample was 50 percent female with a mean age of 43.2 years and mean education of approximately seven to nine

years (Corcoran & Fischer, 2000b). The alpha coefficient of reliability for the CDS is .89; CDS scores significantly correlated with measures of quality of life factors and life events, providing evidence of the criterion and predictive validity of the scale, respectively (Corcoran & Fischer, 2000b).

An example of a culture-specific measure is the Vietnamese Depression Scale (VDS; Kinzie et al., 1982). This 15-item Vietnamese-language measure assesses cognitive, affective, and somatic aspects of depression in adult Vietnamese refugees. Respondents indicate the frequency of depressive symptoms using three-point scales. Scores can range from 15 to 45, with higher scores indicating greater depressive symptomatology. The VDS was jointly developed by a psychiatrist who had been trained in cross-cultural psychiatry and had lived in Vietnam, an anthropologist, and four Vietnamese mental health workers. The measure was validated by comparison of the test results of two groups: a psychiatric clinic index group ($N = 21$) who met DSM-III criteria for the diagnosis of depression and a matched community sample of Vietnamese refugees living in the United States ($N = 44$). A cutoff of 13 points on the VDS identified 91 percent of depressed patients and 95 percent of the community control sample (Lin, Ihle, & Tazuma, 1985). The sensitivity of the measure was validated in a primary care study that found 89 percent of patients identified as depressed by the VDS were confirmed to have major depression through psychiatric evaluation (Buchwald et al., 1995). Other examples of culture-specific measures are shown in Table 5.

PROCEDURES FOR DEVELOPING MEASURES

The clinical social worker can use standardized instruments to make comparisons among many clients or for a single client. Often it may be impossible to locate standardized instruments relevant to the clinical social worker's tasks and objectives with a particular client. In that case, the social worker can develop an instrument that is unique to the client. Easily developed instruments include self-anchored rating scales, rating scales, systematic observations, and questionnaires.

Self-Anchored Rating Scales

A self-anchored rating scale is a scale in which the client rates a dimension chosen by the client and his or her social worker. The scale represents a continuum ranging from a very low point to a very high point. There could be as few as three points and as many as 100. However, it is recommended that the range of scalar points be as low as five and as high as nine (Bloom, Fischer, & Orme, 2006). For example, a female client who has difficulty expressing feelings (positive or negative) toward her adult daughter may use a five-point scale in which 1 = I cannot tell my daughter how I feel about anything concerning her; 3 = Half of the time I can tell my daughter how I feel about many things concerning her; and 5 = I can tell my daughter how I feel about anything concerning her. The client also might use a nine-point scale in which 1 = I can never tell my daughter how I feel about her; 5 = Sometimes I can tell my daughter how I feel about her; and 9 = I can always tell my daughter how I feel about her. The client can use either scale to rate the degree to which she can express her feelings about her daughter to her daughter. Bloom and colleagues (pp. 207–216) have recommended the following procedures for constructing self-anchored rating scales:

Prepare the Client. Explain the concept of a continuum representing the lowest and highest points of a problem on which the social worker and the client have agreed. The client should understand the lowest and highest points of the scale. Therefore, the client should define the points with the social worker's assistance. If the social worker and the client follow this procedure, the content validity is high because it is relevant to the client's perception of the problem.

Select the Number of Scale Points. Use an odd number of points, with the middle point representing the halfway point on the scale. Scales with five, seven, or nine points are preferable because clients can effectively discriminate among the various points. Discriminating scale points is much more difficult and ambiguous with scales that have more points.

Use Equal Intervals. The client should regard distances between adjacent numbers, say points 5 and 6 on a nine-point scale, as equal to distances between any other adjacent numbers on the scale, such as between points 1 and 2, 2 and 3, 8 and 9, and so on.

Use One Dimension. Refer to only one attitude, behavior, or mood. Using more than one dimension (for example, intelligent–unintelligent or rigid–flexible) is less accurate than using one, and it leads to ambiguity in interpretation.

Anchor the Scale Points. At a minimum, the clinical social worker should define through concrete examples the extreme ends (for example, points 1 and 9 on a nine-point scale) and the middle value of a scale. The examples should be from the client's point of view, hence the notion of self-anchoring. The clinical social worker should ensure that the client understands how the scale works. Moreover, he or she should refer to the client's specific situation, thinking about how the client might feel if he or she selects any of the scale points.

Decide When, Where, and How Often to Use the Scale. The clinical social worker discusses with the client when to use the scale, where to use it, and how often to use it. When using such an instrument for assessment at baseline, it is important to use standardized procedures. For each measurement, the social worker should follow the same procedures. For example, the client may make a rating once per day at the same time, right after dinner, and at the same place, in the living room. In addition, the practitioner should specify the frequency of measurement, such as once a week for one week. Adhering to the same specific procedures aids in increasing the instrument's reliability.

Use as Repeated Measures. The clinical social worker can use self-anchored rating scales for repeated measurements. If he or she uses these scales at

baseline without introducing an intervention, then he or she can obtain an estimate of reliability. A consistent pattern that is parallel to the horizontal axis would indicate stability or test–retest reliability. For example, Figure 9 shows the relative differences between reliable and unreliable data over time. Figure 9a is relatively stable and is parallel to the horizontal axis, whereas Figure 9b is relatively unstable and is not parallel to the horizontal axis.

Rating Scales

Rating scales are scales used by persons other than the client, typically the clinical social worker or persons important to the client. The rater uses rating scales as measures during baseline, intervention, and follow-up and for assessment, monitoring progress, and evaluation. Just as in a self-anchored rating scale, a rating scale represents a continuum of ordinal measurement ranging from a low to a high degree on a specified dimension. Many standardized instruments comprise items to which a client responds with the same scale; then the scale's values are added to form a variable. These rating scales differ from self-anchored rating scales in that they use the same reference points with the same ostensive meaning for all people responding to each item. An example is the revised Connors' Parent Rating Scale (CPRS-R; Connors, Sitarenios, Parker, & Epstein, 1998) for assessing parental reports of the following

---

figure 9   *Stable (A) and Nonstable (B) Graphic Patterns for a One-Week Interval on a Nine-Point Expression of Feelings Scale*

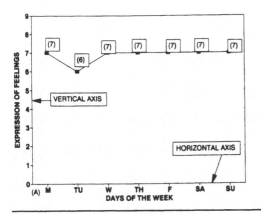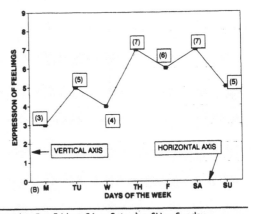

NOTE: M = Monday, TU = Tuesday, W = Wednesday, TH = Thursday, F = Friday, SA = Saturday, SU = Sunday.

ADHD-related childhood behavior problems: cognitive problems, oppositional behavior, hyperactivity-impulsivity, anxiety and shyness, perfectionism, social problems, and psychosomatic behavior. For each area, parents rate their child's behavior using four-point Likert scales ranging from 0 = not at all true to 4 = very much true. The social worker can use a scale for each area or obtain a total score of ADHD-related behavior problems by adding the scores for each item, with a possible range of 0 to 228.

When standardized rating scales for measuring client problems are unavailable, the clinical social worker can devise a rating scale to measure an identified problem over time. Vonk and colleagues (2006) have discussed several of the following principles for constructing rating scales when standardized rating scales are unavailable.

Specify Treatment Objectives. Measures should be relevant to the treatment objectives that the social worker and client have selected as the object of intervention. The social worker should then operationally define the treatment objectives and determine whether change is expected in client attitudes, moods, behaviors, relationships, and so forth. Having specified a mood change—for example, anxiety—the clinical social worker should consider what indicators he or she wants to use. The social worker could define anxiety globally with respect to the client's perception of it or could create various indicators of anxiety, constructing rating scales for each indicator, such as sleep disturbances, loss of appetite, feeling of "butterflies" in the pit of one's stomach, dryness of mouth, and so forth. This process results in the specification of one

or more dimensions to be rated on an ordinal measurement scale.

Determine the Availability of Existing Rating Scales. The social worker should use existing rating scales if available. He or she should consult professional journals, compendia of research instruments, research centers, and so forth.

Determine Who Will Do the Ratings. The person other than the client who does the rating should be one who is in a position to observe the client, is relatively objective, and has the time and the inclination to make ratings. If the clinical social worker is not making the ratings, then he or she should explain the dimensions being rated to the rater, who might be the client's spouse or other significant relative, friend, employer, or teacher. The conditions for rating should be the same from rating to rating, and the social worker should instruct the rater on how often to make ratings. For example, a group worker may make ratings of cooperation for a particular client at the end of each group session.

Construct Stimulus and Response Systems. In rating scales, the stimulus refers to the question, set of instructions, or statements to which the rater is supposed to respond. Stimuli can take the form of narratives that describe sets of behaviors, single sentences, phrases, words, or questions. Response systems represent the formats within which the ratings are made. They are similar to the response systems in closed-ended questions. In the Severity of Depression Scale (Figure 10), severity of depression is the stimulus, and the numbers 1 through 9 are the response categories. The statements under scale steps 1, 3, 5, 7, and 9 are the anchoring illustrations—they promote the reliability of the ratings.

figure 10 *Severity of Depression Scale*

Severity of Depression

1	2	3	4	5	6	7	8	9
+		+		+		+		+
Not Depressed		Slightly Depressed		Moderately Depressed		Strongly Depressed		Severely Depressed

MEASUREMENT

As with closed-ended items, the response categories are mutually exclusive and exhaustive. The following are six possible stimuli and response systems for rating a client's level of anxiety (Vonk et al., 2006, pp. 77–78):

1. **Presence or absence of symptom**
   Appearance of anxiety
   0 = Absent
   1 = Present

2. **Adverbial scales of frequency of symptom**
   How often is the client anxious?
   1 = Very infrequently
   2 = Infrequently
   3 = Frequently
   4 = Very frequently

3. **Adverbial scales of severity of symptom**
   How anxious is the client?
   1 = Not at all anxious
   2 = Slightly anxious
   3 = Moderately anxious
   4 = Strongly anxious
   5 = Severely anxious

4. **Frequency scales by percentage**
   About what percentage of the time is the client anxious?
   0 = 0%
   1 = 1%–10%
   2 = 11%–20%
   3 = 21%–30%
   4 = 31%–40%
   5 = 41%–50%
   6 = 51%–60%
   7 = 61%–70%
   8 = 71%–80%
   9 = 81%–90%
   10 = 91%–100%

5. **Frequency designated by time intervals**
   About how often does the client appear anxious?
   1 = Once a month or less
   2 = Once every two weeks
   3 = Once a week
   4 = Twice a week
   5 = Every other day
   6 = Daily

6. **Likert scale (with or without neutral category)**
   The client appears anxious.
   1 = Strongly agree
   2 = Agree
   3 = Uncertain
   4 = Disagree
   5 = Strongly disagree
   or
   1 = Strongly agree
   2 = Agree
   3 = Disagree
   4 = Strongly disagree

The clinical social worker might construct these suggested formats. He or she should use only one dimension (concept) for each scale and avoid having too few or too many response categories; scales from four to nine categories are preferable. Furthermore, the raters should completely understand the dimension and the response system.

Minimize Bias in the Stimulus and Response Systems. The social worker should avoid bias in instructions to the rater; instructions must be clear and direct. As much as possible, the social worker should avoid value-laden terms in the stimuli and should instruct raters to be honest and objective in their ratings. The social worker should balance the response systems, with no obvious biases favoring any of the response categories.

Write Instructions. The practitioner should provide the rater with clear instructions and examples of how to use the scales. The more specific the instructions (for example, "Circle the response that most clearly reflects your opinion"), the greater the degree of reliability in using the rating scale.

Pretest and Implement the Rating Scales. The social worker should test the rating scales before using them. He or she should look for clarity of instructions, ambiguity in concepts, lack of understanding in their application, and possible biases. The practitioner can use the scales in an actual situation similar to the one for which they are designed or in a role-play situation. After use, the clinical social worker should seek the opinions of the raters on how to make the scales more standardized; if necessary, the social worker should modify the scales. On implementation of the scales, the clinical social worker should ensure that the conditions for rating are as standardized as possible.

Systematic Observations

Clinical social workers are participant observers of the treatment or intervention process. However, it is not recommended that social workers make systematic observations—that is, observations of behaviors during specified time segments that social workers rate on a measurement scale in the form of rating scales, tally sheets, or checklists—so they may measure while simultaneously conducting practice. The reasons are that they may distort the observations and may not adequately implement the intervention. Systematic observations, however, are useful under three conditions: (1) the social worker makes a videotape or audiotape of clinical sessions to later observe behaviors or events that occurred in those sessions; (2) the clinical social worker teaches a significant person in the client's life (such as a relative, friend, or employer) to systematically observe during specified periods; and (3) the clinical social worker teaches the client to self-monitor his or her behavior during specified periods.

Through systematic observations, the clinical social worker might observe the frequency of themes in interviews, the extent to which the client makes eye contact, the degree to which a client's utterances (sentences) about himself or herself or others are positive or negative, the attentiveness of members in group sessions, and so forth. He or she can enlist the support of relevant others, for example, a child's teacher at school, to obtain repeated measurements of such client variables as attendance, time on task, and disruptive classroom behaviors. He or she can also engage the client in observations of his or her own behavior, for example, the number of minutes that he or she arrives late to work for a specified interval. The social worker applies the same principles for developing rating scales when constructing rating scales for systematic observations. For example, a group worker might use a tally sheet—a paper on which ob-

servers indicate how many times an event occurs—to record how many times a particular member leaves the group and returns or the amount of time that a client talks or is silent. Individual participants could use the tally sheet to self-monitor their behavior during the group. On a checklist, the social worker or client indicates whether a behavior occurs. A checklist for observing client interactions with other group members and with the group leader might look like the following:

Gazes at leader	X
Talks to leader	
Listens to leader	X
Gazes at a group member	
Talks to a group member	
Listens to a group member	

The pattern indicates that the client gazed and listened to the leader, but did not engage in any other behaviors.

Systematic observations can be accompanied by the use of counting devices such as stop watches, tape recorders, coins or beads that are moved from one pocket to another, and so forth when it is impractical or inconvenient to record information directly on a checklist or tally sheet. For example, a teacher observing a child's time on task in the classroom might use a wristwatch timer to record the length of time that he or she observes the child working on classroom assignments. He or she may then record this information on a form developed for this purpose at the end of the class period. Similarly, a college student who is concernd about his or her excessive cellular phone use could keep track of the number of minutes he or she spends on the phone using a counter built into this device, and transfer this information to a log at the end of each day. Behavioral byproducts can also be used to quantify behaviors. For example, a diabetic client who wishes to monitor his or her intake of foods and beverages high in sugar such as candy bars and soda could collect wrappers and soda can tabs from the foods and beverages that he or she has had throughout the day and record this information in a log at the end of the day.

Clinical social workers can use systematic observations in single-case design to develop measures within sessions or to have the client or others collect repeated measurements of a behavior between sessions. The social worker should apply several of the following principles adapted from Vonk et al., (2006) when constructing an instrument for systematic observations.

Determine the Object of Observation. The clinical social worker and client or supervisor can independently observe their participation in a session that the social worker has tape-recorded or videotaped. Suppose, for instance, that a clinical social worker wishes to observe aspects of family interaction in a segment of a clinical interview with a father, a mother, and their son. What the social worker wishes to observe is how much time each person speaks and how many utterances each person makes within the first half hour of an hour session. Similarly, a teacher can observe a child's time spent on academic tasks in each of four 40-minute class periods during which the teacher has the opportunity to observe the child's behavior. In the self-observation example above, the client can record the time that he or she arrives at work over the course of a five day workweek.

Specify the Source of the Information. The source of information in the preceding family interaction example is a tape recording. However, video, live observations, or process notes might be other sources. Live observations are the sources of information in the preceding classroom and employment examples. The source the social worker uses should be relevant to what he or she is observing.

Indicate the Unit of Analysis. The unit of analysis is the segment of information from the source being observed. When the source is a recording, the unit is a work unit that could range from single words or sentences to interview segments or the entire interview. In the family interaction example, the unit is a sentence. For example, the social worker could observe the number of

sentences each of the family members uttered within a half-hour interview segment, as well as the amount of time each family member spent talking. In the classroom example, the unit is the duration of the child's on-task performance or the amount of time that he or she spends completing classroom assignments. In the employment example, the unit is tardiness or the amount of time that passes between when the employee is due at work and his or her actual arrival time.

Operationally Define the Variables. The social worker operationally defines variables when he or she observes them on a measurement scale. In the family interaction example, the amount of time each family member spends talking can be operationally defined as the length in minutes per person spent talking in a half-hour interview; the number of utterances each person makes can be operationally defined as the number of sentences spoken by each family member in a half-hour interview. Time on task in the classroom example can be operationally defined as the length in minutes spent completing classroom assignments in each of four classroom periods. In the employment example, tardiness can be operationally defined as the number of minutes late the employee arrives to work each day.

Develop the Recording Plan. Together with the client, the social worker develops forms and procedures for systematically recording observations of the client's behavior. In the family interaction example, the clinician listens to the tape recording after the first 30 minutes of the hour interview and counts the number of sentences spoken and the amount of time each family member spent talking. This information would then be recorded on a form developed for this purpose. The social worker might note that the father speaks most of the time (50 percent), followed by the mother (45 percent), and then the son (5 percent). An objective of treatment may be to increase the talk time for the son; the social worker would discern this objective from repeated measurements at baseline and during intervention. In the classroom example, the teacher uses a wristwatch timer to record the duration of the child's time on task during each of four class periods and documents this information on a form developed for this purpose at the end of each period for a specified interval, for example, one week. The clinician may find that the child's time on task decreases as the day progresses. A goal of intervention may be to increase the child's time on task during later classroom periods. In the employment example, the clinician and client devise a simple form for the client to keep in his or her desk at work. For a one-week interval, the client notes the time that he or she arrives at work each day and records this on the form. The clinician and client can use the resulting information to determine the number of minutes the client was late to work on each day. They may find, for example, that the client was 20 minutes late to work on each of the five days for which observations were made. A goal of intervention may be to gradually decrease the client's tardiness from 20 minutes to zero. Sample recording forms are shown below.

Number of sentences spoken in a half-hour interview:

Father _____
Mother _____
Son _____
Therapist _____
Total _____

Amount of time spent talking in a half-hour interview:

Father _____
Mother _____
Son _____
Therapist _____
Total _____

Length of time on task during each of four class periods for a one-week interval:

| | Time on task (minutes) | | | |
Weekday	Period 1	Period 2	Period 3	Period 4
Monday				
Tuesday				
Wednesday				
Thursday				
Friday				

Number of minutes late to work each day for a one-week interval:

Weekday	Arrival time (hours: minutes)	Difference from expected arrival time (minutes)
Monday		
Tuesday		
Wednesday		
Thursday		
Friday		

A number of factors can influence the success of the recording plan. A recording plan that is too demanding may be difficult for the client or others to follow through (Kopp, 1989). For example, continuous recording (documenting each occurrence of a behavior) is more reliable and provides more information; however, the task can be demanding when applied to behaviors that occur frequently. For frequently occurring behaviors, time sampling (recording during preset intervals) may be preferable. The degree of precision and extent of information sought should be based on clinical objectives and the client's concerns and goals (Kopp). Measurement procedures should be carefully planned to ensure that they are acceptable to the person whose behavior is being observed. Unobtrusive procedures are less likely to be distracting or embarrassing to the client (Bloom et al. 2006). When individuals other than the client will observe the client's behavior, the individuals selected should be those who are in a position to observe the behavior when it occurs, willing participants in the measurement process, and whose involvement is acceptable to the client. Ensuring that observers are unaware of expected changes in the client's behavior is important for minimizing the likelihood that their observations will be distorted based on their expectations about change (Bloom et al., 2006). Ideally, recording procedures should be accessible, portable, and easy for the client or others to use (Bloom et al.).

Train Observers. Review measurement procedures with observers in advance of recording. Ensure that they have a clear understanding of the unit of observation and the procedures for documenting their observations. When possible, have observers conduct a set of observations for a brief interval when the clinician can also be present. In the classroom example, the clinical social worker and teacher could observe the child's behavior for a single class period and compare their observations to ensure that the relevant behaviors are the focus of observation. When behavioral self-monitoring is used, the clinician and client should discuss hypothetical situations in which the behavior is manifest and review the steps for recording the behavior in these situations. Initiating a follow-up contact with observers after the recording plan has been implemented is useful for assessing progress and identifying problems they may be having with it (Kopp, 1989).

Test for Reliability. Because the social worker will use the measures to detect changes over time, the relevant type of reliability is test–retest reliability, which is consistency in observations over time. The clinical social worker can test reliability by listening to the tape recording and by classifying a sample of sentences—say 20 with respect to who (that is, father, mother, or son) is uttering them. The social worker can repeat the same task one week later and then classify the 20 sentences as shown in Table 6. A comparison of time 1 and time 2 reveals agreement on 19 out of 20 sentences. The social worker would then calculate percentage agreement as follows: Percentage agreement = $100 \times (19/20)$. The result is 95 percent. This is an acceptable degree of reliability.

In the classroom and employment examples, test–retest reliability is attained when there is horizontal stability in measures of time on task and tardiness at baseline. In the classroom example, the clinician could also determine interobserver reliability if more than one observer, for example, the teacher and a classroom aide, was enlisted to conduct observations using the procedures described earlier in the chapter. The reliability of observations would be considered acceptable if there was agreement between 70

| table 6 | *Test–Retest Reliability Information for Classifying Speakers of Sentences as Father, Mother, or Son* |

Sentence	Time 1	Time 2
1	F	F
2	M	M
3	F	F
4	M	M
5	F	F
6	M	M
7	S	S
8	F	F
9	F	F
10	F	F
11	M	M
12	F	M
13	M	M
14	F	F
15	M	M
16	F	F
17	M	M
18	F	F
19	M	M
20	M	M

NOTE: F = father; M = mother; S = son.

percent or more of teacher and aide assessments of the child's time on task.

Gather and Analyze the Information. The last step in the systematic observation process is to gather and analyze the data. The social worker could show on a bar graph (Figure 11) the amount of time each person spends talking. The figure indicates that the son talked more in interviews 3, 4, and 5 than in interviews 1 and 2. The social worker can also plot on a line graph the number of sentences spoken (Figure 12). Systematic observations of student and employee behaviors are shown in Tables 7 and 8, respectively. A line graph depicting the student's time on task for

each of four class periods over a one-week interval is shown in Figure 13. The extent of the employee's tardiness for a five-day workweek is plotted in Figure 14.

Questionnaires

Questionnaires—sets of instructions, questions, and response systems that contain open-ended or forced-choice responses—are useful when the clinical social worker wishes to obtain information from more than one client. The social worker can obtain data from groups of clients at intake, from a caseload, or from clinical practice with a group. In single-case design, he or she can create measures for group practice by averaging information for all of the group members.

The social worker should adhere to the following principles when constructing questionnaires for group practice measures (the principles have been adapted from Vonk et al., 2006).

---

figure 11

Time Father, Mother, and Son Talk in Therapeutic Interviews

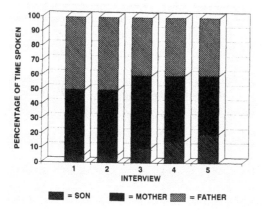

---

figure 12

Number of Sentences Spoken by Son during Five Interviews

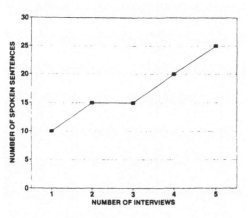

---

table 7   *Student Time on Task During Each of Four Class Periods for a One-Week Interval*

	Time on task (minutes) per period			
Weekday	Period 1	Period 2	Period 3	Period 4
Monday	15	15	10	8
Tuesday	14	15	9	9
Wednesday	15	14	9	8
Thursday	14	15	9	9
Friday	15	14	8	9

---

table 8   *Employee Tardiness over a One-Week Interval*

Weekday	Arrival time (hours: minutes)	Difference from expected arrival time (minutes)
Monday	9:20	20
Tuesday	9:18	18
Wednesday	9:19	19
Thursday	9:21	21
Friday	9:20	20

MEASUREMENT

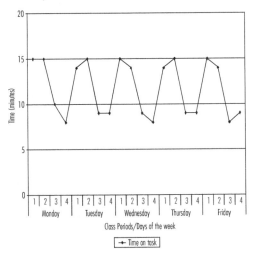

figure 13

Student Time on Task During Each of Four Class Periods for a One-Week Interval

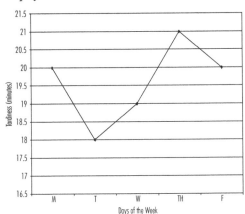

figure 14

Employee Tardiness over a One-Week Interval

Specify the Purpose. The purpose is to obtain information from clients who are members of a group. For example, a clinical social worker may construct a questionnaire to gather information from five clients about their satisfaction with the discussion of their problems in a group devoted to problem solving.

Decide on the Information Desired. The social worker should know what type of information he or she needs to develop measures. For group practice, at a minimum, the social worker needs identifying information: name of the client, date, and the session number for the group. Other infor-

mation he or she obtains should pertain to the purpose. For example, the social worker might obtain data about a problem a client wishes to discuss, the amount of time spent on the problem, and the client's satisfaction with the group process in discussing the problem.

Decide on the Format. The format of the questionnaire includes a description of the purpose of the questionnaire and how the social worker will use it, directions for answering the questionnaire, and the questions or stimuli and the response system. It is preferable to use mostly forced-choice questions and only a few open-ended questions so that the social worker can tabulate responses more easily. Vonk and associates (2006) provide several examples of response systems for the same question about a homemaker:

- An open-ended question might be as follows: In what ways would a homemaker be most useful to your family? _____
- Closed questions might be as follows:
  (1) Would a homemaker be helpful to you in dealing with your current family problems? Yes _____ No _____
  (2) Indicate how much you agree or disagree with the following statement: A homemaker would be helpful to me in dealing with my current family problems (Check one):
  Strongly agree _____
  Agree _____
  Disagree _____
  Strongly disagree _____
- Frequency of response scales could have:
  (1) adverb modifiers: If a homemaker were available, how frequently would you need that person's services? (Check one)
  Frequently _____
  Occasionally _____
  Never _____
  (2) numerical modifiers: If a homemaker were available to you, on how many days of the week would you need that person's services? (Check one):
  Seven _____
  Six _____
  Five _____
  Three or Four _____
  One or Two _____
  None _____

(3) percentages: If a homemaker were available to you, what percentage of your family problems would be solved? (Check one):

0–24% _____
25–49% _____
50–74% _____
75–100% _____

- Comparative response scales might be: Compared with other services you currently need, how important are homemaker services? (Check one):

Very important _____
Somewhat important _____
Unimportant _____

- An identification response question could be stated: Below is a list of ways in which a homemaker could be helpful to you. Please check those areas in which you could most use that person's help. (Check as many as apply):

Help with housecleaning _____
Help with budgeting _____
Help with child management _____
Help with prepared meals _____

The clinical social worker should only use one or two response systems. Note that the response alternatives should be clear and mutually exclusive (that is, they should not overlap). The format for the questionnaire on group practice might be open-ended responses and a closed (multiple choice) response system such as follows:

Strongly agree _____
Agree _____
Disagree _____
Strongly disagree _____

Construct the Questionnaire. The questions and responses should be unbiased and clear, and each question should contain only one thought. The questionnaire should be geared to the vocabulary of the client, and it should be understandable and easy to complete in a relatively short period. For example, a questionnaire for group practice might look like the following:

The purpose of this questionnaire is to provide information about the extent to which the group discusses your problems and your satisfaction with the group process. The group leader will use the information only to provide feedback to you and the other group members. Please respond to each of the following questions.

1. Including today's session, how many group meetings have you attended? _____
2. (a) Describe the problem you wanted to discuss today. _____
_____
_____

(b) How much time was spent on your problem in the group session (approximately, in minutes)? _____

(c) Indicate the extent to which you were satisfied or dissatisfied with the following statements by checking that response that best describes your opinion:

My problem was thoroughly discussed.
Strongly agree _____
Agree _____
Disagree _____
Strongly disagree _____

I received good ideas from the group leader.
Strongly agree _____
Agree _____
Disagree _____
Strongly disagree _____

The members of the group gave me useful information.
Strongly agree _____
Agree _____
Disagree _____
Strongly disagree _____

I was satisfied with the group process today.
Strongly agree _____
Agree _____
Disagree _____
Strongly disagree _____

3. Please fill in your name and the date.
Name _____
Date _____

After you have completed this questionnaire, give it to the group leader. Thank you.

Pretest the Questionnaire. After constructing the questionnaire, the clinical social worker should pretest it with group members to see whether they understand the instructions and whether the task of completing the questionnaire is reasonable. If necessary, the social worker should modify the questionnaire to facilitate client responses.

Administer the Questionnaire and Tabulate the Results. The social worker should administer the questionnaire in the same way for each group session. For example, he or she could give it at the end of the group session; the group would return the completed questionnaire to the social worker. At the beginning of the next session, the social worker would present responses from group members in terms of satisfaction. For example, the results of the first session might be as follows:

• Two of five members agreed or strongly agreed that the group thoroughly discussed their problem.
• Four of five agreed or strongly agreed that they received good ideas from the group leader.
• One of five agreed or strongly agreed that the members of the group gave them useful information.
• Four of five agreed or strongly agreed that they were satisfied with the group process.

Guidelines for selecting useful measures for practice are summarized in Table 9. For examples of instruments included in the book by Corcoran and Fischer (1987), refer to Appendixes 2, 3, 8, and 12. Clinical social workers who work in substance abuse programs, EAPs, child and family agencies, and psychiatric and medical social work settings can use these instruments. All of them form variables that social workers can use in single-case designs.

TEACHING SUGGESTIONS

1. Distribute a rapid assessment inventory and rating scale to the class. Describe the steps for completing these measures. For each, review the measurement scales of variables assessed by the measure and the relevance, reliability, validity, feasibility, nonreactivity, cultural relevance, and utility of the instrument for use in clinical practice. Illustrate the ways in which these measures can be presented to clients in clinical practice.

2. Demonstrate the development of a self-anchored rating scale for assessing a culture-specific client variable.
3. Compare and contrast two measures for assessing the same problem—one that was culturally adapted for use with a specific group and one that was developed for measuring the variable in this population. Discuss the strengths and limitations of each measure for use in cross-cultural social work practice.
4. Break the class into three groups. Using examples from their practice, ask students in each group to identify a client variable relevant to their practice and develop one of the following measures for assessing this variable: (1) a self-anchored rating scale, (2) a rating scale, or (3) a recording plan for the client, social worker, or relevant other to systematically observe the variable. Have each group of students present the measure to the class and describe the steps taken to develop it.
5. Demonstrate the development of a questionnaire for measuring a set of variables that are of interest to agency administrators for program planning and evaluation purposes. Illustrate the ways in which this measure can be used for making comparisons across individual clients served by the agency and generating aggregate-level measures of the variables assessed.

STUDENT EXERCISES

1. Drawing from your practice, identify a variable relevant to work with one of your cases. Operationally define the variable using a nominal, ordinal, interval, and ratio scale. Describe procedures you might use to measure the variable based on each of the definitions you have provided.
2. Using the published single-case design study selected for purposes of completing Exercise 1 in chapter 1, identify the dependent variables targeted by the research. Provide conceptual and operational definitions of each variable. How did the authors measure these variables? Assess strengths and limitations of the measurement plan described drawing from concepts presented in the chapter and in Appendix 1.

table 9 *Guidelines for Selecting Useful Measures for Practice*

				Criteria			
Type of Measure	Relevance	Reliability	Validity	Feasibility	Nonreactivity	Cultural Relevance	Utility
Standardized rapid assessment instruments (RAIs) and rating scales	High if items are congruent with the clinical definition of the variable studied	Adequate when reported internal consistency, test-retest, and parallel forms reliability coefficients are .8 or higher	Content validity is adequate when the contents of the measure are pertinent to all clients for whom the clinician is measuring the variable; empirical validity is attained when the clinician observes significant correlations between scores on the measure and scores from a similar measure of the variable (concurrent), scores on a measure of the future occurrence of a behavior the variable has been shown to predict (predictive), and scores on measures of variables that are theoretically related to the behavior (construct)	High with instruments that can be completed in a relatively short period of time, use language that is easily understood by the client, and when the purpose of and procedures for completing the measure are explained to the client	Attained when there is horizontal stability in repeated measurements of the variable over time	High when selected in cooperation with well-informed members of the client's culture of origin; normative data are based on the scores of a group that shares the client's culture of origin and the client and group are similar on such characteristics as degree of acculturation, gender, age, and language proficiency; the contents of the measure are relevant to the client and response formats are meaningful to and understood by him or her; adapted measures have been modified for the group in question and items have been translated and back-translated to ensure their semantic equivalence; the location	Allows for comparisons between data provided by the client and norms derived from the group that was previously scored on the measure (RAIs and rating scales); allows the clinician to collect information when the client is unable to rate himself or herself, when an additional perspective on the problem is needed, or to rate an artificially created situation, such as a role play, that the clinician sets up to evaluate client progress on a selected behavior (rating scale)

| Self-anchored rating scales and rating scales (clinician developed) | High when geared toward the client's perceptions of the problem | Test–retest reliability is attained when there is evidence of horizontal stability in repeated measurements of the variable over time | Content validity is adequate when the measure is based on the client's definition of the problem and indicators are relevant to the client's perception of problem severity | High when measures are brief; geared to the language of the client (or rater in the case of a rating scale); developed in consultation with the client; and measurement procedures are explained in advance of recording | Attained when there is horizontal stability in repeated measurements of the variable over time | High when developed in collaboration with the client (or rater, in the case of a rating scale); items and response formats are understood by and acceptable to the client; and characteristics of the measurement process are geared to client preferences and abilities and are fully understood by and acceptable to him or her | and frequency of measurements and steps for completing the measure are understood by and acceptable to the client; and the client understands the types of data the measure will generate and the purposes for which these data will be used | Provides information unique to the client's problems, needs, and resources (self-anchored rating scales and rating scales); allows the clinician to collect information when the client is unable to rate himself or herself, when an additional perspective on the problem is needed, or to rate an artificially created situation, such as a role play, that the clinician sets up to evaluate client progress on a selected behavior (rating scale). |

(table continues)

table 9 *Guidelines for Selecting Useful Measures for Practice (continued)*

				Criteria			
Type of Measure	Relevance	Reliability	Validity	Feasibility	Nonreactivity	Cultural Relevance	Utility
Systematic observations	High when behavioral targets are relevant to the problem the clinician is measuring and to the goals the client and social worker have selected for intervention	Test-retest reliability is high when there is at least 80% agreement between clinician observations of the behavior at two time points; interobserver reliability is acceptable when there is 70% to 80% agreement between the observations of two independent observers; the reliability of observations is enhanced when observers are unaware of the expected change in the client's behavior	High when observed behaviors are direct manifestations of the client's problem	High when observation and recording procedures are not overly demanding; the degree of precision and extent of information sought are based on clinical objectives and the client's concerns and goals; measurement procedures are acceptable to the person whose behavior is being observed, unobtrusive, accessible, portable, and easy to use; and observers are persons in a position to observe the behavior when it occurs, willing participants in the measurement process, and whose involvement is acceptable to the client	Attained when there is horizontal stability in repeated measurements of the variable over time	High when behavioral targets are consistent with the client's definition of the problem; observation and recording procedures are understood by and acceptable to him or her; and when characteristics of the measurement process are geared to client preferences and abilities and are fully understood by and acceptable to the client	Provides information on variables unique to the client or generalizable across clients (provided the same behavioral target is measured across clientele); and enables capture of the direct expression of a problem the client is experiencing
Questionnaires	High when items and/or scales in the measure are geared toward problems encountered in practice	Same as for standardized instruments, rating scales, and systematic observations described above, depending on the type(s) of measures included in the questionnaire					Allows for comparisons between clients and can provide aggregate measures of a client variable for a couple, family, or group

CHAPTER 4

Phase 1: Baseline

DEFINITION OF BASELINE

The first phase of single-case design is constructing the baseline. In this phase, the clinical social worker takes repeated measurements of variables related to treatment objectives typically at equally spaced intervals over time. The social worker then interconnects and displays the repeated measurements on a graph; the resulting pattern is the baseline, which the social worker uses to make inferences pertinent to assessment and evaluation. Measurements can reflect magnitude (or severity), frequency, duration, or existence of a problem. Baselines can consist of as few as three measurements or can contain as many measurements as necessary to achieve horizontal stability, that is, a line that is parallel to the x-axis on a graph (Barlow & Hersen, 1984). This chapter discusses the basic principles clinical social workers can use to construct baselines and graphs that depict baselines.

Figure 15 provides six examples of baseline graphs—three each for each partner in a married couple seeking counseling. After the first exploratory session, the clinical social worker asked Jack and Jill, the married couple, to each complete three instruments—the Index of Marital Satisfaction (Corcoran & Fischer, 2000a, pp. 119–120); the Index of Self-Esteem (ISE) (Appendix 2); and the Self-Rating Anxiety Scale (SAS) (Corcoran & Fischer, 2000b, pp. 693–694)—every day for one week. The social worker scored each instrument and plotted graphs that reflected the magnitude of the problem.

The social worker observed that both Jack and Jill are dissatisfied with their marriage; both their scores are higher than the critical score of 30 for all of their measurements, which indicates a clinical problem (Figure 15a). Moreover, their graphic patterns are relatively horizontal, that is, parallel to the x-axis, indicating a persistent problem for the seven days of measurements. However, Jack has relatively low self-esteem compared with Jill, who has a high degree of self-esteem (Figure 15b). Yet, Jack does not show he is anxious, whereas Jill's anxiety has been increasing so that it is becoming a clinical problem (Figure 15c). These graphic patterns provide information the clinical social worker can use to probe further in his or her assessment of the clinical situation, formulation of treatment goals, and the evaluation of treatment effectiveness. The social worker, for example, may have goals of reducing the anxiety in Jill, increasing self-esteem in Jack, and increasing marital satisfaction for both Jack and Jill.

PURPOSE OF BASELINE

The two basic functions of baselines are (1) to provide information for assessment and (2) to serve as a frame of reference for evaluation (Bloom, Fischer, & Orme, 2006). For assessment purposes, baseline graphs can provide information on the magnitude of the problem and its persistence, assuming that the variables the social worker is measuring indicate relevant problems. From Figure 15, it is clear that marital satisfaction inventories are pertinent to marital counseling. However, anxiety and self-esteem

figure 15

Baselines of Marital Dissatisfaction (A), Self-Esteen (B), and Anxiety (C) for Jack and Jill over One Week

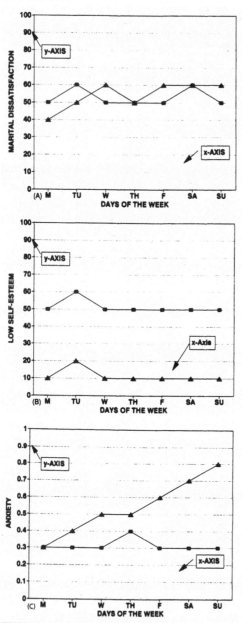

NOTE: ■ = Jack's scores; ▲ = Jill's scores

nor Jill may have complained about anxiety, but the social worker might have asked Jack and Jill to complete the SAS because, in the social worker's experience with marital couples seeking marital counseling, one partner or both often exhibit signs of anxiety. That anxiety is becoming a problem for Jill is clinically relevant because it is of high magnitude and is becoming worse (Figure 15c). However, the social worker cannot discern from the graphs other possible problems such as depression, spouse abuse, or extramarital affairs. These problems, if they exist, would emerge in the clinical interview when the social worker would notice discrepancies in Jack and Jill's graphic patterns regarding self-esteem and anxiety. The social worker would explore with them the reasons for their marital dissatisfaction and what they want to do about it.

The second major function of a baseline is to serve as a frame of reference or benchmark against which to appraise the effectiveness of the clinical social worker's intervention. Hence, the social worker must compare observations he or she made during the second phase-intervention (see chapter 5) with those in the first phase. To illustrate, suppose one goal of intervention is to decrease marital dissatisfaction for both Jack and Jill. Suppose also that the social worker provides a brief cognitive-therapeutic intervention three times per week for four weeks. The intervention is apparently effective because marital dissatisfaction has steadily decreased for both Jack and Jill (Figure 16). Moreover, the magnitude of the problem has decreased so that it is relatively stable in the last week of intervention and is below the cutoff point of 30 (Corcoran & Fischer, 2000a), indicating that it is not a clinical problem. In contrast, the intervention shown in Figure 17 is ineffective: The magnitude of marital dissatisfaction is the same or maybe more than it was at baseline for both Jack and Jill.

OBTAINING INFORMATION FOR BASELINES

The clinical social worker obtains information for constructing baselines in four ways:

1. Making observations during assessment before any intervention takes place

may or may not have been relevant. Jack may have complained about his lack of self-esteem in the first interview, and the clinical social worker may have used the ISE (see Appendix 2) to verify his complaint. On the other hand, neither Jack

figure 16

Using Baseline as a Frame of Reference to Depict an Effective Intervention for Increasing Marital Satisfaction: ■ = Jack, ▲ = Jill

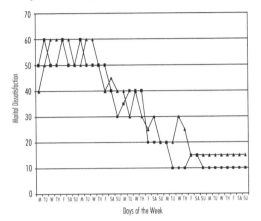

figure 17

Using Baseline as a Frame of Reference to Depict an Ineffective Intervention for Increasing Marital Satisfaction: ■ = Jack, ▲ = Jill

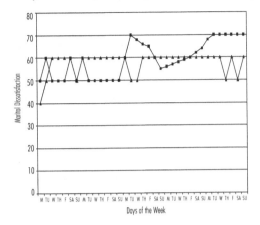

2. Making observations on a specific problem while intervention is being carried out to address a different problem than the one being baselined
3. By reconstruction based on archival data and available records
4. By retrospection based on questionnaires with clients and/or significant others (Blythe & Tripodi, 1989, p. 77).

The first method requires that the social worker withhold intervention until he or she constructs a baseline with stable characteristics. Typically, one to two weeks is a minimum period for observing trends in the time series of repeated measurements, assuming the time interval is in days. For moods, attitudes, and behaviors, this period is feasible. However, this does not mean that the clinical social worker cannot see clients. Rather, if the first interviews are exploratory and devoted to assessment, the social worker can arrange for clients to do homework and rate themselves on standardized scales or self-anchored scales or observe themselves on a daily basis, as the social worker in the previous example instructed Jack and Jill to do. In many situations, however, the clinical social worker may make a relatively quick assessment during the first interview and begin with an intervention. The social worker still can baseline after the first interview provided the intervention is less intense than it might be in subsequent interviews. The social worker

can graph observations on important variables ostensibly related to client problems to show whether there is a problem (magnitude); that the problem is persistent (the baseline graph is horizontal to the x-axis); that the problem is getting worse; or that the client solves the problem before more intensive intervention.

Although many proponents of single-case design would like to believe that the social worker makes observations at baseline without the presence of any intervention because the particular social worker is withholding intervention until he or she makes an assessment, this requires a heroic assumption—that is, that the client has not had any previous interventions or the client has not been exposed to materials and information that are identical, similar, or akin to the planned intervention. For example, many clients have received services from a variety of professional and social agencies. Moreover, the substance of many interventions is present in forms other than the clinical social worker's treatment modality, such as the ministrations of clergy with their parishioners or popular books or newspaper articles on positive thinking similar to some tenets of cognitive therapy; possible discussions with friends and relatives on topics and feelings similarly encountered in therapeutic sessions; or client involvement in recreational or self-help group situations, such as Parents without Partners or Adult Children of

Alcoholics. Hence, the social worker can know whether he or she provides intervention during baseline, but the social worker may not be able to discern whether the client has received intervention similar to the one the social worker is offering. Of course, through clinical interviews, the social worker can estimate current or previous interventions the client has received or is receiving by asking the client.

The second way the social worker gathers information for baseline construction is to obtain the information on a problem other than the one with which he or she is dealing during an intervention. For example, if the clinical social worker is working with Jack and Jill on their marital dissatisfaction, he or she might obtain information on another problem such as attendance at work or school, following prescribed medical regimens, or depression for either spouse. However, the social worker assumes that the intervention for a problem—marital dissatisfaction in this instance—does not also influence the other problem the social worker is baselining. The social worker can infer the independence or dependence of data by observing and comparing graphic patterns. For example, Figure 18a shows a baseline pattern of horizontal stability with a high magnitude of marital dissatisfaction, followed by an increase in marital satisfaction following intervention. Baselining depression during the intervention for reducing marital dissatisfaction can result in a baseline that depends on, is influenced by, the intervention (Figure 18b) or is independent of, and not influenced by, the intervention (Figure 18c). The social worker can use the baseline for depression in Figure 18c for subsequent analysis and evaluation of an intervention focused on depression. However, the social worker should use only the baseline in Figure 18b for assessment, when it is clear that the problem is being reduced without any further intervention.

A third way to gather data is to use available information that the social worker or others might have systematically recorded. Such data might include employment records such as absences, school tardiness and attendance records and grades, delinquency records such as arrests or convictions, and hospital records regarding

figure 18

Independent (A and C) and Dependent (B) Baseline Patterns for the Same Client

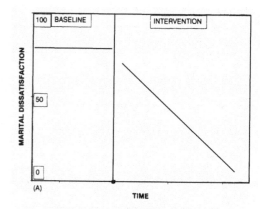

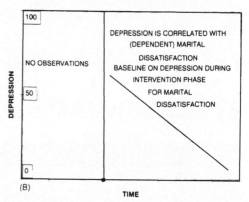

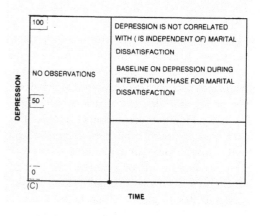

physical and medical characteristics. The social worker should use this information only if it was previously recorded and if the social worker believes that the data were gathered consistently and are reliable and valid. The clinical social worker can use the information, however, only if he or she has the client's permission and the permission of the organization that keeps the records to gain access to the data. Suppose that, in the illustration of Jack and Jill, the clinical social worker was interested in Jack's employment. Jack might have indicated that he had a problem with work, and he did not like his job. With his permission, the clinical social worker might gain access to his work records, for example, of his attendance and visits to the company's Employee Assistance Program. Such records are available in large national corporations and, once tabulated, can serve as baselines. If the social worker finds that Jack has an attendance problem at work, he or she might use that variable as an objective of treatment. The social worker might hypothesize, for example, that Jack may not regularly attend work for other reasons such as substance abuse, and might also hypothesize that an increase in marital satisfaction might be associated with increased attendance at work.

A fourth way to obtain information for constructing baselines is to ask the client to remember information from the past. The client's recollections generally are more accurate when the client is recalling extreme quantities, such as smoking two packs of cigarettes every day for one year rather than remembering lesser quantities, such as smoking five to 10 cigarettes per day. The clinical social worker might make estimates from the client's recollections. For example, in response to "How often did you drink liquor in the past week?" the client might indicate that he or she drank at least four shots of whiskey per day and has done so for the past month. The clinical social worker may estimate that the client drank some amount of alcohol every day during the past month, drank more than four shots a day during the past 30 days, and so forth. The estimate used should be based on the operational definition of the problem. If, for example, the client's alcohol consumption is defined as the number of shots of whiskey he or she had each day and the clinician is constructing a baseline for the preceding week, the estimated daily number should be used to represent the client's alcohol consumption on each of the seven days.

Behaviors that clients can easily recall because of their extreme positions include spouse abuse or child abuse, substance abuse, cigarette smoking, and yelling at the dinner table. If a client is unable to recall such data, the social worker may enlist a spouse, a friend, a relative, or other important person to help provide the desired information. The chief danger in this method of obtaining information is that of retrospective falsification, that is, the client alters his or her recollection of the past so that it more likely will coincide with the present. Or, clients may want to please the social worker by telling him or her what they think the social worker wants to hear—that is to say, there may be a bias of social desirability.

Overall, the social worker obtains the most accurate information by making observations over a designated period before applying the intervention. In contrast, the social worker procures the least accurate information through client retrospection. The clinician should use the data source or sources that provide the most accurate information for constructing the baseline phase of single-case design, as long they can be reasonably obtained. If it is unethical to delay intervention, for example, in work with a client who is having thoughts of suicide, the most accurate information is obtained through the use of archival data or client retrospection, for example, treatment records from another provider documenting the client's suicidal ideations or attempts in the recent past, or the client's retrospective recall of these events.

TIME-SERIES DATA

Time-series data are the patterns of measurements within specified periods, such as in the baseline, intervention, or follow-up phases of single-case design. Measurements over time for the same client are useful for determining patterns at baseline. The clinical social worker develops a measurement plan—a blueprint—for guiding the collection of time series data in the baseline phase of single-case design. For making comparisons between repeated measurements of a client variable at baseline with repeated measurements of the variable in intervention and follow-up phases of the model, the same measurement plan should be used. Thus, care should be taken in developing the plan because it will guide the collection of time-series data before (that is, in the baseline phase), during (that is, in the intervention phase) and after (that is, in the follow-up phase) treatment.

Critical decisions in developing the measurement plan include the variable or variables to be measured, the tools and procedures for measuring variables, the time interval between measurements, and the number of measurements. When baseline data are collected prospectively or when questionnaires will be used to facilitate retrospective recall of the problem by the client or others, the first two decisions will be informed by such factors as the relevance, reliability, validity, feasibility, nonreactivity, and cultural relevance of the instruments and procedures for collecting measurements as discussed in chapter 3. When baseline data are reconstructed based on archival data or available records, the availability and accuracy of these records should be considered.

The social worker should base the decision for selecting time intervals on clinical judgment; that is, the interval chosen should make sense in relation to the problem as described by the client. If there is daily spousal abuse in a marital relationship, it makes sense to obtain daily measurements. On the other hand, if the abuse occurs once a week, then weekly measurements are appropriate. The interval chosen should be sufficient for capturing variations in the occurrence of the problem. Suppose, for example, that the clinician is working with a client to reduce the frequency of panic attacks that occur several times a day. Recording these attacks on a weekly basis would be insufficient for measuring changes in their daily occurrence; daily measures are appropriate. The time interval between measurements should also be consistent with treatment objectives. If the social worker's treatment objective is to reduce the number of family arguments from every day to no arguments, then he or she should measure the arguments daily.

The number of measurements the social worker makes is based on the amount of time required to obtain a sample of observations that are representative of the problem and the number of measurements required for determining trends in the data. Suppose, for example, that the clinician is working with a client to address binge-drinking episodes that occur primarily on weekends. The timeframe selected may need to span several weeks to allow the clinician and client to obtain a representative picture of the client's weekend drinking pattern. If, on the other hand, the clinician is working with a client to address angry outbursts that occur several times a day, fewer measurements will be needed to discern the nature and extent of the problem.

For determining trends in the data, Jayaratne and Levy (1979) and Barlow and Hersen (1984) suggest that at least three points are sufficient. This criterion is useful for the graphs in Figures 19a–19d but not for 19e–19f. Figure 19a shows a steady decline in anxiety at baseline; 19b, a steady increase; 19c, a horizontally stable graph of high anxiety; 19d, a horizontally stable graph of low anxiety; and 19e and 19f, fluctuating patterns with too few data points to characterize a trend. Another criterion is to take measurements continually at baseline until there is a discernible stable trend. Stability means that a straight line will connect all the points at baseline; the more variation there is from a straight line, the less stable the data. Figure 20 provides examples of relatively stable and relatively unstable baseline data when appraised by the eye ("eyeball"). Ideally, horizontal stability in baseline measurements of the variable for which a client is seeking treatment should be attained. This pattern is evident in 20a.

Achieving horizontal stability in baseline measurements of a problem variable is important for several reasons. First, a horizontally stable pattern indicates that the presence, frequency, magnitude or duration of the client's problem is consistent over time. The observed pattern may reveal that the problem occurs consistently but not to a degree that warrants clinical concern. On the other hand, the pattern may reveal the presence of a consistently occurring and clinically significant problem, for example, bouts of depression that occur three times a day and severely limit the client's daily functioning. Second, baseline horizontal stability provides evidence of nonreactivity, a threat to internal

figure 19

Baseline Graphs of Anxiety over Three Time Points

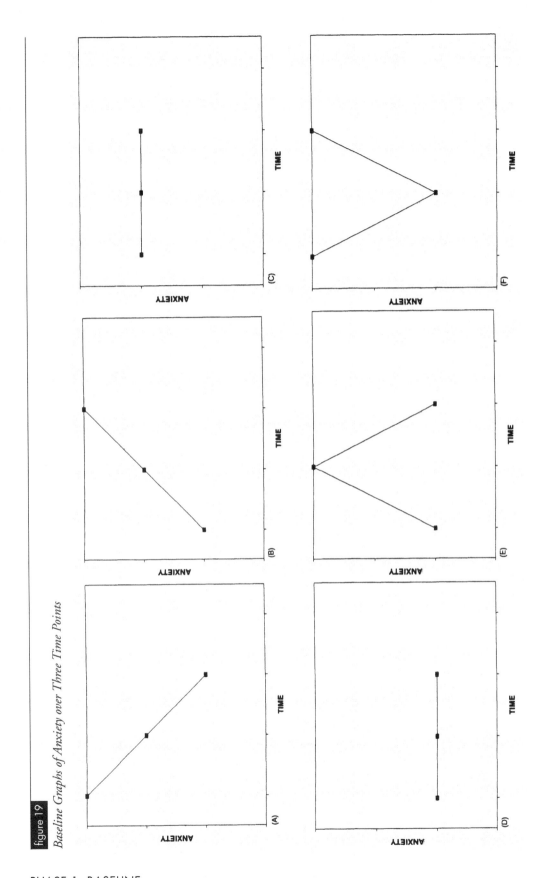

figure 20 *Stable and Unstable Baseline Patterns: (A) Horizontally stable, (B) Horizontally unstable, (C) Ascending stable, (D) Ascending unstable, (E) Descending stable, (F) Descending unstable*

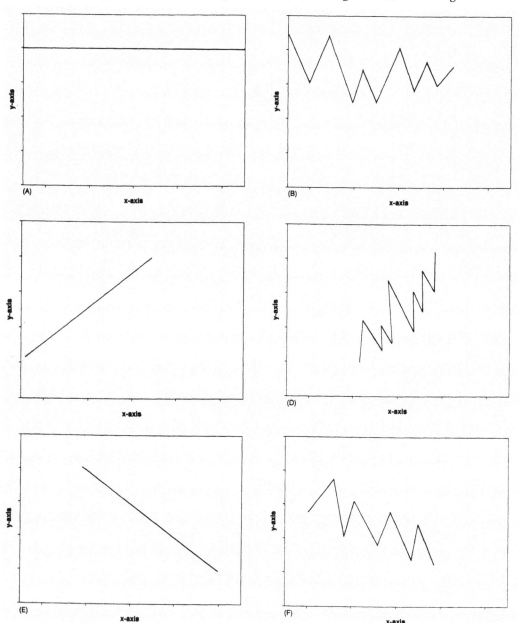

validity discussed in chapter 3. The presence of horizontal stability in baseline measurements of a variable affords the clinician confidence that the process of measurement has not influenced the behavior measured. Third, and perhaps most important, baseline horizontal stability facilitates inferences regarding correlational and causal knowledge. The clinician can infer correlational knowledge of the intervention and problem severity, for example, by comparing observations in the intervention phase with those taken during baseline or follow-up. If the clinician observes a positive trend in the data during intervention (that is, a change in the desired direction) and there is evidence of horizontal stability at baseline, the clinician can infer correlational knowledge of the intervention and problem severity because the observed shift occurred after the intervention was implemented. When changes are already occurring in the problem prior to intervention (that is, when there is a trend in baseline data), the clinician cannot discern if changes observed during intervention are related to the intervention that he or she provided or some other factor.

The reader will recall that in group experimental research designs, scores for a group of individuals who were not exposed to an intervention serve as the comparison against which scores for the group who received the intervention are compared. In single-case design, the client's preintervention level of functioning is the comparison against which subsequent changes in his or her functioning are compared. When there is no change in a measured variable prior to intervention (that is, when baseline data are stable), the clinician has greater confidence that observed changes following intervention are related to the intervention that he or she is providing.

Ideally, for purposes of making clear inferences when comparing patterns of measurements at intervention and follow-up with those at baseline, stability should be horizontal. The clinical social worker can estimate horizontal stability by eye, or, when there are at least eight measurements, he or she can assess horizontal stability by using the C statistic (Tryon, 1982). The C statistic is one of two statistical methods used in this book; the other is the binomial test for horizontal baseline. The binomial test can be used when there is evidence of horizontal stability in time-series data gathered at baseline. Because it is used for making comparisons between phases of the model, we present this statistic in chapter 5. For simplicity, we refer to the C statistic as the primary method for evaluating time-series data throughout this book. However, there are limiations to its use.[1] For overcoming these limitations and increasing the precision and statistical power of this statistic, we advocate the use of a conservative approach that encompasses the collection of the minimum number of measurements required to calculate C (eight) in each phase of the the basic model of single-case de-

sign. The use of this approach can provide valid estimates for interpreting time-series data when data patterns are difficult to determine based on visual inspection. For a wide array of other statistical procedures for evaluating time-series data, the reader should refer to Franklin, Allison, & Gorman (1997), Barlow and Hersen (1984), and Kazdin (1992).

Suppose the social worker obtains the following 10 measurements of marital satisfaction (the higher the number, the less the satisfaction) for a client over eight days: 68, 66, 64, 60, 56, 55, 53, 50, 46, and 40. The social worker can construct a graph with these data and discern by eye a downward trend in the data. But is there really a trend or is it horizontally stable? The C statistic can inform whether these time series data are on an upward or a downward trend beyond a five-in-100 chance or are horizontally stable.

The first step is to put each score (x) in column 1; the sum of these scores is 558, and the mean (average) is the sum of the scores divided by the number of scores (n = 10), or 55.8 (Table 10). In column 2, the mean of 55.8 is subtracted from each score, and in column 3, each value from column 2 is squared, for example, 12.2 × 12.2 = 148.84 and 10.2 × 10.2 = 104.04. All of the values in column 3 are added to produce the sum of squares (SS) of x [S(x)] or $(x - M)^2$. Column 4 consists of adjacent scores (xi): beginning with the first score of 68 (column 1), the next score—66—is adjacent to 68 and is the first score in column 4; the adjacent score for 66 is 64; for 64, it is 60, and so on. In column 5, the adjacent scores are subtracted from the scores, $x - x_i$, and in column 6, the $x - x_i$ values are squared $[(x - x_i)^2]$. The sum of the $(x - x_i)^2$ values in column 6 produces D^2. The C statistic then is calculated as shown in Table 10. The standard error (SE) of C is: $Sc = \sqrt{n - 2} / (n + 1)(n - 1)$, where n equals the number of scores. The probability of the C statistic is evaluated by Z, which is C divided by Sc. The critical value for the .05 level of significance is 1.64. When Z is greater than 1.64, there is evidence of a statistically significant trend in the time-series data. When Z is less than 1.64, the clinician can infer that there is horizontal stability in the time-series data.

			table 10	*Computing S, Sc, and Z to Evaluate Time-Series Data*	

Score (x)	$x - M$	$(x - M)^2$	x_i	$x - x_i$	$(x - x_i)^2$
68	12.20	148.84	66	2	4
66	10.20	104.04	64	2	4
64	8.20	67.24	60	4	16
60	4.20	17.64	56	4	16
56	.20	.04	55	1	1
55	−.80	.64	53	2	4
53	−2.80	7.84	50	3	9
50	−5.80	33.64	46	4	16
46	−9.80	96.04	40	6	36
40	−15.80	249.64	–	–	–
$558 = \Sigma x$		$1725.601 = SS(x)$	$1106 = D^2$		

$M = \Sigma x / n$ $= 558/10$ $= 55.80$

$C = 1 - D^2/(2SS(x))$ $= 1 - 106/2(725.60)$ $= .92$

$Sc = \sqrt{(n - 2)/(n + 1)(n - 1)} = \sqrt{(10 - 2)/(10 + 1)(10 - 1)} = .28$

$Z = C/Sc$ $= .92/.28$ $= 3.32$

NOTE: If $Z > 1.64$, there is a trend in the time-series; otherwise there is horizontal stability. Because $Z = 3.28$ is greater than 1.64, there is a trend in the time-series.

The result of these calculations is the determination of whether the time series at baseline is horizontal. In the example shown in Table 10, it is not, meaning that the data are on a downward trend, indicating increasing marital satisfaction.

Developing the Measurement Plan

The development of the measurement plan comprises a series of interrelated steps. First, the clinician and client identify and operationally define the variable or variables to be measured. Second, planned procedures for collecting measurements are specified. If measurements will be gathered prospectively (that is, for the problem with which the clinician is dealing or one other than the problem that is the focus of intervention) or through the use of questionnaires to facilitate retrospective recall of the problem by the client, the clinician and client identify the tools and procedures to be used as outlined in chapter 3. This includes a discussion of the protocol for returning completed instruments (that is, rapid assessment instruments, rating scales, self-anchored rating scales, forms documenting systematic observa-

tions of a problem variable, and questionnaires) to the clinician. If the source of measurements is archival data or available records, the types of records that will be used (that is, employment, school, probation) and the procedures for obtaining these records (for example, steps for securing the required permissions to access the records, the person or persons who will provide them, and the frequency with which they will be obtained) are determined. If measurements will be reconstructed based on questionnaires with clients or others, the questionnaires and persons involved are identified. Third, the time interval between measures is determined. The interval chosen should make clinical sense in relation to the problem and be geared toward the frequency with which it occurs and clinical objectives for addressing it. When archival data are used, the frequency of original measurements will determine the available intervals. Suppose, for example, that a client's employer records his or her attendance at work daily. The clinician can select a daily interval between measurements or any less frequent interval (for example, weekly or monthly). Fourth, the number of baseline measurements, or, the length of the baseline phase, is determined. When baseline data are gathered prospectively, the clinician and client should select the number of measurements based on the amount of time required to capture the manifestation of the problem and determine the presence or absence of a trend in baseline data. The number of measurements for establishing a baseline based on archival records will depend on the information that is available in those records. If, in the example above, the client's attendance at work was recorded for a one-week interval only as part of a company assessment of work performance, then five measurements is the maximum number that the clinician can use to construct the baseline. When baselines are constructed by retrospection, the number of measurements will depend on the client's ability to recall the presence, frequency, severity, or duration of the problem, or the availability and willingness of others such as his or her spouse, friend, or relative to provide the desired information. The clinical social worker can develop a simple form for organizing details of the measurement plan as it is developed, as shown in the example that follows.

In chapter 3, we presented the hypothetical case of a male client who sought treatment for his low self-esteem. In clinical interviews with the client, the clinical social worker learned that the client frequently made self-deprecating remarks. The client's spouse was enlisted to monitor the daily frequency of his self-deprecating remarks. A rating scale was devised that included the question, "How often does your spouse make self-deprecating statements?" and Likert response options for recording the frequency of his remarks ranging from 1 = rarely, if ever to 5 = very frequently. The wife was instructed to observe her husband's behavior from the time he returned home from work through the end of the day for one week and to record, by circling the aproporate response, the frequency of his self-deprecating remarks. Based on clinical interviews with the client, the clinician determined that ratings at or greater than 4 on this scale would indicate the presence of a clinially significant problem. Furthermore, suppose that the clinician and client decided to have the client self-monitor the magnitude of his self-esteem each day, operationally defined as his daily score on the Index of Self-esteem (ISE) shown in Appendix 2. The client is instructed to reflect, at the end of each day, on his level of self-esteem throughout the day, and to complete the ISE before going to bed. The completed forms for this hypothetical case might look like the form on pages 86 and 87.

Implementing the Measurement Plan

After the measurement plan is developed, the clinical social worker prepares the client and others to conduct measurements. Because the plan developed will guide measurements in intervention and follow-up, preparing those involved in the process is critical to the success of the plan. The clinician reviews planned procedures in advance of recording to ensure that they are clearly understood by the persons involved and acceptable to the client. If the clinician has documented details of the measurement plan using the form described above, her or she can use the completed form to guide his or her discussion of the plan with the client and others.

Continuous recording can be a demanding task, even when planned procedures are straightforward and easy to use. It is therefore important for the clinician to enlist the support of the client and others to participate in the measurement process. He or she can enhance their motivation to do so by communicating to those involved that the baseline data they provide will inform understanding of the presence, frequency, severity, or duration of a problem the client is experiencing and facilitate the development of a treatment plan for addressing the problem. It is equally important for the clinician to recognize those involved as valuable partners in the treatment process by conveying his or her understanding of and appreciation for the time and effort each is willing to invest on the client's behalf. The clinician should review the measurement plan and reiterate these sentiments at the start of subsequent phases of the model. After the plan has been implemented, follow-up contacts should be initiated with the persons providing measurements to assess their progress and discuss any problems they may be having with the plan.

Variable:	Self-deprecating remarks
Operational definition	Daily frequency of statements made by the client in which he undervalues his worth or abilities
Data source (prospective measurements/archival data or available records/reconstruction)	Prospective measurements

PROSPECTIVE MEASUREMENTS	
Instrument(s)	Five-point rating scale with response options ranging from 1 = rarely, if ever to 5 = very frequently.
Administration and scoring procedures	Client's behavior will be observed from the time he returns home from work through the end of the day. The frequency of his self-deprecating statements will be recorded daily on the rating scale. Blank copies of the scale (one each for collecting the designated number of measurements) will be distributed at the start of baseline. Completed forms will be returned to the clinician at the end of the recording period. Scores at or above 4 on the scale indicate the presence of a clinically significant problem.
Individual(s) providing data	Client's spouse
Location of measurements	Client's home
Time interval between measurements	
Number of measurements	

ARCHIVAL DATA AND/OR AVAILABLE RECORDS	
Type of record(s)	
Procedures for obtaining permission(s) to access the record	
Individuals(s) who will provide record(s)	
Frequency with which records will be provided	
Time interval between measurements	
Number of measurements	

RETROSPECTIVE RECALL BY THE CLIENT AND/OR OTHERS	
Questionnaire(s) for gathering data	
Individual(s) who will provide measurements	
Variable	Self-esteem

Operational definition	Daily magnitude of the client's self-esteem as indicated by his score on a measure of self-esteem
Data source (prospective measurements/ archival data or available records/reconstruction):	Prospective measurements

PROSPECTIVE MEASUREMENTS	
Instrument(s):	Index of Self-esteem (ISE).
Administration and scoring procedures	Client's self-esteem will be measured through self-administration of the ISE at the end of the day. Blank copies of the ISE will be distributed at the start of baseline (one each for collecting the designated number of measurements). The client will bring the completed forms to his next session with the clinician for scoring. ISE scores at 30 ± 5 indicate the presence of a clinically significant problem; scores higher than 70 indicate severe stress with a clear possibility that some type of violence could be considered or used to deal with problems.
Individuals(s) providing data	Client
Location of measurements	Client's home

ARCHIVAL DATA OR AVAILABLE RECORDS	
Type of record(s)	
Procedures for obtaining permission(s) to access the record	
Individuals(s) who will provide record(s)	
Frequency with which records will be provided	
Time interval between measurements (daily)	
Number of measurements (seven)	

RETROSPECTIVE RECALL BY THE CLIENT OR OTHERS	
Questionnaire(s) for gathering data	
Individuals(s) who will provide measurements	
Time interval between measurements (daily)	
Number of measurements (seven)	

Graphs serve two purposes: (1) they facilitate data analysis based on visual inspection, and (2) they provide a means for presenting the results of data collection to the client. The clinical social worker may or may not use graphs for data analysis purposes, depending on the number of measurements and their observed values. For example, baseline measurements of a variable with identical values indicate the presence of horizontal stability; the clinician would not need to graph these data for making that determination. However, when values vary, graphs can facilitate visual inspection and analysis of data provided by the client and others. Regardless of whether the graphs are used for this purpose, the clinician should use graphs to present the results of data collection to the client, and, with his or her permission, others involved in the measurement process. Because of the considerable time and effort the client and others have invested in the collection of repeated measurements of a variable or variables at baseline, graphically depicting these measurements and sharing graphs with the client can be an empowering experience for him or her. In addition to allowing the client to see the results of his or her efforts and those of others, graphs can confirm the presence or absence of a problem for which he or she has sought treatment.

The following material on graphs is adapted from Blythe and Tripodi (1989, pp. 67–75). Before constructing a graph, it is helpful to know the basic terminology. In Figure 21, the vertical line with units zero through 12 is the y-axis; the horizontal line with units zero through 10 is the x-axis. The variable that indicates problem magnitude, existence, frequency, or duration is the dependent variable; it is subject to change under the possible influence of intervention. During baseline, the social worker constructs a graph to show trends in the dependent variable, which he or she plots on the y-axis. The y-axis is divided into equal units, and the nature of the units depends on the particular variable chosen. If the dependent variable is the Index of Marital Satisfaction, for example, the units range from zero to 100 (Corcoran & Fischer, 2000a, pp. 119–120), whereas, the units may range from zero to

figure 21

Basic Terminology for Constructing Graphs

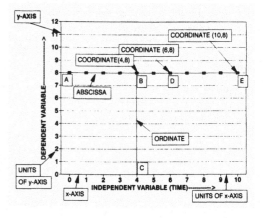

10 on a self-anchored rating scale of marital satisfaction. Correspondingly, the x-axis contains equal units of time; the specific units depend on the clinical relevance of the time points, which may be hours, days, weeks, and so forth. The range of units can differ from graph to graph.

To plot a graph, the social worker must know the coordinates for each point. The coordinates for point b in Figure 21 are (4, 8): 4 represents the time unit and 8 represents the value of the dependent variable. Count to 4 on the x-axis, and then draw line bc, a line perpendicular to the x-axis at time unit 4. Extend the line to the intersection of line ab, which is perpendicular to the y-axis at the dependent variable value 8. Line ab represents the abscissa and line bc the ordinate. Following the same procedure, coordinates (6, 8) form point d and (10, 8) point e. A line connecting points b, d, and e is a graph consisting of the coordinates to points b, d, and e.

Graphs may reflect magnitude, the severity or strength of a phenomenon; magnitude shows the intensity of beliefs, feelings, moods, or attitudes, typically on standardized scales. For example, the data obtained from a client's self-ratings of depression (on a scale ranging from 0 = no depression to 10 = the greatest degree of depression possible) for 10 successive days are as follows: 9,9,10,8,8,5,8,9,8,8. These data are the coordinates for Figure 22. The social worker should construct the graph on graph paper with equal units and compare it with the graph in

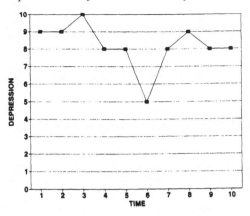

Depression Scores for 10 Successive Days

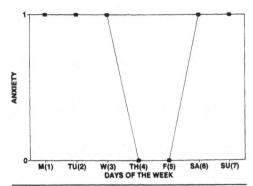

Problem Existence of Anxiety for One Week;
0 = No anxiety, 1 = Anxiety

NOTE: M = Monday, TU = Tuesday, W = Wednesday,
TH = Thursday, F = Friday, SA = Saturday, SU = Sunday.

Figure 22. He or she should label each axis and include a heading above the graph as shown in Figure 22. Except for the sixth day of measurement, the graph in Figure 22 represents a high intensity of depression for a client, 8 or higher on the 10-point self-anchored scale. As a general rule, the clinician should ascertain if it is possible based on visual inspection of the graph, to determine the number of measurements, the time interval between measurements, and the observed values of the plotted scores. If he or she is able to do that, then the graph appropriately summarizes data provided by the client.

Problem existence refers to the presence or absence of a behavior, symptom, or problem within a particular period such as a day, a week, and so forth. The client may have a symptom of depression, but that differs from the intensity of a feeling of depression. Clinical social workers might observe common behaviors such as feelings of anxiety, indicated by excessive perspiration and heart palpitations; hitting a child; abusing a spouse; skipping school; frequenting a neighborhood bar; complying with a medical regimen-taking medication or monitoring blood pressure; practicing safe sex; abusing substances; or seeking employment. Graphs depicting problem existence typically have two points on the y-axis: 0 = the absence of the problem and 1 = the presence of the problem or symptom. A baseline for a client measured daily for one week with respect to whether the client had symptoms of anxiety is depicted in Figure 23.

In that figure, the x-axis is in days and the y-axis reflects the presence or absence of anxiety, with the following coordinates: (1,1), (2,1), (3,1), (4,0), (5,0), (6,1), and (7,1). With this baseline, it is clear that the client had symptoms of anxiety five out of the seven days during the week. Stability would represent a straight line connecting all the points at either 0 = no problem or 1 = a persistent daily problem. The clinical social worker's objective would be to achieve stability at zero, which he or she would simply evaluate visually; statistical procedures are unnecessary for evaluating this type of baseline because there are only two points on the graph.

Problem frequency refers to the number of times a problem occurs within a specified period. The social worker can transform problem existence into problem frequency when he or she changes the time unit. For example, in Figure 23, days are the time unit. Changing the unit to weeks, the social worker can count the number of times the problem exists within a week. Thus, anxiety occurred five times out of seven possible days during that one week. Figure 24 illustrates a baseline for three weeks. The coordinates for graph ABC are (1, 5), (2, 5), and (3, 4), respectively. It is unnecessary for the divisions or time intervals on the x-axis to be equal to the divisions on the y-axis.

Problem duration is the length of time the problem occurs during a designated time interval.

figure 24

Problem Frequency of Anxiety for Three Weeks

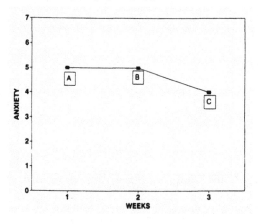

To illustrate the relationships among problem existence, frequency, duration, and magnitude, suppose that a client is prone to having attacks of acute anxiety during which the client feels jittery, with butterflies in his or her stomach, nauseous, and extremely apprehensive. The clinical social worker asks the client to record information about the anxiety attacks each day. If the client has any attacks during a day, there is evidence of problem existence. Problem frequency would refer to the number of attacks during the day; if there were more than one attack, the variable of frequency would differ from that of existence: two versus one. Problem duration would refer to the total length of time for attacks. If the first attack lasted for 15 minutes and the second lasted for 20 minutes, the problem duration for that day would be 35 minutes. Problem magnitude would refer to the intensity of each attack; on an intensity scale ranging from 0 = no anxiety to 10 = high anxiety, the magnitude for the first attack might have been 10 and for the second attack, 9. The clinical social worker might plot on a graph the magnitude of each attack or the average of the magnitudes for the attack (10 + 9/2 = 9.5), depending on what is most related to the objectives of the clinical social worker and the client.

Graphic Patterns

One forms a graph by connecting all adjacent coordinates by straight lines. The resulting shape is linear, nonlinear, or a combination of both.

It is impossible to characterize all possible patterns of graphs, but a rough estimate of possible shapes is depicted in Figure 25. Linear shapes are simple straight lines that are ascending (Figure 25a1), horizontal to the x-axis (Figure 25a2), or descending (Figure 25a3). Nonlinear or curvilinear graphs are ascending (Figure 25b1), cyclic (Figure 25b2), and descending (Figure 25b3). Figures 25c1–3 illustrate combinations of linear and nonlinear shapes or patterns.

Shapes or patterns of graphs indicate trends. Hence, Figures 25a1, 25b1, and 25c1 represent an increase or an acceleration of the problem over time, whereas Figures 25a3, 25b3, and 25c3 indicate a declining problem. An acceleration of the problem is cause for concern because it indicates the problem is getting worse; the clinical social worker would attempt to intervene with the objective of ameliorating the problem. In contrast, a descending or decelerating trend indicates the problem is diminishing. If this is occurring at baseline, intervention may be unnecessary. When there is evidence of a trend in baseline data, the clinical social worker should use clinical interviews with the client to determine if the trend is due to circumstances or events that are coinciding with baseline measurements or if the trend is occurring on its own. If outside circumstances or events are influencing baseline measurements and they are expected to be short lived, the clinician can extend the baseline phase to account for their potential effects, as long as delaying intervention is feasible based on the time interval between measurements and would not expose the client or others to harm. If the interval is weekly, for example, and the clinician wishes to obtain three additional measurements of the problem, he or she would need to weigh the utility of extending the baseline for an additional three weeks against his or her assessment of the degree to which intervention to address the problem is warranted.

An example of a situation in which the clinician might extend the baseline phase to account for the effects of a known situation or event that coincides with baseline measurements of a problem follows. Suppose the clinician is working with a client to reduce his or her anxiety. A two-week baseline is established during which

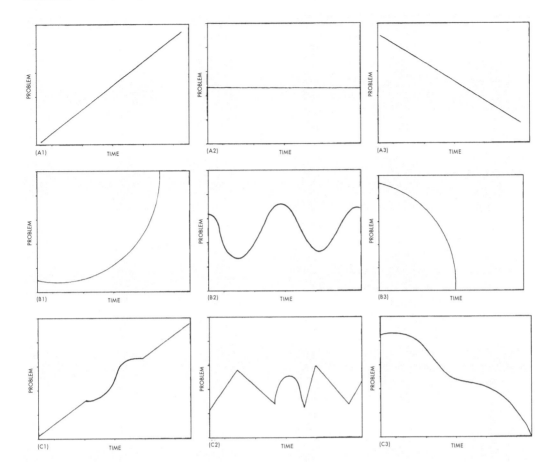

the client records daily measurements of the severity of his or her anxiety. During the second week of baseline, the client returns home for the holidays—an event that increases the client's anxiety. The clinician calculates the C statistic using the 14 measurements provided by the client. The data reveal that there is a negative trend in the data—an indication that the client's anxiety is increasing over time. The clinician and client decide to extend the baseline phase for an additional week. The additional measurements will allow the clinician to determine if, after the client has returned home, his or her level of anxiety is similar to that observed prior to the trip. This would be indicated by horizontal stability in the 21 measurements of anxiety provided by the client. If horizontal stability is achieved, the clinician can prepare for intervention to address the client's anxiety in situations other than those involving family-related events.

The patterns in Figures 25a2, 25b2, and 25c2 represent constancy at a particular level horizontal to the x-axis; if the magnitude or frequency indicates there is a problem, then the social worker should plan intervention. In contrast, a horizontal pattern with little evidence of a problem may indicate that intervention is not warranted for that particular problem. If the observed pattern is indeterminate based on available information and it is possible to delay intervention to collect additional baseline measurements, the clinician should consider doing so, and reevaluate data from the extended baseline phase.

Transforming Graphs

Often graphs are not smooth lines—they are full of jagged edges, peaks (maximum points), and valleys (minimum points). When they serve as benchmarks at baseline and the social worker uses them for comparisons with graphs at intervention or at follow-up, they can be transformed. Transformations serve to smooth the graphs to make the patterns more horizontal, which leads to easier interpretations on comparison. However, if the social worker transforms baseline graphs, he or she must transform the graphs for intervention and follow-up; otherwise, the comparisons would be inaccurate. When transforming the data, the social worker must carefully report the data, noting the transformation that he or she made. In addition to rendering it easier for the clinical social worker to make comparisons, transformations also can lead to a better understanding of feedback in the form of graphs when the social worker presents them to clients.

The social worker can transform graphs in four ways so that they become more horizontal. Graphic analysis for statistics, business, and economics commonly follows the first procedure, which is averaging across adjacent points. For example, in Figure 26a, the pattern of a cyclic linear graph is shown by ACFGHIJ, whose coordinates are A (1, 1), C (2, 3), F (3, 1), G (4, 3), H (5, 1), I (6, 3), and J (7, 1). To transform the graph, take the average of each adjacent pair of coordinates. Following this procedure, the new coordinates are depicted in Figure 26b as A' (1.5, 2), B' (2.5, 2), C' (3.5, 2), D' (4.5, 2), E' (5.5, 2), and F' (6.5, 2). The transformed graph is a horizontal straight line but has one point less than the graph in Figure 26a. Also, it is a graph of averages of the first two weeks, the second two weeks, and so on.

A second way to transform a graphic pattern is to change each problem value by a constant amount. One way to flatten or make a linear curve more horizontal is to take the common logarithm of each value; another way is to take the square root of each value. Figure 27a shows three problem values of 1, 3, and 2 over three successive periods. Figures 27b and 27c show two transformations of the graph. In the figure, the common logarithms of 0, .30103, and .47712 are taken of 1, 3, and 2, respectively, to produce a graph that is more horizontal than the one shown in Figure 27a. The square roots of each value (1, 3, and 2) yield new points of 1,

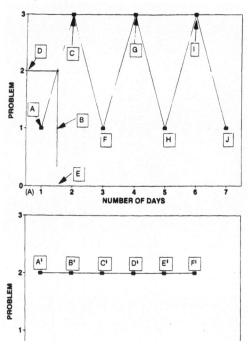

<figure>figure 26</figure>

Transforming Graphs by Averaging Adjacent Points: (Top) Cyclic Linear Pattern, (Bottom) Transformed Horizontal Linear Pattern

1.732, and 1.414 (Figure 27c); this graph is more horizontal than the original graph. These transformations are only for purposes of comparing other patterns at intervention or follow-up to baseline, and only if those graphs use the same algorithm for transforming data. For purposes of assessment only, the social worker would use the original graph and not its transformation.

A third way to flatten a graph and make it more horizontal is to shrink the y-axis by reducing the size of its units. The original values remain the same but the distance between adjacent time units on the y-axis is made shorter. Figure 28b shows a flatter graph than Figure 28a by shrinking the units on the y-axis while keeping the units on the x-axis constant.

Correspondingly, a fourth way of making a graph more horizontal is to change the units of

figure 27

Transforming Graphs by Changing Values by Common Logarithms and Square Roots; (A) Original Values, (B) Common Logarithms of Original Values, (C) Square Roots of Original Values

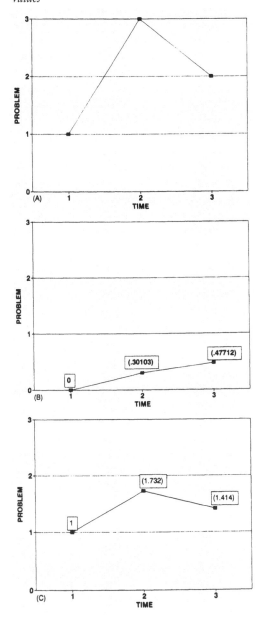

figure 28

Transforming Graphs by Changing Values of the y Axis; (A) Original units, (B) Changing units in the y axis but not in the x axis, (C) Changing units in the x axis but not the y axis

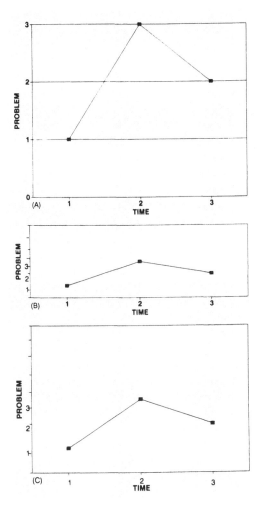

ANALYZING BASELINE DATA

Colleagues, supervisees, clients, and other professionals can produce graphs of baselines at meetings, workshops, in the literature, and so forth. When analyzing graphic patterns at baseline, the social worker should consider several criteria:

- Determine whether clinical objectives exist. An implicit objective might be to reduce symptomatic behavior (such as child abuse) to nonsymptomatic behavior (that is, the behavior no longer occurs). Knowledge of

the x-axis. By increasing the length of the units on the x-axis and keeping the units of the y-axis constant (compare Figures 28c and 28a), the resulting graph in Figure 28c becomes more horizontal.

possible objectives will assist in determining whether the baseline data suggest practice intervention. Life-threatening behavior such as child abuse, spouse abuse, or suicide attempts warrant intervention with relatively few occurrences during a baseline period, whereas mild feelings of anxiety during a situation (an examination for a professional license, for instance) that normally provokes anxiety may be insufficient to warrant intervention. On the other hand, no precise clinical objectives may be evident in the baseline period. However, the decision to gather information that the social worker can baseline suggests that a problem for the client may exist; if it does, then the social worker should reduce or eliminate it through intervention.

- Determine whether a point on the problem variable is regarded as clinically significant. Standardized tests such as Hudson's Index of Marital Satisfaction (see Corcoran & Fischer 2000a, pp. 119–120) might have a cutoff above which a score indicates a problem for the client. Alternatively, the clinical social worker and the client might have agreed that a rating at or above a point on a self-anchored rating scale indicates a problem. For example, the social worker and client might regard as clinically significant 7 on a 10-point scale of depression ranging from 0 = no depression to 10 = very depressed.

- Analyze the problem variable and the y-axis. In analyzing the y-axis, the social worker should determine whether the problem variable is one of magnitude, existence, frequency, or duration. Furthermore, the clinician should assess whether the problem variable relates to any articulated objectives (for example, to reduce anxiety). The social worker also needs to determine whether the intervals on the y-axis are equally spaced. If they are not, the graphic picture will be distorted and will be more difficult to visually examine. In addition, the social worker should examine how the baseline was constructed. Retrospective data are apt to be less reliable and valid than data collected prospectively.

- Analyze the time dimension and the x-axis. Through an analysis of the x-axis, the social worker should determine whether the time interval appears to be of sufficient length to allow for baseline stability. He or she also should ensure that time intervals are equally spaced; otherwise, the graphic picture will be distorted. The social worker also should determine how many measurements were made. Eight measures are necessary to determine the statistical significance of a trend at baseline, whereas three measures are sufficient for eyeballing the data.

- Describe the data. The social worker should determine the mean (the average of the baseline scores), the mode (the most frequently repeating score in the time-series) and the range of scores (the difference between the highest and lowest score) to characterize the data. If there is a cutoff score or a point on the measured variable that indicates the presence of a clinically significant problem, the social worker should count the number of measurements that are clinically significant or problematic out of the total number of measurements. For example, if 30 or greater represents a clinically significant score, out of 10 measurements over 10 days, the social worker might observe that nine out of 10 have scores of 30 or higher. If possible, the practitioner also should describe the number of measurements that indicate a problem. For example, the concern may be the client's binge-drinking, and the data may reveal that the problem occurred once over a seven-day interval. However, the social worker must consider that information with respect to the nature of the problem occurrence. One alcoholic binge in a baseline of one week is a serious problem and, more than likely, considering other available information, would still warrant intervention.

- Analyze the graphic pattern. The practitioner should look for trends in baseline measurements. Is there stability? Is the pattern horizontal, ascending, or descending, or is it indeterminate on the basis of available information? To assist in eyeballing a possible trend, the practitioner can draw a straight line that is an estimate of the average of the points and reflects the trend as shown in line AB in Figure 29. Line AB is extended to point A on the y-axis; at point A, draw another line—AC—that is parallel to the x-axis. The angle, 14 degrees, measured with

figure 29

Baseline of Marital Dissatisfaction; a = 14; Line AC is Parallel to x-axis; Line AB is the Estimated Straight Line that is the Average of the Eight Points

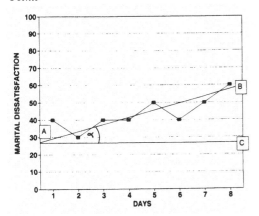

a protractor, indicates the slope of the line. The higher the number of degrees (up to 90 degrees), the greater the apparent acceleration in the graph.

- Eyeballing graphs can be deceiving. A slight observable trend might be evident, but there might not be a statistically significant trend. When there are eight or more measurements,

the clinician can compute *C*, *Sc*, and *Z* to verify whether there is horizontal stability or evidence of an accelerating or decelerating trend in the data. In Table 11, there is no statistical evidence of a trend for the graph in Figure 29.

- Use the resulting information to determine the circumstances under which intervention is warranted. The clinician should review findings from analyses of baseline data to determine the presence or absence of horizontal stability and assess whether the magnitude of the measured variable is sufficient to warrant clinical concern. He or she can use a typology based on baseline measurements of a problem variable to determine the circumstances under which intervention is warranted. The information consists of the presence or absence of horizontal stability in the measured variable and the judgment as to whether the magnitude of the problem is sufficient to warrant clinical concern (Table 12).

Type 1 is one in which there is horizontal stability in baseline measurements of the variable and the observed pattern indicates that the problem is of sufficient magnitude to warrant clinical concern. The clinician and client should establish treatment objectives for addressing the

table 11	*Computing S, Sc, and Z for Figure 29*				
Score (x)	x − M	$(x - M)^2$	x_i	$x - x_i$	$(x - x_i)^2$
40	−3.75	14.06	30	10	100
30	−13.75	189.06	40	−10	100
40	−3.75	14.06	40	0	0
40	−3.75	14.06	50	−10	100
50	6.25	39.06	40	10	100
40	−3.75	14.06	50	−10	100
50	6.25	39.06	60	−10	100
60	16.25	264.06	–	–	–
350 = Σx		|587.48| = SS(x)	|600| = D^2		
$M = \Sigma x/n$	= 350/8	= 43.75			
$C = 1 - D^2/(2SS(x))$	= 1 − 600/2(587.48)	= .48			
$Sc = \sqrt{(n-2)/(n+1)(n-1)}$	$= \sqrt{(8-2)/(8+1)(8-1)}$	= .30			
$Z = C/Sc$	= .48/.30	= 1.60			

NOTE: Because Z < 1.64, there is no statistical evidence of a trend.

table 12 *Typology Based on the Presence or Absence of Horizontal Stability in Baseline Measurements of a Problem and the Observed Magnitude of the Problem*

	Problem Magnitude	
Presence or Absence of Horizontal Stability	Clinically Significant	Not Clinically Significant
Horizontal Stability Present	Type 1	Type 3
Horizontal Stability Absent	Type 2	Type 4

problem and prepare for the intervention phase of single-case design.

Type 2 is one in which there is evidence of a negative trend in baseline measurements of the variable and the observed pattern indicates that the problem is accelerating at a rate that is of sufficient magnitude to warrant clinical concern. The clinician and client should establish treatment objectives for addressing the problem and prepare for the intervention phase of single-case design.

Type 3 is one in which there is horizontal stability in baseline measurements of the variable but the observed pattern indicates that the problem is of insufficient magnitude to warrant clinical concern. If, in clinical discussions with the client, the client indicates that the problem was not of the magnitude he or she originally thought and he or she no longer wishes to address it, the clinician should determine if there are other problems or issues the client wants to address. If, on the other hand, the client reports that the observed pattern was atypical based on his or her experience of the problem, the clinician can extend the baseline phase to collect additional measurements, re-evaluate the time-series data for the extended baseline, and plan accordingly based on the results of that analysis.

Type 4 is one in which there is a positive trend in baseline measurement of the variable but the magnitude of the observed trend is of insufficient magnitude to warrant clinical concern. The clinician can extend the baseline phase to collect additional measurements of the variable and reevaluate the time-series data for the extend baseline to determine if horizontal stability is achieved or there is a continuing trend. If the continuing trend is positive, intervention may be unnecessary because the problem is improving on its own. If, on the other hand, horizontal stability is achieved, the clinician should evaluate whether the magnitude of the observed pattern is sufficient to warrant clinical concern and proceed accordingly.

If the observed pattern is indeterminate based on available information, the clinical social worker should consider extending the baseline phase to collect additional measurements of the variable when it is possible to do. He or she should use clinical interviews with the client to obtain additional information for making such judgments.

The clinician should develop a tentative plan that details the clinical course of action that is implicated by the data. The plan, graphs of baseline measurements, and findings from analyses of baseline data should then be reviewed with the client. Together, the clinician and client determine the appropriate course of action and prepare for work on the agreed-upon tasks.

EXAMPLES

For each of the following graphs and their accompanying tables, the reader should apply principles learned in this chapter for describing baseline data. The reader should then compare the reading of the graphs with comments made in the text.

Figure 29 represents a graph constructed on the basis of eight daily measurements on Hudson's Index of Marital Satisfaction (Corcoran & Fischer, 2000a, pp. 119–120), in which a score greater than 30 indicates a clinical problem of marital dissatisfaction. The index ranges from zero to 100; the higher the score, the greater the degree of marital dissatisfaction. Assume that a clinical objective would be to increase marital satisfaction (that is, reduce the score) per the client's expressed wish. In Figure 29, clearly all eight of the measurements are at the cutoff score of 30 or higher, which is strong evidence of a clinically significant problem. The coordinates of the eight measurements are (1, 40), (2, 30), (3, 40), (4, 40), (5, 50), (6, 40), (7, 50), and (8, 60). Line AB shows a slight ascending curve; however, the calculations in Table 11 indicate that there are no statistical trends in the data. On the basis of the information presented in the graph, intervention is warranted.

Figure 30 displays the baseline for a client over 10 successive days of the week, from Monday through Wednesday. The intervals on both the x- and y-axes are equally spaced. The problem variable, anxiety, has a possible range of magnitude from 0 = absence of anxiety to 10 = the highest degree of anxiety. The client, a male adolescent, records his ratings of anxiety at the same time each day, just before bedtime. The client and the clinical social worker should have thoroughly discussed the operational definition of anxiety before the client makes his ratings.

The graph representing anxiety (Figure 30) appears to be relatively horizontal. Except for Saturday and Sunday, for which the magnitude of anxiety is a score of 2 each day, the other eight measurements are at a magnitude of 6 or higher, which, assuming that the social worker and the client agreed on this number, is clinically significant. The graph indicates that the client's anxiety is high during the week while he is at school, but not during the weekend, presumably while he is at home. Obviously, the clinical social worker needs to explore with the client this possible relationship of school, home, and anxiety. Intervention to reduce anxiety appears to be warranted. Calculations indicate that the baseline of anxiety is horizontally stable because the calculated Z of 1.14 is less than 1.64 (Table 13). The calculated Z can be considered statistically significant only if Z is equal to or greater than 1.64.

figure 30

Magnitude of Self-Anchored Ratings of Anxiety

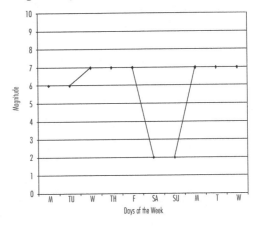

Figure 31 shows the baseline of an adult child abuser who, in his interview with a clinical social worker in private practice, indicated that he spanked his child too often and believed the spankings were abusive. The social worker asked him to obtain a baseline of abuse generated by his daily observation of abuse for eight successive days. Any abusive incident is considered clinically significant. The intervals on the frequency of abuse scale are equally spaced (Figure 31). The time intervals for the x axis also are equally spaced. The first three measurements are recorded as five abuses daily; then there is a rapid deceleration, with one less abuse in each successive day until there is no abuse on the eighth day. The statistics in Table 14 verify that there is a decelerating trend in the data because the calculated Z of 3.00 is greater than 1.64, indicating a statistically significant shift in the time series. Because child abuse is a serious problem and there was only one day without abuse, the clinical social worker may decide to extend the baseline period, still noting whether child abuse recurs.

GUIDELINES FOR DEVELOPING BASELINES

The clinical social worker constructs the baseline phase of single-case design by taking repeated measurements of a client variable or variables related to treatment objectives. Together, with the

table 13 *Computing S, Sc, and Z for Figure 30*

Score (x)	x − M	(x − M)²	x_i	x − x_i	(x − x_i)²
6	.2	.04	6	0	0
6	.2	.04	7	−1	1
7	1.2	1.44	7	0	0
7	1.2	1.44	7	0	0
7	1.2	1.44	2	5	25
2	−3.8	14.44	2	0	0
2	−3.8	14.44	7	−5	25
7	1.2	1.44	7	0	0
7	1.2	1.44	7	0	0
7	1.2	1.44	−	−	−

58 = Σx		137.601 = SS(x)	151 = D²		
M = Σx/n		= 58/10	= 5.80		
C = 1 − D²/(2SS(x))		= 1 − 51/2(37.60)	= .32		
Sc = √(n − 2)/(n + 1)(n − 1)		= √(10 − 2)/(10 + 1)(10 − 1)	= .28		
Z = C/Sc		= .32/.28	= 1.14		

NOTE: Because Z < 1.64, there is no statistical evidence of a trend.

client, the social worker makes decisions regarding the variables to be measured, the procedures for collecting measurements, the time interval between measurements, and the number of measurements, or duration of the baseline phase. The resulting measurements are plotted on a graph. Graphic patterns are analyzed based on visual inspection and/or the use of statistical data anal-ysis procedures. The clinician formulates tentative conclusions regarding the observed patterns and their implications for treatment planning. He or she shares the graphs, findings from statistical analyses, and his or her tentative conclusions with the client. The appropriate course of treatment is determined based on their shared agreement regarding what the baseline data reveal. The clinical social worker should apply the following principles when constructing the baseline phase of single-case design:

figure 31

Baseline of Frequency of Abuse

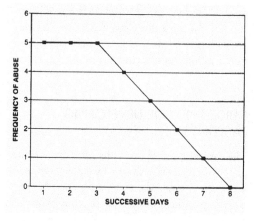

- Develop a measurement plan. Together, with the client, identify and operationally define the variables related to treatment planning and determine the data source(s) for obtaining measurements, the tools and procedures for collecting measurements, the time interval between measurements, and the number of measurements to be made. In developing the plan, consider such factors as the relevance, reliability, validity, feasibility, nonreactivity, and cultural relevance of the tools and procedures for collecting baseline data, prospectively or retrospectively, and

table 14	*Computing S, Sc, and Z for Figure 31*					

Score (x)	$x - M$	$(x - M)^2$	x_i	$X - x_i$	$(x - x_i)^2$
5	1.88	3.53	5	0	0
5	1.88	3.53	5	0	0
5	1.88	3.53	4	1	1
4	.88	.77	3	1	1
3	−.12	.01	2	1	1
2	−1.12	1.25	1	1	1
1	−2.12	4.49	0	1	1
0	−3.12	9.73	–	–	–

$25 = \Sigma x$		$126.841 = SS(x)$	$151 = D^2$		
$M = \Sigma x / n$		$= 25/8$	$= 3.12$		
$C = 1 - D^2/(2SS(x))$		$= 1 - 5/2(26.84)$	$= .90$		
$Sc = \sqrt{(n - 2)/(n + 1)(n - 1)} = \sqrt{(8 - 2)/(8 + 1)(8 - 1)}$			$= .30$		
$Z = C/Sc$		$= .90/.30$	$= 3.00$		

NOTE: Because $Z > 1.64$, there is evidence of a trend.

the availability and quality of existing records for reconstructing baseline data. The time interval between measurements should make clinical sense in relation to the problem described by the client, be sufficient for capturing variations in the occurrence of the problem, and be consistent with treatment objectives for addressing it. The number of measurements should be sufficient for obtaining a sample of observations that is representative of the problem and determining trends in the data.

- Implement the plan. Prepare the client and others to collect measurements in advance of recording. Communicate to the individuals involved that the measurements they provide will inform understanding of the presence, frequency, severity, or duration of the client's problem and facilitate the development of a treatment plan for addressing it. Convey an understanding of and appreciation for the time and effort that each is willing to invest on the client's behalf. After the plan is implemented, initiate follow-up contacts with the individuals involved to assess their progress and discuss any problems they may be having with the plan.

- Graph the results. Identify the coordinates for each measurement of the variable on the x-and y-axes. Using these coordinates, plot each measurement. Draw a line connecting the points. Label each axis and include a heading above the graph. Confirm that the graph appropriately summarizes data provided by the client by assessing if it is possible, based on visual inspection, to determine the number of measurements, the time interval between measurements, and the observed values of the plotted scores. Transform graphs that are difficult to interpret by averaging adjacent pairs of coordinates, changing each problem value by a constant amount, reducing the size of the units on the y-axis, or increasing the length of the units on the x-axis.

- Analyze the data. Determine whether clinical objectives exist. Assess whether a point on the problem variable is regarded as clinically significant (that is, above a cutoff score that indicates a problem for which intervention is warranted). Analyze the problem variable and the y-axis to determine whether the variable is related to any articulated objectives. Confirm that the intervals on the y-axis are equally spaced. Analyze the time dimension and the x-axis to determine if the interval is of sufficient length to allow for baseline stability and if intervals on the x-axis are equally spaced. Describe the mean, mode, and range of observed scores, the number of measurements that are higher than the clinical cutoff score out of the total number of measurements taken, and the number of measurements that indicate a problem. Analyze the graphic pattern to determine if it is horizontal, ascending, descending, or indeterminate based on available information. When there are eight or more measurements, calculate the C statistic to verify if there is evidence of horizontal stability.

- Determine the circumstances under which intervention is warranted. Use information regarding the presence or absence of horizontal stability and clinical judgment as to whether the magnitude of the problem indicates that it is clinically significant to determine the appropriate course of action. If there is horizontal stability in baseline data and the presence of a clinically significant problem, prepare for the intervention phase of single-case design. If there is horizontal stability in baseline data and the absence of a clinically significant problem, determine whether it is appropriate to continue work on the problem or extend the baseline phase to collect additional measurements of it. If there is evidence of a trend, analyze the trend to determine if it is positive, negative, or indeterminate based on available information. Plan for the intervention phase if there is a negative trend in the data and the presence of a clinically significant problem. Intervention may be unnecessary when there is evidence of a positive trend. If it is possible to delay intervention when the observed pattern is indeterminate based on available information, extend the baseline phase to collect additional measurements of the variable and re-evaluate the time-series data.

TEACHING SUGGESTIONS

1. Review the procedures for constructing a baseline using repeated measurements of a client variable prior to intervention, by reconstruction based on archival data and available records, and by retrospection based on questionnaires with clients and/or others. Discuss the advantages and disadvantages of each approach using concepts presented in the chapter.

2. Prepare graphs depicting baseline data for a hypothetical client that illustrate the following: (1) a stable pattern, (2) a positive trend, (3) a negative trend, and (4) an ambiguous pattern. Have students interpret the graphs and discuss the courses of action that are implicated by the observed patterns.

3. Develop a measurement plan for a hypothetical case that will engage the client and another person in the data collection process and additionally make use of available records for measuring the selected variables. Demonstrate the procedures for presenting the plan to the client and others involved, including the statements that a clinician would use to prepare these individuals to begin measurements and initiate follow-up contacts with them after the plan has been implemented. Ask students to role-play actors in the case by raising questions or obstacles that the client or others might express in discussions of the plan developed. Provide suggestions for addressing client questions and overcoming the identified obstacles.

STUDENT EXERCISES

1. Develop a measurement plan for self-monitoring one of your behaviors using the form presented in the chapter. Implement the plan and graph the results. Analyze baseline data for the behavior you have self-monitored. Discuss the results of your findings and the clinical course of action that is implicated by the data.

2. Using the published single-case design study selected for purposes of completing Exercise 1 in chapter 1, material presented in Appendix 1, and the sample form presented in this chapter for developing a measurement plan, outline the plan used in this study.

3. Evaluate the plan. Discuss whether sufficient information was provided for determining

the presence or absence of stability in the time-series data at baseline. Critically assess strengths and limitations of the plan.

ENDNOTE

1. Using data sets of four points each for baseline and intervention phases, Blumberg (1984) expressed three concerns that pertain to the case in which a statistically significant trend is evident at baseline and the data analyst wishes to determine if the trend changes or continues in the treatment phase. She articulated a fourth concern regarding the erroneous conclusions that can result when a small number of baseline observations are used to evaluate time-series data. Her arguments and Tryon's (1984) responses to them are summarized below.

1. When a linear baseline trend is compared with a linear treatment phase trend having a different slope, the C statistic will have the same value regardless of the actual values of the slopes of the baseline and treatment phase lines. In this case, the value of C is totally dependent upon the number of observations taken. Tryon agrees that C would be dependent on the number observations in the situation described by Blumberg, but adds that the presence of data points that form an exact linear sequence is very unlikely. He also argues that C is not a measure of effect size, but instead, an evaluation of the probability that the time-series is random. He further states that given eight data points all lying on the same line, C will be significant because this is such an unlikely random result.

2. When there are linear trends in both the baseline and treatment phases with the same slopes but different intercepts, C will not be significant even though the treatment has had an effect. Tryon argues that this is not true if the treatment series is appended to the baseline series and the composite series is analyzed, noting that a shift in slope alone produces a significant C value. It follows that changes in both slope and intercept would produce significant C values.

3. It is possible to get a statistically significant Z value when there is no change in the trend

of the data between the baseline phase and the intervention phase. Tryon argues that this condition exists when the behavioral data equal the square or some other power of the session number. He provides sample data with an average slope of 5 at baseline and 13 during intervention, noting that the average change during treatment is 260% of that during baseline. Although the C statistic is significant under these conditions, he states that few behavior analysts would erroneously conclude that no change has occurred because the exponent remains constant from baseline to treatment.

4. Using an example with three baseline data points (for which no trend is evident) and two intervention data points (for which a trend is evident), the behavior analyst would wrongly conclude that: (1) baseline data are stable, and (2) a treatment effect is evident. Tryon responds that the power of C is directly proportional to the number of data points in the series and that the baseline plus treatment analysis is more powerful than the baseline alone analysis. He argues that because statistical power is always a function of the size of the data set, any statistic will be significant if it is based on a large enough set of data, and hence, Blumberg's concern is with statistical analysis in general rather than the C statistic in particular. He offers the following solution: Use the standard error calculated during the baseline analysis to test for the presence of a trend during the baseline plus treatment analysis. This ignores that more information provides more data, resulting in greater precision and statistical power; however, the proposed resolution allows for greater equivalence between the baseline alone and baseline plus treatment analyses.

Jones (2003) citing Crosbie (1989) states that although Tryon (1984) largely countered concerns raised by Blumberg (1984), Crosbie identified an additional reason for concern when using the C statistic to evaluate time-series data. Based on Monte Carlo simulations, Crosbie reported significant limitations on the use of C in data sets with statistically significant autocorrelation, notably the lag 1 autocorrelation. Crosbie reported that as autocorrelation approaches zero, the risk of Type I error with the C statistic was within satisfactory limits. According to Jones, given the similarity between the formulae for calculating the C statistic and lag 1 autocorrelation, a baseline series evaluated with C as having no trend would also be expected to have a low autocorrelation index. Reframing Tryon's (1982) suggestion regarding the most effective use of C (when there is no trend in the time-series data at baseline) as a rule, Jones argued that C should be performed only if no trend is evident at baseline. He further suggested as a practical guideline that the baseline analysis should comprise at least eight observations, an approach that is consistent with that advocated in this text.

CHAPTER 5

Phase 2: Intervention

DEFINITION OF THE INTERVENTION PHASE

The intervention phase is the second phase in the basic model of single-case design methodology. Following the establishment of a baseline, the clinical social worker introduces an intervention—a set of actions, behaviors, or activities the clinical social worker arranges or exhibits to achieve one or more prescribed objectives. He or she takes repeated measurements, ideally in the same periods as at baseline and of the same problem variables that the social worker measured during baseline.

The purpose of the intervention is to achieve change or, in the case of prevention or maintenance, absence of change. For example, a clinical objective with a client who is an alcoholic may be to change the amount of his or her daily intake of alcohol; on achievement of the change objective, another clinical objective might be to prevent the recurrence of alcoholic consumption at the same rate as at baseline—another way of indicating prevention of relapse. Correspondingly, an objective with a child of the alcoholic client might be to prevent the occurrence of alcoholic consumption.

An intervention may be as simple as a direct verbal communication to make a telephone call or as complex as an interactive mode of psychotherapy. Thus, interventions are broadly conceived and can represent the full range of approaches, principles, and techniques clinical social workers use, such as group psychotherapy, reinforcement schedules, task-centered treat-ment, cognitive therapy, advice giving, insight development, social support, and communication. Interventions are described in and derived from social work theories and assumptions about human behavior and the conditions and factors that can change behavior.

Social workers learn interventions in schools of social work, continuing education classes, seminars and workshops on particular problems and techniques, from the literature, and from their own and shared experiences with colleagues and supervisors. In an analysis of the direct practice literature pertaining to the use and generalization of principles that guide practice, Nurius, Wedenoja, and Tripodi (1987) reported that authors who used practice prescriptions or proscriptions were most likely to base them on their own experiences or others' experiences. They defined prescriptions and proscriptions as follows:

> A prescription mandates a specific action, intervention or treatment structure to be performed or implemented by a social work practitioner in the context of interpersonal practice when working with a specific client or defined client population. This may involve direct practitioner and client interaction in a clinical setting or interventions carried out by the practitioner on behalf of the client (for example, case management, advocacy, and so forth). Prescriptions are identified by statements directed toward the practitioner's actions by means of words such as "should," "must," "need to," "is mandatory," "is required," "essential," or "vital" and sentence

structures describing what practitioners are "to do." Proscriptions follow the same definitional guidelines as prescriptions except that they mandate what actions, interventions, or treatment structures the practitioners should not perform or implement. (pp. 590–591)

CLINICAL INTERVENTION OBJECTIVES

Intervention objectives for clinical social workers can be roughly classified as those that deal with change, maintenance, prevention, or care (Blythe & Tripodi, 1989; Ivanoff, Blythe, & Tripodi, 1994; Vonk, Tripodi, & Epstein, 2006). Change refers to an increase, a decrease, or a qualitative difference in problem variables measured at intervention and compared with baseline. Hence, shifts in the time-series data indicate change. Of course, the objective is that change be clinically desirable. Thus, a reduction in anxiety, an increase in problem solving behavior, and a change from living in a situation that discourages social interaction to one that encourages it are examples of clinically desirable change objectives. Change that occurs in the desired direction is referred to as positive change. When the problem is exacerbating, the change is referred to as negative change. Changes are registered in knowledge, attitudes, beliefs, skills, living situations, places of residence or employment, clinical symptomatology, and so forth. For example, a teenager may learn about safer sex practices. Parents may change their attitudes about the use of punishment in child rearing. An introverted person might learn social skills for developing and nurturing social relationships. An abused child may function better in a foster home environment than in the home where he or she is abused by his or her natural parents. And a person with bipolar depression may not exhibit symptoms with persistent use of appropriate medication.

Maintenance and prevention are both change objectives as long as there is no change within a specified period. For example, if the objective is to prevent the incidence of substance abuse, baseline measurements should indicate no substance abuse. To accomplish the clinical objective, there should be no change in substance abuse after the social worker has initiated

an intervention. Undesirable changes possibly may occur during a person's lifetime, but that is typically too long a period for evaluation. The social worker should specify the clinical timeframe for objectives more precisely. The clinical social worker, for example, may seek no change in substance abuse behavior for a particular year that a teenage client is enrolled in school. The problem of relapse among alcoholics, child abusers, schizophrenics, and so forth is severe. The purpose of maintenance intervention is to maintain such clients (who previously had the undesirable symptomatology) in a symptom-free state, showing no reversion to their previous problems.

Another area that represents clinical objectives is difficult to define in terms of change: care. Care refers to the humaneness in showing care for the welfare and humanity of clients; its intent is to show the client that people do care—they will listen to the client's opinions and beliefs. Care overlaps with the maintenance and prevention intervention objectives and may lead to measurable objectives in specific situations. For example, the elderly person in a hospice may feel lonely; the social worker's intervention might help meet that need. The social worker can measure change in loneliness if the practitioner and the client can define the change to produce, for example, a decrease of two points in the client's degree of self-reported loneliness as measured by a self-anchored rating scale.

CHOOSING INTERVENTIONS

The clinical social worker chooses interventions that are relevant to the accomplishment of clinical objectives, consonant with the clinical social worker's experience, feasible, ethical, effective, and efficient (Blythe & Tripodi, 1989; Ivanoff, Blythe, & Tripodi, 1994; Vonk, Tripodi, & Epstein, 2006). Relevance is based on the clinical social worker's knowledge and perception of the utility of interventions for accomplishing clinical objectives. Although the social worker chooses interventions that are consistent with his or her experience in working with a variety of clients or are based on the experience of seasoned consultants and supervisors, the clinician also needs to choose realistic interventions. The social worker might use such interventions, depending on the specific clinical situation, within a specified time period with a limited number of interviews. Interventions designed for long-term therapy, for example, to induce insight about the relationship of past relationships to present social interactions, would be inappropriate for emergency, short-term, crisis interventions (Ivanoff et al.).

Correspondingly, a short-term intervention would be inappropriate for sustaining supportive psychotherapy and medication for a chronic schizophrenic client living in a group home. Furthermore, a clinician should use interventions only if the social worker, the client, and the community perceive them as ethical. Using negative reinforcement or punishment in the form of electroshock in a therapy based on theories of classical conditioning is unethical. Chief guidelines for the ethical use of interventions are promulgated in the *NASW Code of Ethics* (National Association of Social Workers, 2000).

When choosing interventions that are based on research or the social worker's experiences, the social worker needs to meet the criteria of effectiveness and efficiency. Empirically based practice is founded on research knowledge about effectiveness and efficiency (Siegel, 1984) and on experiential knowledge gained through cumulative practice experiences (which also are empirical, that is, amenable to the senses). Basically, the social worker requires the knowledge that the intervention will lead to or has led to the accomplishment of clinical objectives with clients with which the clinical social worker is engaged. When choosing among competing interventions, the social worker can meet the criterion of efficiency, that is, the relationship of effectiveness to the cost of implementing an intervention (Tripodi, 1983). For example, a single-session discussion group designed to reduce preoperative anxiety in patients would be more efficient than individual interviews with each group member if the practitioner can achieve the same reduction in anxiety using either method and the cost to implement the group is lower than the cost to conduct the individual interviews.

SPECIFYING INTERVENTIONS

Specifying interventions will clarify when an intervention is or is not occurring. In this way, the clinician can more appropriately apply the logic of single-case design methodology for evaluating the effectiveness of an intervention. Furthermore, the clinical social worker can accumulate a repertoire of interventions and their relative successes and failures for individual practice and can communicate this knowledge to colleagues and other professionals.

The practitioner should first specify clinical objectives with respect to their emphases on change, maintenance, prevention, or care, or a combination of these. The social worker can then further delineate the objectives by considering parameters related to the clinical objectives and factors that describe the intervention. Parameters that further specify the clinical objectives are the variables related to the problem: an indication of when the social worker expects change (or no change) to occur and an estimate of how long the change will last if it occurs. These parameters involve measuring problem indicators as discussed in chapters 3 and 4. For example, the clinical objective may be to reduce symptomatology about depression; the variable may be a 10-point self-anchored rating scale ranging from 0 = no depression to 10 = severe depression. The clinical social worker bases his or her expectations on an assessment of the client and on whatever knowledge the social worker has of client anxiety and the intervention. For example, the practitioner may expect change as defined in the clinical objective, from an average rating of 8 to an average rating of 2, within two months after six to eight interviews. If change occurs, the social worker may expect it to endure for a minimum of three months. The specificity of these objectives guides the social worker in evaluating the effectiveness of the intervention. If no change occurs after two months of intervention, the social worker would need to determine, if possible, the reasons and then decide whether to continue or modify the intervention or substitute intervention alternatives. Assuming change occurs after two months, the social worker would want to build in plans for follow-up (see chapter 6) to determine whether changes persist after three months.

To make decisions about intervention modifications, the social worker must have detailed descriptions of intervention. He or she can specify in advance factors that might characterize the essence of simple interventions such as straightforward verbal communications, behaviors, and actions, for example, a directive to complete an activity, contact a person, or initiate a discussion or a verbal positive reinforcement and a smile for positive interactions in a family interview. However, it is impossible to specify in advance the contents of interactive psychotherapeutic interventions. With more complex forms of intervention, it is possible to specify a few factors, but the practitioner can determine the contents only after the interventions occur; thus, interview notes, process and summary recordings, and tape-recorded interviews are mechanisms for obtaining more complete descriptions of the interventions.

General factors the practitioner can specify in advance include the intervenors, location of the intervention, frequency of the intervention, duration of the intervention, and information about the contents of the intervention (Tripodi, 1983). The clinical social worker typically is the intervenor, but he or she also may work with colleagues or enlist the services of significant others. For example, intervention may require "homework assignments" the clinical social worker gives to the client which the client's spouse monitors daily. Or, the clinical social worker may engage in the contents of the intervention during interviews, while the client's spouse ensures that the client takes prescribed dosages of medication, another aspect of the intervention.

The location of the intervention is another factor that defines general characteristics of the intervention. The clinical social worker's office, the client's home, a waiting room, and so forth are possible sites. The frequency of the intervention refers to the number of different contacts the clinical social worker makes with the client. Contacts may be in the form of interviews, telephone calls, or group meetings, among others. Contacts may range from complete 24-hour-per-day availability for six weeks, as in the Homebuilders model of family preservation (Ivanoff et al., 1994), to routine once-per-month maintenance contacts.

The duration of the intervention indicates the length of time the social worker has planned for the intervention. An intervention may be for an indefinite period, for example, with parolees or with severely mentally disturbed children in residential care. Or the intervention may be for a prescribed duration such as one month while a client is in an observational setting such as juvenile court or for the time necessary to include a prescribed set of interviews, as in the conveyance of instructional materials regarding health-promoting behavior.

These factors, though, do not describe the essence of an intervention, which is contained in its contents. Information about the contents of intervention might include as much detail as possible about the behaviors, statements, and protocols the clinical social worker uses to implement the intervention. Ideally, the clinician should present enough information so that any other clinical social worker could replicate the intervention. The social worker can easily articulate contents that are didactic or instructional. Furthermore, he or she can only specify contents for interactions by referring to guidelines, that is, principles that inform the social worker but do not bind him or her to act in specific ways. These guidelines might include procedures such as the following: directives on when to probe, to gather information, to listen, to allow the client to vent feelings, and so forth; directions for developing role-play situations with the client; and identification of themes to discuss in individual interviews or group discussions.

Examples of simple to more complex forms of interventions are as follows:

- a daily telephone call to a client to take medication
- an instruction to follow up on a referral to a particular agency

- advice to a parent to meet his or her child after school every evening
- five educational sessions over a three-week period, including didactic presentations and discussions about specific areas
- use of role-play situations in four group meetings with eight clients over a one-month period; clients select interpersonal conflict situations; they carry out role plays under the guidance of the group leader; and group members discuss ways to deal with the conflict situations
- a prescribed series of interviews of a short-term psychotherapy (such as cognitive therapy or task-oriented social work) as prescribed by proponents of the therapy and illustrated in the literature and in case vignettes and videotapes.

IMPLEMENTING THE INTERVENTIONS

After establishing a baseline and indicating a need to ameliorate the existing problem, the clinical social worker should introduce the intervention in accordance with his or her plan. The experience of the client who receives the intervention should be discernibly different from the client's experience before the intervention. Distinguishing the presence of an intervention from other possible interventions, however, may be difficult, especially in complex settings in which the client may interact with professionals from a variety of related disciplines, such as psychiatry, psychology, social work, nursing, education, and occupational therapy. The following questions, though, may help the social worker make the distinction:

- Who provides the intervention? Is the provider similar or different from the client's other intervention providers?
- Where is the intervention provided? Is the location of intervention similar to or different from the location of other interventions?
- What are the contents of the intervention? Are they similar to or different from the contents of other interventions?
- What are the frequency and duration of the intervention? Are they similar to or different from the frequency or duration of other interventions?

- What is the client unit (individual, couple, family, or group)? Is it similar to or different from the client unit in other interventions?

The more differences there are between the new intervention and other interventions currently in operation, the more likely the clinician can analyze the additional effect of the new intervention. If more similarities than differences among the interventions exist, then the social worker can analyze the joint effectiveness of all the interventions only as a package. To apply single-case design methodology for evaluating interventions, it is imperative that the clinical social worker and the client can distinguish the presence or absence of the intervention. For example, a Veterans Affairs (VA) neuropsychiatric hospital may refer a client to the clinical social worker who will plan the client's departure from the hospital as well as make the necessary arrangements to enable the client to adjust to his or her community. Posthospital planning is one of many interventions, but the social worker and the client can clearly distinguish it from many other hospital interventions that focus on hospital adjustment, diagnoses, and symptom reduction rather than on adjustment in the family and the community. The client unit is the family in posthospital planning in contrast to the individual as client unit in interventions concerned with hospital adjustment. Moreover, the focus of the contents is on behaviors and attitudes pertaining to family and community adjustment.

Monitoring Intervention Implementation

The social worker determines whether an intervention has been implemented by monitoring the implementation. An intervention is valid if implemented as planned and reliable if implemented consistently for the clients in question (Blythe & Tripodi, 1989). The clinical social worker can construct a checklist to monitor the extent to which he or she has followed certain guidelines, prescriptions, and behaviors for implementing the intervention (Blythe & Tripodi). Also, the clinical social worker can devise a questionnaire whereby he or she asks the client whether the social worker followed the guidelines. The checklist in Figure 32 and

Item	Implemented or Not
Filled out all necessary insurance and discharge forms	Yes _____ No _____
Discussed medication regimen	
• With client	Yes _____ No _____
• With family	Yes _____ No _____
Considered whether client can live with family	
• With client	Yes _____ No _____
• With family	Yes _____ No _____
Considered alternative living arrangements in community	Yes _____ No _____
Made contacts with family	
• Face to face	Yes _____ No _____
• Telephone	Yes _____ No _____
Planned contact with community social worker	Yes _____ No _____
Discussed employment	Yes _____ No _____
Discussed educational possibilities	Yes _____ No _____
Arranged for follow-up contact	Yes _____ No _____

questionnaire (see Appendix 4), for example, indicates whether the social worker has implemented the intervention of posthospital planning in a VA neuropsychiatric hospital.

The items in Figure 32 and Appendix 4 are illustrative rather than exhaustive. The more that the social worker or the client checks "yes," the more likely it is that the social worker has implemented the intervention. Furthermore, social worker and client agreement on specific items provides evidence of the validity of the intervention. If the social worker were to use the same intervention for a caseload of clients, then consistency in responses across clients would indicate that the social worker is reliably implementing the intervention.

In addition, the clinical social worker can create forms that are specific to interviews or that refer to the ingredients of the intervention, which may cover several contacts between the clinical social worker and the client. The more specific the items in terms of observable behaviors, the more useful the form for distinguishing between the presence or absence of an intervention. Such

forms serve as useful reminders of functions that the clinical social worker needs to carry out. More important, they can indicate whether the client is aware of the social worker's efforts in delivering the intervention.

Measuring during the Intervention Phase

Suppose that a clinical social worker in private practice is beginning to work with a young female client who is disturbed by her obsessive behavior. The client wanted to marry her boyfriend, but he did not want to make that commitment. Their relationship ended, but the client continued to phone her former boyfriend and hang up the phone without leaving any messages or identification. She also knew how to access his answering machine and would listen to his phone messages at least once per day when she knew he was not home. The social worker asked the client to construct a baseline of calls she made each day to her former boyfriend. The social worker then engaged in short-term cognitive therapy with the client, focusing on the reasons for the phone calls, the client's anger, the possibility of police intervention, realistic alternatives, and so forth.

A daily measurement of the number of phone calls during baseline and three weeks of intervention, two interviews per week, is depicted in Figure 33. Measurement, obtained by the client's self-reports of daily phone calls during intervention, shows a decline in phone calls; hence, the social worker achieved the clinical objective of no phone calls after three weeks of intervention. The clinician also might have constructed a graph to show the number of times the client accessed her former boyfriend's answering machine during baseline and intervention.

Advantages. As shown in Figure 33, measurement during intervention allows the clinical social worker to compare the magnitude of variables at intervention with baseline when there is no intervention. The social worker can use the results of this comparison to evaluate the effectiveness of the intervention in terms of achieving client–social worker clinical objectives. Without measurements at baseline, though, there will not be any comparisons. However, the clinician can use the graphs (Figure 33) to assist in assessment, for example, as determined by high magnitudes on the problem variable such as 5, 4, 5, and 4 telephone calls on the first four days of intervention. Furthermore, the clinical social worker can observe whether he or she is making progress toward achieving the clinical objectives. A reduction in the number of phone

calls over time (Figure 33) indicates progress. In contrast, there might not have been any change in the first three weeks of intervention, and the therapeutic interactions might even have led to an increased number of phone calls. If the social worker has not made progress within a designated period, then he or she would have to rely on his or her clinical experience and knowledge to decide whether to continue the intervention, modify it, discard it for a substitute intervention, seek consultation for assistance in the decision-making process, refer the client elsewhere, or terminate the intervention.

The clinical social worker also can use measurements at intervention to provide feedback to the client and as stimuli for additional therapeutic discussion. For example, after the first week of intervention (Figure 33), there is a decline in the number of phone calls, with a plateau of three phone calls per day on Friday, Saturday, and Sunday. Suppose the client and the social worker had an interview on Tuesday of the second week of intervention. The social worker might point out the pattern to the client, reinforcing verbally the progress the client has made and asking about the reasons for the plateau of three calls per day. Overall, measurements at intervention can serve as brief summaries of progress on specified problem variables. The practitioner can use graphs and therapy notes when he or she gives case presentations for consultation, professional workshops, and community presentations to interested groups.

Disadvantages. One disadvantage of obtaining measurements during intervention is that such a process can detract from the intervention, especially when complicated measurements require a great deal of time for data collection. For example, the completion of a long personality inventory during every social worker–client contact would be excessive. Contrariwise, the client's daily recording of measurements outside of the intervention contact with the social worker would not seriously reduce the time devoted to intervention. However, the social worker would require a brief moment to construct the graphs.

Another disadvantage involves incorporating into the intervention the discussion of progress

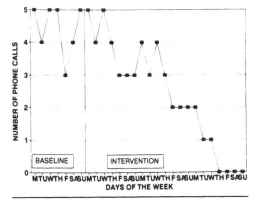

Number of Client Phone Calls per Day for Four Weeks

NOTE: M = Monday, TU = Tuesday, W = Wednesday, TH = Thursday, F = Friday, SA = Saturday, SU = Sunday.

as depicted by graphic trends. If the clinical social worker sees little use for graphic portrayals of progress, then the time he or she devotes to measurements during the intervention might be wasteful. On the other hand, such information can be useful in making decisions about progress toward the achievement of clinical objectives.

That the clinical social worker could view the results of measurements mechanically, not attending to important features of the client's life and to client-social worker interactions, is another disadvantage. During intervention, unanticipated events occur; the clinical social worker makes himself or herself aware of these events by observing qualitative differences in the transactions. For example, the client's progress shown in Figure 33 might not have resulted from the intervention; rather, it might have been the result of the client's positive interactions with another person and the fact that she had become more active socially compared with her relatively sedentary life in the past. Hence, the social worker's observations of other events in the client's life can provide a context for interpreting the measurements on one problem variable.

Characteristics. The measurement process during intervention must be consistent with that during the baseline phase. The operational definitions are identical and the procedures for gathering data are equivalent. Moreover, standards of feasibility, reliability, and validity continually apply. Two especially important characteristics are space between successive measurements and the number of measurements that the social worker should obtain. The distance or space between measurements, for example, days (Figure 33), should be identical at baseline and at intervention so that comparisons between intervention and baseline measurements are of the same units of analysis. If the time units in measurements are not equivalent (for example, comparing days versus weeks), distortions among the graphs are possible and may lead to erroneous conclusions about clinical progress.

The number of measurements the clinician makes during intervention depends on the clinical objective with respect to when the so-cial worker expects changes to occur (or for how long changes are not expected to occur, as in maintenance or prevention). If the social worker predicts changes after a designated period and they do not occur, then the clinical social worker has to decide whether he or she will modify the objective regarding when change will occur. Otherwise, the criterion for the number of measurements is the number obtainable during the designated period. As shown in Figure 33, if the practitioner expects changes during three weeks of intervention, then 21 measurements is the required number.

The number of measurements made also depends on the extent to which there is deterioration in the magnitude of problem variables during intervention. An intervention possibly might exacerbate the problem. For example, the client might not have made progress (Figure 33) if she felt the social worker thought she was "crazy" or "pathological." Instead, after the first week, the number of calls might have increased to 10 or more calls, indicating a strong aversive reaction to the therapist. Of course, the social worker might have considered an initial exacerbation of the behavior as part of the clinical plan. Then the social worker's decision making about the number of measurements—given ethical constraints involved in clinical practice—would depend on the length of time the clinical social worker's theory would allow for an increase in undesirable deteriorative behaviors. Many practitioners would seriously consider modifying or changing the intervention if the number of phone calls increased immediately.

The number of measurements a practitioner makes also depends on the attainment of clinical objectives. If, in the example of the female client with obsessive behavior, the number of phone calls decreased to zero after the first week of intervention and she did not make any phone calls during the second week of intervention, then the social worker could suspend measurements for that problem variable during intervention and simultaneously stop the intervention.

Generally, as indicated by Barlow and Hersen (1984), a criterion for the number of measurements during intervention is to attain repeated measurements of the variable showing persistent achievement of the clinical objective regarding the magnitude of the problem variable. For example, in Figure 33, this pattern is illustrated by the last four measurements from Thursday through Sunday during the third week of intervention. The clinical objective of no phone calls was achieved, and persisted for the four-day interval shown. If, on the other hand, the pattern fluctuated from zero to one to two and then back to one on these four days, the clinician should consider gathering additional measurements (and continue the intervention) until there is evidence that the observed change persists.

The clinical social worker should review the measurement plan with the client and others who will provide measurements at the beginning of the intervention phase. As in the baseline phase, the clinician should communicate to those involved that the information they provide will facilitate the establishment of treatment goals for addressing the client's problem and the development of a treatment plan for achieving the selected goals. Additionally, the clinician should convey his or her understanding of the time and effort each is willing to invest on the client's behalf and articulate his or her appreciation for their continued participation in the measurement process.

GRAPHING THE MEASURES

Intervention without a Baseline

Even when a baseline is unattainable, there is utility in graphing the problem variables (measures) during the intervention phase. The measurements can verify the clinical social worker's initial assessment and indicate the extent to which positive or negative change in the existence, frequency, severity or duration of the problem variable is occurring.

Suppose a male client of a clinical social worker at a community mental health center has just returned to the community after a three-month psychiatric hospitalization for an acute episode of depression. Suppose also that the hospital refers the client to intervention immediately on release to the community. Before hospitaliza-

tion, the client had difficulty attending his job and the clinical social worker decided to use supportive therapy in addition to the client's prescribed medication for depression. One clinical objective was to increase weekly job attendance to 100 percent attendance. The social worker made 12 measurements, each recording the percentage of attendance on the job (Figure 34). Using the same principles for graphic construction and analysis as used for baseline, the social worker plotted the problem variable on the y-axis, and time (in number of weeks) on the x-axis. During the first five weeks, the client's job attendance oscillated between 10 percent and 20 percent, measurements that verify the assessment of an attendance problem at work. The social worker arranged to obtain, with the client's consent, attendance information from the client's employer. If the client was supposed to be at work 20 hours per week, and he attended only for four hours, his weekly percentage of attendance would be 100 percent times $(4/20) = 20$ percent. From the sixth week to the 10th week, attendance increased steadily from 50 percent to 100 percent. In addition, the client achieved the clinical objective of 100 percent attendance, which stabilized during the last three weeks; hence, the graph indicates progress during intervention.

It is apparent visually that change occurred during the intervention. However, it is unclear

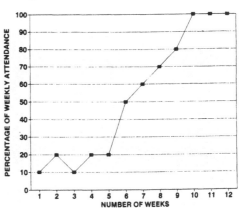

figure 34

Percentage of Weekly Attendance in Client's Job during Clinical Intervention

whether change is linked to the intervention or if it would have occurred without the intervention because a baseline was unavailable. What the clinical social worker can infer is whether there is a change in the time series of measurements during intervention, using the same principles of visual and statistical analysis (see chapter 4). There is a statistically significant trend in the time series of measurements, as indicated by the C statistic (Table 15). Hence, the data, which show there is not horizontal stability but rather an acceleration over time, support the visual perception. The absence of change during intervention would indicate no clinical progress when the clinical objective is to achieve change.

Comparing Intervention to Baseline

To construct graphs that contain measurements plotted for both baseline and intervention, the clinical social worker should follow the same principles for constructing baseline graphs, as

well as the following suggestions for extending the time series to interventions.

The social worker should use the measurement plan that was introduced in the baseline phase for collecting measurements during intervention. As is evident from Figure 35, vertical line AB separates measurements at baseline from those at intervention. Each phase should be labeled to facilitate visual inspection and analysis of the observed measurements. The social worker has plotted the first eight measurements of anxiety on a 10-point scale ranging from 0 = no anxiety to 10 = high anxiety during baseline when there was no intervention; he or she plotted the next eight measurements during intervention. The practitioner has plotted measurements for intervention using the same range of possible magnitudes as at baseline. The ordinate of each point can range from 0 to 10 (y-axis) for both baseline and intervention. The practitioner plotted measurements for each point on

table 15	*Computing S, Sc, and Z for Data in Figure 34*				
Score (x)	$x - M$	$(x - M)^2$	x_i	$x - x_i$	$(x - x_i)^2$
10	−43.33	1877.48	20	−10	100
20	−33.33	1110.88	10	10	100
10	−43.33	1877.48	20	−10	100
20	−33.33	1110.88	20	0	0
20	−33.33	1110.88	50	−30	900
50	−3.33	11.08	60	−10	100
60	6.67	44.48	70	−10	100
70	16.67	277.88	80	−10	100
80	26.67	711.28	100	−20	400
100	46.67	2178.08	100	0	0
100	46.67	2178.08	100	0	0
100	46.67	2178.08	–	–	–

$640 = \Sigma x$		$114,666.56 = SS(x)$	$11,900 = D^2$	
$M = \Sigma x/n$		$= 640/12$	$= 53.33$	
$C = 1 - D^2/(2SS(x))$		$= 1 - 1,900/2(14,666.56)$	$= .93$	
$Sc = \sqrt{(n-2)/(n+1)(n-1)}$		$= \sqrt{(12-2)/(12+1)(12-1)}$	$= .26$	
$Z = C/Sc$		$= .93/.26$	$= 3.57$	

NOTE: Because $Z > 1.64$, there is a change in the time-series.

figure 35

Baseline and Intervention Measurements of Daily Anxiety over 16 Days

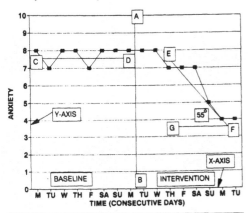

NOTE: M = Monday, TU = Tuesday, W = Wednesday, TH = Thursday, F = Friday, SA = Saturday, SU = Sunday.

clinician could compare baseline with intervention after five months, omitting the graph for the first five months of intervention. The social worker also should know the clinical objectives with respect to the degree of change expected. For example, the client and clinical social worker might have agreed that a change in magnitude of four points on a self-anchored anxiety scale would be clinically significant.

In reading the graphs comparing intervention with baseline, the clinical social worker must keep the following points in mind. For one, he or she should look for a change in degree from the baseline series of measurements to the intervention series of measurements. In Figure 35 at baseline, anxiety ranges from 7 to 8, but during intervention, the magnitude of anxiety decreases from 8 to 4.

In addition, the practitioner should look for a change in the slope of the time series. At baseline, the slope is virtually 0 degrees as shown by line CD, which is an estimated average line of the measurements (Figure 35). During intervention, line EF shows an average estimated slope of 55 degrees (formed by drawing a line parallel to the x-axis and intersecting it with point F). These average estimate lines are not completely accurate; instead, they help indicate whether there is a change in the time series (a section later in this chapter discusses how statistical methods can more precisely indicate change). The series of measurements at baseline are relatively stable horizontally; the series of measurements during intervention are decelerating downward, with the last two measurements stable at a magnitude of 4.

In reading graphs, the clinician should look for achievement of clinical objectives. If the objective is to reduce anxiety by four points, then the last two measurements in Figure 35 are clinically significant-the social worker has achieved the objective. The clinician also should assess whether the achieved change is persisting. For example, in Figure 35, the third, fourth, and fifth measurements during intervention are at a magnitude of 7, but all the other measurements are below that point. The consistency of the last two measurements at a magnitude of 4 also may

the x-axis, which has the same time intervals for intervention and for baseline (each interval is one day).

The number of measurements during intervention should be at least the same number as at baseline. Typically, there are many more measurements at intervention. In Figure 35, the number of measurements at baseline and at intervention is identical. However, the social worker could have extended the measurement to include more measurements so they would be consonant with clinical objectives.

Furthermore, the clinician should know the clinical objectives with respect to when he or she expects the intervention to have an impact. For example, the social worker might not expect anxiety to be reduced until there are five or more clinical sessions over a two-week period; if that is the case, he or she would extend the graph to cover that period. If the clinical social worker did not expect change until five months, he or she would continually take measurements for more than five months, without expecting change until five months had elapsed. Then, the social worker could graph the baseline and compare it with intervention after five months, determining whether the expected change occurred at the expected time. That is, if no change had occurred during the five-month period, the

change with subsequent measurements that also might decelerate downward. The clinical social worker should assess the clinical utility of extending the intervention phase to collect additional measurements for determining if the observed change persists. Finally, the social worker should describe the highest and lowest points. In Figure 35, the range of magnitude is 8 to 7 at baseline and 8 to 4 during intervention. The drop of four points in magnitude during intervention represents a change in a desirable direction, that is, in relation to the clinical objective of reducing anxiety.

Examples of Change and No Change

Suppose that a clinical social worker is engaged in short-term cognitive therapy with a female client who is having a great deal of difficulty in her marital relationship. Although both she and her husband have indicated that the husband has not had nor is having an extramarital relationship, the client complained of obsessive thoughts about his infidelity. According to the client, she has these thoughts several times per day. The social worker asks the client to record on a daily basis the number of obsessive thoughts for eight consecutive days to form a baseline.

Figure 36 shows the baseline measurements and eight measurements during intervention in which there was only one treatment session, with no change expected. The magnitude of measurement is roughly the same at baseline and during intervention. At baseline, there are six 5s and two 4s; at intervention, there are five 5s and three 4s. Both intervention and baseline have slopes near 0 degrees without evident change. If a clinical objective were to reduce the number of obsessive thoughts to 1 or 0 per day, then it is evident in the figure that the social worker did not achieve the clinical objective. However, no change is a clinical objective when there is an intervention to stabilize maintenance, thus preventing relapse. If the client achieved the objective of having no obsessive thoughts, a maintenance objective might be to continue to show no obsessive thoughts or to register no change.

Negative change or deterioration occurs when the client shows change from baseline to a greater degree of the problem following the

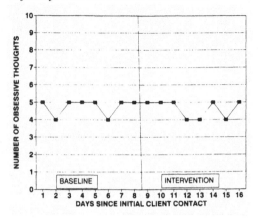

figure 36

Daily Nunber of Obsessive Thoughts about Infidelity, at Baseline and at Intervention

introduction of intervention. Deterioration is unplanned; it is an unexpected consequence the clinical social worker must be prepared to confront. To illustrate this type of change, Figure 37 shows that the client with obsessive thoughts about infidelity increased her obsessive thoughts during the first week of intervention, nine days after initial contact with the clinical social worker. The magnitude of the number of obsessive thoughts increased from 5 on the eighth day of baseline to 7 on the first day of intervention, nine days after initial contact with the client at intake. Moreover, the number of obsessive thoughts during intervention increased at

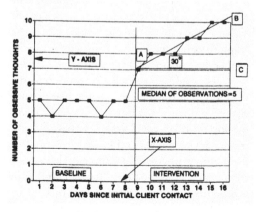

figure 37

Deterioration in the Daily Number of Obsessive Thoughts about Infidelity, from Baseline to Intervention

a slope of approximately 30 degrees (the angle BAC is formed by intersecting the estimated average line of the measurements, AB, with line AC, parallel to the x-axis) to 10 obsessive thoughts per day.

Positive change is a change in the desired direction with respect to clinical objectives. In Figure 38, positive change is evident because there is a decelerating slope, which indicates a decrease in the number of obsessive thoughts. Line AB represents the median (the point below which 50 percent of the observations fall) of the baseline observations. The social worker calculates the median by rank ordering all of the baseline observations (that is, listing observed scores in ascending or descending order) and selecting the point that is halfway as follows:

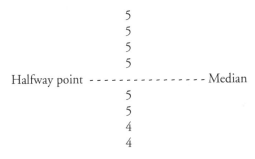

The halfway point is the average of the fourth and fifth ranked observations; the median is 5.

In Figure 38, all of the observations in the fourth week of intervention, beginning with 22 days since initial contact with the client at intake, are below the baseline median, assuming there are no changes from baseline to the first three weeks of intervention. During the fourth week, the number of obsessive thoughts decreased from 2 to 0 per day. The slope, shown by angle CDE is 26 degrees, which indicates a decelerating trend. The social worker has attained the clinical objective of no obsessive thoughts on day 27 of measurement and has maintained the objective on days 28 and 29.

Calculating Statistical Significance

The clinical social worker can follow two procedures for calculating statistical significance: (1) the C statistic and (2) the binomial test for horizontal baseline. Other procedures are available

figure 38

Positive Change in the Daily Number of Obsessive Thoughts about Infidelity, from Baseline to Three Weeks after Intervention

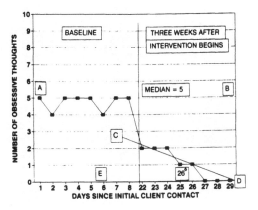

in Kazdin (1992), Bloom, Fischer, and Orme (2006), and Blythe, Tripodi, and Briar (1994). Using the data in Figures 37 and 38, the social worker calculates the C statistic for comparing the time series at baseline and intervention in the same way that C was calculated using baseline data only. The social worker uses all of the observations from baseline and intervention, as long as there are eight or more observations, to make the calculations. In Table 16, $C = .88$, $Sc = .23$, and $Z = 3.82$. Because Z is greater than 1.64, the probability of this occurrence is less than five times out of 100, a statistical criterion indicating a shift in the time series of observations from baseline to intervention during the fourth week. If Z were less than 1.64, it would indicate no change from baseline to intervention.

To evaluate whether there are any statistically significant shifts from baseline to intervention, the social worker can use the binomial test for horizontal baseline (Blythe & Tripodi, 1989, pp. 127–130). The social worker can only use this procedure when there is no evidence of change in the baseline series of observations (that is, when baseline data are horizontally stable), which he or she can determine by using C as described in chapter 4.

First, the social worker calculates the median of the baseline observations (which is 5; see Figure 38). Then, he or she draws a dotted line

table 16	*Computing S, Sc, and Z for Data in Figure 38*				
Score (x)	x – M	(x – M)²	x_i	x – x_i	(x – x_i)²
5	2.13	4.53	4	1	1
4	1.13	1.27	5	–1	1
5	2.13	4.53	5	0	0
5	2.13	4.53	5	0	0
5	2.13	4.53	4	1	1
4	1.13	1.27	5	–1	1
5	2.13	4.53	5	0	0
5	2.13	4.53	2	3	9
2	–.87	.75	2	0	0
2	–.87	.75	2	0	0
2	–.87	.75	1	1	1
1	–1.87	3.49	1	0	0
1	–1.87	3.49	0	1	1
0	–2.87	8.23	0	0	0
0	–2.87	8.23	0	0	0
0	–2.87	8.23	–	–	–

$46 = \Sigma x$	$63.64 = SS(x)$	$15 = D^2$
$M = \Sigma x/n$	$= 46/16$	$= 2.87$
$C = 1 - D^2/(2SS(x))$	$= 1 - 15/2(63.64)$	$= .88$
$Sc = \sqrt{(n-2)/(n+1)(n-1)} = \sqrt{(16-2)/(16+1)(16-1)} = .23$		
$Z = C/Sc$	$= .88/.23$	$= 3.82$

NOTE: Because $Z > 1.64$, and $p < .05$, there is a statistically significant change in the time-series.

through point 5 on the y-axis parallel to the x-axis (line AB). The social worker subsequently determines what is a success and what is a failure. Successes should be on that side of the line that is consonant with the clinical objective. In Figure 38, any observation below line AB is considered a success, and observations above the line are failures. If an observation fell exactly on the median, then the social worker would not use it. The next step is to count the number of successes and the number of observations during intervention. Because all eight observations (Figure 38) are below the median, there are eight successes out of eight observations. Table 17 indicates the minimum number of successes required out of specified numbers of observations ranging from 5 to 25 to indicate a statistically significant shift from baseline to intervention

beyond the .05 level of probability. For eight observations, the minimum number of successes is seven; this means that there are statistically significant changes with seven or eight successes out of eight observations. Hence, this method also shows statistically significant differences for the data in Figure 38.

The calculation of C for the data in Figure 37 is shown in Table 18. The statistics $C = .92$, $Sc = .23$, and $Z = 4.00$ indicate a statistically significant shift in the time series from baseline to intervention because Z is greater than the criterion of 1.96. Because the observations are not in the predicted direction, the criterion shifts from a one-tailed probability test with Z greater than 1.64 to a two-tailed probability test with Z greater than 1.96. Refer to any standard statistics

table 17 *Minimum Number of Successes for Statistical Significance at* $p \leq .05$

Number of Observations during Intervention	Minimum Number of Successes Required
5	5
6	6
7	7
8	7
9	8
10	9
11	9
12	10
13	11
14	11
15	12
16	12
17	13
18	14
19	14
20	15
21	16
22	16
23	17
24	17
25	18

text for a discussion of one-tailed and two-tailed probability tests. That the criterion value is 1.96 instead of 1.64 reflects that deterioration is not predicted whereas positive change is. Hence, the social worker should use $Z = 1.64$ when predicting positive change and $Z = 1.96$ when testing for negative change. These data indicate that deterioration (or negative change) is associated with the intervention.

The binomial test also indicates negative change. In Figure 37, the median is 5. During intervention, eight out of eight observations are failures because the observations are in an opposite direction from the clinical objective of reducing the number of obsessive thoughts.

Judging Change

The clinical social worker determines whether there is change from baseline to intervention by using clinical judgment or statistical significance. Clinical judgment is based on the clinical social worker's observations of whether there is a significant shift in the client's behaviors, attitudes, or moods. A reasonable criterion is one the client and social worker have agreed on after the social worker has assessed the problems for that particular client. The social worker might make a judgment with respect to a general objective such as an unspecified reduction or increase in the problem variable, for example, a decrease in the number of obsessive thoughts, a decrease in the number of drinks, or an increase in the number of positive interactions. A more specific objective would indicate the expected magnitude of the problem variable, for example, a decrease to zero obsessive thoughts, a decrease to two drinks per day, or an increase to four positive interactions per day. When the expectation is close to baseline, it is difficult to determine whether change is meaningful or whether it occurs on a chance basis. Suppose there is a baseline of five obsessive thoughts per day. An objective of four thoughts per day could result from an error in the data collection or might occur on a chance basis. In that event, the criterion

Score (x)	x – M	$(x - M)^2$	x_i	$x - x_i$	$(x - x_i)^2$
5	−1.68	2.82	4	1	1
4	−2.68	7.18	5	−1	1
5	−1.68	2.82	5	0	0
5	−1.68	2.82	5	0	0
5	−1.68	2.82	4	1	1
4	−2.68	7.18	5	−1	1
5	−1.68	2.82	5	0	0
5	−1.68	2.82	7	−2	4
7	.32	.10	8	−1	1
8	1.32	1.74	8	0	0
8	1.32	1.74	8	0	0
8	1.32	1.74	9	−1	1
9	2.32	5.38	9	0	0
9	2.32	5.38	10	−1	1
10	3.32	11.02	10	0	0
10	3.32	11.02	–	–	–

Table 18 *Computing S, Sc, and Z for Data in Figure 37*

$107 = \Sigma x$ $\qquad$ $169.401 = SS(x)$ $\qquad$ $111 = D^2$

$M = \Sigma x / n$	$= 107/16$	$= 6.68$
$C = 1 - D^2/(2SS(x))$	$= 1 - 11/2(69.40)$	$= .92$
$Sc = \sqrt{(n - 2)/(n + 1)(n - 1)}$	$= \sqrt{(16 - 2)/(16 + 1)(16 - 1)}$	$= .23$
$Z = C/Sc$	$= .92/.23$	$= 4.00$

NOTE: Because $Z > 1.96$, there is a change in the time-series.

of statistical significance can help to solidify the conclusion of clinical significance if the result is both clinically significant as specified by an a priori judgment and statistically significant.

Statistical significance may or may not indicate clinical significance. To illustrate, the binomial test might indicate statistical significance with all observations below a median of 5 as in the example about obsessive thoughts; however, all of the observations may be at a magnitude of 4, and the reduction of 5 to 4 may not be sufficiently clinically significant to represent progress to the clinical social worker and the client. Hence, to be certain whether or not change has occurred, it is strongly recommended that, along with graphic analysis, the social worker use clinical significance in relation to the clinical objectives for the client.

Making Inferences about Correlational and Causal Knowledge

Correlational Knowledge. Graphs and statistical techniques along with clinical objectives can serve as tools that assist the clinical social worker in making inferences about correlational knowledge. Correlational knowledge describes the relationship between an intervention and observed change in a problem variable. Hypotheses about correlational knowledge include clinical examples such as follows: Group cognitive therapy reduces animal phobias in children or short-term psychotherapy increases the number of positive comments that family members make about each other. Evidence to substantiate hypotheses about correlational knowledge includes accurate, reliable, and valid measurements of the problem variable (see chapter 3) and a significant shift in the time series of measurements from baseline to intervention.

Inferences about correlational knowledge are essentially judgments that there is sufficient evidence to support the correlational hypotheses. A statistically significant change in time series at baseline with no intervention to time series of measurements during intervention provides evidence of a correlation. If the time series shows an increase with the introduction of the intervention, then the correlation is positive; correspondingly, a decrease in the time series indicates a negative correlation. The social worker may evaluate either negative or positive correlations as positive change (improvement) or negative change (deterioration). The evaluation depends on whether the direction of change is consistent with the clinical objectives of intervention. Hence, a positive correlation between short-term psychotherapy and an increase in confidence about a decision to divorce indicates positive change, whereas a positive correlation between group cognitive therapy and an increase in animal phobias is evidence of deterioration or negative change.

Graphs that provide evidence of correlations should show a stable horizontal baseline, followed by an acceleration (positive correlation) or a deceleration (negative correlation) during intervention. Specific clinical objectives such as reducing alcoholic consumption from five drinks to zero drinks per day provide evidence of correlational knowledge if, without intervention, the client consumes five drinks daily and, during intervention, consumes zero drinks.

Causal Knowledge. Causal knowledge provides substantiating evidence that an intervention is solely responsible for changes in a problem variable. Not only must there be a verified correlation between intervention and changes in the problem variable, but there also must be evidence that the intervention has preceded (in time) changes in the problem variable and that no other variables are responsible for the changes.

The structure of single-case designs provides evidence of correlational knowledge and the occurrence of the intervention before the prob-

lem variable has changed. The social worker accomplishes the correlation by achieving a horizontally stable baseline on the time series of measurements on the problem variable, followed by introducing the intervention and significant change in the problem variable during intervention.

Single-case design methodology also can provide evidence of the control of variables other than the intervention that might be responsible for change. These other variables are internal validity threats (Campbell & Stanley, 1963; Cook & Campbell, 1979). According to Blythe and Tripodi (1989, p. 142), the social worker needs to control or minimize the following relevant internal validity threats so he or she can make inferences of causality between an intervention and problem variable changes for a single client: history, maturation, initial measurement effects, instrumentation, statistical regression, multiple treatment interference, expectancy effects, interactions, and other unknown factors.

History refers to any variables or events outside of the intervention that occur between the first measurement of the problem variable at baseline and the last measurement during intervention. It does not include events usually considered history that have preceded the measurements. Factors such as natural disasters, changes in employment and occupational status, and changes in family income or health are variables subsumed under history. Suppose a male client reduces the number of negative comments to his spouse during one week of intervention. This change may result from a historical factor between measurements, such as the illness of his spouse. He may have made his negative comments during dinner, but his wife's illness may have reduced the opportunities for this negative exchange. The clinical social worker would want to know whether he will continue to reduce his negative comments in situations in which he and his wife have dinner together.

The basic single-case design phases of baseline, intervention, and follow-up do not control historical factors. When applicable, the social worker can achieve control of historical factors by using design variations such as multiple baseline, graduated intensity, and withdrawal-reversal designs (see chapter 7). In addition, the clinical social worker can use qualitative data obtained from clinical interviews to make inferences about the extent to which events that could affect changes in the problem variables have occurred. For example, the clinical social worker, through interviews, may know whether family composition, economic status, or jobs have changed. If there are no qualitative changes in these apparent factors that could influence change, the clinical social worker can make an inference that, although historical factors are not controlled, their effects on the observed changes appear to be minimal.

Maturation refers to events that occur within the client; such events result from changes in growth, physiological mechanisms, illness, and so forth. Design variations also can control these factors (see chapter 7); however, the basic single-case design model cannot control these factors. As with historical factors, the social worker can make inferences about the potential influence or lack of influence of maturation effects on problem variable changes by using information gained during clinical interviews and from other available sources such as family members, medical charts for patients in a hospital, or school records of health. Of course, the social worker needs easy access to such data. We can assume that the social worker would use his or her knowledge from clinical interviews but would not actively seek other data simply to minimize the threat of maturation. However, if changes occur quickly, for example, within several weeks, and there apparently are not any changes in health, growth, medication, or fatigue, then it is plausible for the social worker to assume that maturational effects are minimal.

Initial measurement effects refer to the influence of the first measurements on subsequent measurements of a problem variable. These effects are controlled if there is a horizontally stable baseline. Instrumentation refers to the possibility that the process of measurement is nonstandardized and observed changes result from nonstandardization rather than the intervention. For example, changes observed in the problem variable may not result from interven-

tion but from measurement at different times of day and by different observers. Standardized measurement controls possible effects of instrumentation in terms of consistent observers and measurement times and places, and by achieving a horizontally stable baseline before intervention. Statistical regression refers to the tendency of either positive or negative extreme scores to move toward the average. It also signifies an accelerating or a decelerating trend over time at baseline. Statistical regression, too, is controlled by achieving a horizontally stable baseline.

Multiple treatment interference indicates that other interventions may occur between initial measurements at baseline and subsequent measurements during intervention. The clinical social worker can observe, by means of clinical interviews, whether the client is receiving interventions other than the one being tested. If there are no apparent competing treatments, then this internal validity threat is minimized. It is essentially a subcomponent of history; hence, by using variations of the basic model of single-case design-multiple baseline, graduated intensity, and withdrawal reversal designs-the social worker can control its effects.

Expectancy effects indicate changes in the problem variable that result from client expectations about interventions, prognoses, and so forth. As with history and maturation, the social worker can control these factors by using design variations (see chapter 7). *Interactions* refer to the combined effects of history, maturation, initial measurement effects, instrumentation, statistical regression, multiple treatment interference, and expectancy effects. By using design variations (see chapter 7), but not the basic model of single-case design, the social worker can potentially control these factors. Other unknown factors may be responsible for changes in the problem variable. The social worker also can control these factors using design variations. In addition, through interviews, the clinical social worker can gain information about the extent to which it appears that other factors are not responsible for observed changes.

The basic single-case design model of baseline, intervention, and follow-up can provide a substantial amount of evidence of a causal relationship between an intervention and problem variables. Evidence may be of the intervention occurring before changes in the problem variable; a positive correlation; the control of initial measurement effects, instrumentation, and statistical regression; and additional information gained through clinical interviews that other factors such as history, maturation, and multiple treatment interference are inoperative between initial measurements of the problem variable at baseline and subsequent measurements during intervention. Hence, the social worker can obtain an approximation to causal knowledge using single-case design methodology.

Making Decisions about Interventions

The clinical social worker can use information based on the attainment of clinical objectives and a comparison of time-series data at intervention to baseline to make decisions about when to change the intervention for a particular client. Changing the intervention involves the social worker's clinical judgment in deciding whether to continue or discontinue the intervention. Berlin and Marsh (1993), for example, have offered intervention guidelines based on the social worker's understanding and use of theoretical perspectives for changing clients' cognitions, emotions, interpersonal interactions, and situations. Although their guidelines provide useful dimensions to consider in planning and implementing interventions, they apparently do not indicate when and how social workers should, if at all, change interventions during the course of treatment. The specific actions ultimately depend on the clinical social worker's judgment, experience, and work with similar clients.

TYPOLOGY FOR CONSIDERING INTERVENTION CHANGES

The clinical social worker can use a topology based on information from single-case designs to describe conditions under which he or she considers making changes during the intervention phase. The information consists of change (or no change), determined by comparing the intervention phase to baseline, and the judgment as to whether the social worker has attained clinical objectives.

A typology produces six types (Table 19). Type 1 is one of no change but in which the social worker has attained the clinical objective of no change. Type 1 may occur when the objective is to maintain a state that the client already has achieved, for example, preventing the occurrence of relapse in an alcoholic client who has quit drinking. Furthermore, a Type 1 phenomenon may occur when prevention is the objective, such as a group intervention with adolescent girls to prevent teenage pregnancy.

If the clinical social worker has attained the objectives within the desired period, say one year, then he or she could discontinue the intervention and prepare for follow-up, or the social worker could continue the intervention, but with fewer contacts to determine whether he or she has maintained the objectives before ultimately discontinuing services. The social worker also could simply continue the intervention; such a decision would imply that the social worker had shifted the clinical objective of time, for example, believing that maintenance of an alcoholic's nondrinking behavior is a long-term

table 19   *Typology Based on Attainment of Clinical Objectives and Comparisons of Intervention to Baseline*

Change Determined by Comparing Intervention Phase to Baseline	Attainment of Clinical Objectives	
	Attained	Not Attained
No change	Type 1	Type 4
Positive change	Type 2	Type 5
Negative change	Type 3	Type 6

investment that should warrant intervention for more than one year.

Type 2 consists of positive change and the attainment of the clinical objective. For example, family therapy with a family may have resulted in increased positive family interactions among family members. Assuming there are no other clinical objectives, and that the social worker has achieved the objective within a desired period, the social worker needs to decide whether to discontinue or to continue the intervention but with reduced contact. The social worker also could continue to provide intervention to determine whether the observed changes persist.

Type 3 is controversial. It occurs when the social worker has attained an objective but the change is negative. Some clinicians would say it is unethical to have an objective of negative change. However, other clinicians might believe that it may be necessary to obtain an instrumental objective of negative change for a particular client before attaining a positive desirable change. For example, in psychotherapy with a male client who desires a constructive relationship with his father, an instrumental clinical objective might be that the client is first able to express hostile feelings to his father. For this type, the clinical social worker must monitor carefully changes that occur if he or she decides to continue the intervention. Discontinuance of the intervention is necessary if the social worker believes there is no relationship between the instrumental goal and the ultimate goal, or if the social worker accepts that he or she has achieved the objective in the specified time. However, the focus of intervention would shift from the promotion of hostile expressed feelings to the consideration of a constructive relationship. The social worker would discontinue the intervention for that particular objective (to express hostile feelings) and modify it to include the ultimate objective (to provide a constructive relationship). Subsequently, there should be a reduction in the magnitude of hostile feelings.

Type 4 consists of no change and nonattainment of the clinical objective. It occurs when the social worker has not achieved an objective of positive change within a specified period. For example, through cognitive therapy coupled with behavior modification, the social worker may have been unable to reduce a 10-year-old child's fear of animals. In this instance, the clinical social worker may continue the same intervention, giving it a longer time to take effect. Or he or she may continue with a modified intervention, adding or subtracting a component, such as adding a token economy system in which the social worker awards points that the client accumulates for a reward as the client increasingly gets closer to petting a tame animal.

The clinical social worker also may continue with a substitute intervention, such as group therapy focused on a discussion of animal fears and methods for coping with those fears. If the social worker believes he or she is unable to help the client, then the social worker should consider discontinuing the intervention, consulting with her or his supervisor or other knowledgeable professionals, or perhaps referring the client to another source.

Type 5 is one of positive change, but without achieving the clinical objective. For example, the social worker might have used behavioral therapy to enable a teenage client to adhere to his or her home curfew. Graphic analysis may have indicated positive change, as did the statistically significant shifts in the number of times the client missed curfew at intervention compared with baseline. However, the clinical objective may have been to not miss any curfews for one week; the social worker did not attain this objective. Because the data indicate progress, the clinical social worker should continue the intervention, either with no change or with modification. For example, he or she might modify the intervention by increasing the frequency and duration of contacts with the client.

Type 6 is the most serious type because it indicates that the problem variable is becoming increasingly severe as the social worker provides intervention, even though the clinical objective might have been one of positive change, maintenance, or prevention. The clinical social worker should discontinue the intervention, carefully reconsider the assessment, and try to discern what went wrong through clinical interviews. Then he or she should consider using a different intervention or referring the client to another source.

The six types are not pure types; that is, they depend on the a priori clinical objectives of the social worker and the client and on the evidence from single-case designs of change. Although the decisions suggested assumed there were no other clinical objectives, the processing of information is obviously more complex given multiple objectives. The social worker could prioritize the objectives (see Blythe & Tripodi, 1989, for a discussion of prioritization of objectives).

Single-case designs can provide information about whether the clinical social worker should make a decision about intervention. Moreover, the six types suggest decisions that the clinical social worker might make. Ultimately, the social worker makes decisions based on the best available information about the client's situation; the assessment of the problem; indications of progress (obtainable from single-case designs); his or her experience and theoretical orientation; a good sense of timing; practicalities affecting the client's life; and sound clinical judgment.

TEACHING SUGGESTIONS

1. Prepare graphs of baseline data for a hypothetical client in which the observed patterns implicate each of the following intervention objectives: change, maintenance or prevention, and care (prepare separate graphs that depict care objectives in terms of achieving maintenance or prevention and change in a selected variable). Ask the class to describe the intervention pattern associated with the attainment of clinical objectives for each example.
2. Using a hypothetical case example, identify at least two interventions in the social work literature for addressing the problem in the case. Review each intervention describing the degree to which it is relevant to the accomplishment of clinical objectives, consonant with your clinical experience with similar clients, feasible, ethical, effective, and efficient.

Specify each intervention by describing the intervenors, the location, frequency, and duration of the intervention, and the contents of the intervention.
3. Review the procedures for analyzing time-series data for the intervention phase and for making comparisons between time-series data provided during baseline and intervention using the C statistic and the binomial test. Reiterate the requirements for using each statistic and describe the procedures for reporting the results of analyses. Ask students to identify the levels of knowledge that can be inferred from analyses of data for the intervention phase only and for the combined baseline and intervention phases. Have them describe the conditions that must be present for inferring the levels of knowledge identified.
4. Break the class into six groups. Using the typology for considering intervention changes presented in the chapter, assign each group one of the six types. Using examples from their practice, have students in each group develop an illustrative example of the type assigned that includes a graph or graphs depicting hypothetical baseline and intervention data for the case. Ask students in each group to present their case to the class and discuss the clinical course of action that is implicated by their analysis of the data.

STUDENT EXERCISES

1. Using a case from your practice, identify a target/problem issue for which your client has sought treatment. Review the intervention literature to identify potential interventions that you might use to intervene in the case. Compare and contrast each in terms of the degree to which the intervention is relevant to the accomplishment of clinical objectives for this case, consonant with your clinical experience with similar clients, feasible, ethical, effective, and efficient. Based on your comparative analysis, identify the intervention for guiding your work in this case. Specify the intervention selected by describing the intervenors, the location, frequency, and duration of the intervention, and the contents of the intervention.

2. Using the intervention identified in the example above, develop a checklist for monitoring the implementation of the intervention.

3. Using the hypothetical data presented in each of the examples below, identify the following: the type of clinical intervention objective that is evident in the case; the presence or absence of baseline horizontal stability in the time-series data; the presence or absence of a trend in the time-series data during intervention; and the presence or absence of a trend in the time-series data from baseline to intervention. Present graphs and findings from statistical analyses used to evaluate the data provided in each example. Discuss your findings in terms of whether clinical objectives were met, and if observed changes were statistically significant. Discuss if additional measurements and intervention may be needed for determining the clinical course of action in each case. Provide a rationale for your conclusion.

• Example 1. The hypothetical problem in this case, A, is measured daily on a 10-point scale in which higher scores indicate greater problem severity. Baseline measurements of A are as follows: 8, 7, 8, 9, 7, 8, 8, 8. The clinical objective is to reduce the severity of A to three over a two-week period. Intervention measurements of A are as follows: 8, 8, 8, 7, 7, 7, 6, 6, 5, 5, 4, 3, 3, 3.

• Example 2. The hypothetical variable in this case, B, is a positive behavior that is measured daily on a five-point scale in which higher scores indicate a greater frequency of occurrence. Baseline measurements of B are as follows: 4, 5, 4, 5, 4, 5, 4, 5. The clinical objective is to maintain the frequency of B at or above four for a one-week period. Intervention measurements of B are as follows: 4, 5, 4, 5, 4, 5, 4, 5.

• Example 3. The hypothetical variable in this case, C, is measured daily using a rapid assessment instrument in which scores can range from 20 to 50, with higher scores indicating greater problem severity. Baseline measurements of C are as follows: 48, 50, 48, 48, 48, 50, 48, 48. The clinical objective is to reduce the severity of C to 20 over a two-week interval. Intervention measurements of C are as follows: 48, 48, 46, 46, 46, 44, 42, 40, 40, 38, 36, 36, 36, 35.

4. Using the published single-case design study selected for purposes of completing Exercise 1 in Chapter 1 and material presented in Appendix 1, describe the intervention or interventions used in the case. Critically assess the data presented for the baseline and intervention phases of the study. Do the data support the conclusions made by the authors? Is sufficient information provided for making this determination?

CHAPTER 6

Phase 3:
Follow-Up

DEFINITION OF FOLLOW-UP

Follow-up is the final phase in the basic model of baseline, intervention, and follow-up for single-case design methodology. The social worker measures the same problem variables at follow-up as at baseline and intervention; for comparative purposes, the social worker uses the same time intervals between measurements. The purposes of follow-up are to determine whether the positive changes during intervention persist on removal of intervention, the problem recurs or relapses, or new problems appear. The discussion in this chapter is based on information from Vonk, Tripodi, and Epstein (2006); Epstein and Tripodi (1977), Blythe and Tripodi (1989), Rubin and Babbie (2001), Corcoran and Fischer (1987), and Fowler (1988).

The two basic types of follow-up are as follows: the first occurs after the social worker has terminated intervention with the client; the second, after the social worker has terminated intervention for a particular objective with the client while another intervention with the same client is occurring (Blythe & Tripodi, 1989). The first type represents a more typical usage of the term follow-up; for example, a clinical social worker in private practice may terminate his or her work with a phobic teenager after accomplishing the objective of reducing the phobia and when there are no other objectives to pursue. The second type of follow-up can occur when there are multiple objectives and the social worker uses multiple interventions. For example, the social worker and the client may have agreed on two clinical objectives: (1) to reduce cigarette smok-

ing, and (2) to reduce anxiety when meeting new people. The clinical social worker might use behavioral modification techniques based on reinforcement theory to reduce cigarette smoking and cognitive therapy and role-playing techniques to reduce anxiety. If the social worker accomplishes the objective of reducing cigarette smoking, then he or she terminates the behavioral modification intervention; however, the social worker still uses cognitive therapy and role-playing techniques to reduce anxiety. Follow-up occurs as the social worker continues to measure the number of cigarettes smoked while using an intervention to reduce anxiety.

Follow-up can be planned or unplanned. When planned, it can be cost-effective in that the client is engaged in the therapeutic process. After accomplishing the clinical objectives, the social worker can make plans such as the following to ease the transition from intervention to no intervention. First, the practitioner could reduce the intensity and duration of the intervention to determine whether, on termination of intervention, the client could maintain the positive results he or she achieved with full intervention. For example, the social worker might have two client contacts per week for one-hour duration at each contact for full intervention; a reduced intervention might consist of one contact per three weeks. Second, the social worker could specify clinical objectives for when to measure the problem variables. For example, he or she might anticipate that there will be no differences in the occurrence of problem variables between full intervention and reduced intervention one month later. Third, the social worker can plan termination with the client with an objective to enlist the client's participation in measurement of the problem variables one month after termination and to obtain other follow-up information from the client in a scheduled appointment. The social worker decides the time of the appointment based on what he or she considers to be a reasonable amount of time to discern whether the problem has recurred. Fourth, the practitioner gathers follow-up data and analyzes them in relation to the clinical objectives for the client. The social worker then decides whether to continue termination or to invite the client to participate anew in the therapeutic process.

Unplanned follow-up refers to the task of obtaining follow-up data when the social worker has not made any previous arrangements with the client or the client's friends or family to engage in follow-up activities. This follow-up procedure is not recommended for single-case designs because it is difficult to use given potential ambiguities and lack of standardization of measurement. However, the social worker can secure useful information from unplanned follow-up that is based on data gathered at one point in time, such as in a survey.

EXAMPLE OF FOLLOW-UP

Suppose that a male client has low self-esteem and believes that he is inadequate for dealing with most activities and relationships in his everyday life. He is an unmarried adult who works as an insurance underwriter, and throughout each day he thinks about his inadequacy. Taking advantage of an EAP, the client engages in a therapeutic process with a clinical social worker. One clinical objective on which both social worker and client agree is that the client should significantly reduce the number of inadequate thoughts on a daily basis following one week of intervention. The social worker asks the client to count the number of times he has inadequate thoughts about himself daily for a one-week baseline and during intervention, which consists of three 45-minute appointments.

Results indicate that the client had nine inadequate thoughts daily at baseline, except on Tuesday, when he had 10 inadequate thoughts (Fig-

ure 39). The intervention was cognitive therapy, emphasizing strategies to overcome self-defeating beliefs and cognitive distortions (Burns & deJong, 1980). The social worker instructed the client to continue counting the number of inadequate thoughts just before going to bed each day. During intervention, there were three days of no thoughts of inadequacy and four days with only one thought of inadequacy. A visual comparison of the time-series of intervention to baseline clearly shows a significant shift in a clinically desirable direction (readers can verify this shift by computing C, Sc, and Z using the seven observations at baseline—9, 10, 9, 9, 9, 9, 9—and the seven observations at week 2—1, 1, 1, 0, 1, 0, 0). Having achieved the clinical objective of no more than one inadequate thought per day at week 2 of contact, the social worker decides to reduce the intervention to one 45-minute session for a two-week interval. This reduced intervention assumes, for purposes of illustration, that there are no other objectives for the client; for example, another objective might have been to increase the client's self-esteem. Furthermore, the social worker would not have reduced the intervention if the clinical objective had been to have no thoughts of inadequacy for at least five out of seven days.

The client continues to count the number of inadequate thoughts on a daily basis and presents his measurements to the clinical social worker. The agreed-on objective was that reduced

figure 39

Baseline, Intervention, and Follow–up Measurements of Client's Thoughts of Inadequacy

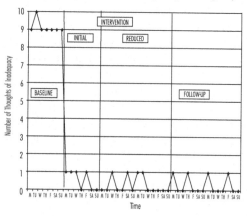

intervention at week 4 would produce the same results as with intervention at week 2. Results indicate four days with one inadequate thought and three days with no inadequate thoughts during intervention, and four days with one inadequate thought and ten days with no inadequate thoughts during reduced intervention (Figure 39). Moreover, Table 20 shows no significant change in the time-series of the number of inadequate thoughts. Hence, the results are virtually identical with those at reduced intervention. At this point, the clinical social worker and the client may decide to terminate inter-

vention, but the client will continue to monitor the number of inadequate thoughts daily. The objective for follow-up is that the results should be the same two weeks later. Hence, the social worker schedules an appointment for that time and asks the client to complete a follow-up questionnaire. The observations at follow-up—1, 0, 0, 1, 0, 0, 0, 1, 0, 0, 0, 1, 0, 0—are similar to the observations at reduced intervention—0, 0, 1, 0, 0, 1, 0, 1, 1, 0, 0, 0, 0, 0 (Figure 39). In addition, there are no statistically significant changes between reduced intervention and follow-up (Table 21), which indicates that the

table 20	*Computing S, Sc, and Z for Intervention and Reduced Intervention in Figure 39*					
Score (x)	$x - M$	$(x - M)^2$	x_i	$x - x_i$	$(x - x_i)^2$
1	.62	.38	1	0	0
1	.62	.38	1	0	0
1	.62	.38	0	1	1
0	−.38	.14	1	−1	1
1	.62	.38	0	1	1
0	−.38	.14	0	0	0
0	−.38	.14	0	0	0
0	−.38	.14	0	0	0
0	−.38	.14	1	−1	1
1	.62	.38	0	1	1
0	−.38	.14	0	0	0
0	−.38	.14	1	−1	1
1	.62	.38	0	1	1
0	−.38	.14	1	−1	1
1	.62	.38	1	0	0
1	.62	.38	0	1	1
0	−.38	.14	0	0	0
0	−.38	.14	0	0	0
0	−.38	.14	0	0	0
0	−.38	.14	0	0	0
0	−.38	.14	−	−	−

$8 = \Sigma x$		$14.861 = SS(x)$	$191 = D^2$		
$M = \Sigma x / n$		$= 8/21$	$= .38$		
$C = 1 - D^2/(2SS(x))$		$= 1 - 9/2(4.86)$	$= .07$		
$Sc = \sqrt{(n - 2)/(n + 1)(n - 1)} = \sqrt{(21 - 2)/(21 + 1)(21 - 1)} = .20$					
$Z = C/Sc$		$= .07/.20$	$= .35$		

NOTE: Because Z < 1.64, there is no change.

results achieved by intervention have persisted in follow-up.

To further verify that the results at follow-up are dramatically different from baseline, the clinical social worker visually compares the observations at baseline—9, 10, 9, 9, 9, 9, 9—with those at follow-up—1, 0, 0, 1, 0, 0, 0, 1, 0, 0, 0, 1, 0, 0 (Figure 39). Furthermore, calculating C, Sc, and Z, the clinical social worker verifies

table 21 *Computing S, Sc, and Z for Reduced Intervention and Follow-up in Figure 39*

Score (x)	x – M	(x – M)²	x_i	x – x_i	(x – x_i)²
0	–.28	.07	0	0	0
0	–.28	.07	1	–1	1
1	.72	.51	0	1	1
0	–.28	.07	0	0	0
0	–.28	.07	1	–1	1
1	.72	.51	0	1	1
0	–.28	.07	1	–1	1
1	.72	.51	1	0	0
1	.72	.51	0	1	1
0	–.28	.07	0	0	0
0	–.28	.07	0	0	0
0	–.28	.07	0	0	0
0	–.28	.07	1	–1	1
1	.72	.51	0	1	1
0	–.28	.07	0	0	0
0	–.28	.07	1	–1	1
1	.72	.51	0	1	1
0	–.28	.07	0	0	0
0	–.28	.07	0	0	0
0	–.28	.07	1	–1	1
1	.72	.51	0	1	1
0	–.28	.07	0	0	0
0	–.28	.07	0	0	0
0	–.28	.07	1	–1	1
1	.72	.51	0	1	1
0	–.28	.07	0	0	0
0	–.28	.07	–	–	–

8 = Σx		|15.48| = SS(x)	|14| = D^2	

$M = \Sigma x / n$ = 8/28 = .28

$C = 1 - D^2 / (2SS(x))$ = 1 – 14/2(5.48) = –.27

$Sc = \sqrt{(n-2)/(n+1)(n-1)} = \sqrt{(28-2)/(28+1)(28-1)}$ = .18

$Z = C/Sc$ = –.27/.18 = –1.50

NOTE: Because Z < 1.64, there is no change.

that the time-series of the number of inadequate thoughts differs from baseline to follow-up, indicating a statistically significant reduction in the number of inadequate thoughts (Table 22). Hence, the results of the time-series show a correlation between the intervention and a shift in the number of thoughts of inadequacy. Moreover, the analysis of data at follow-up indicates that the results persist when there is no intervention. Because the baseline measurements indicated horizontal stability, the internal validity threats of statistical regression, instrumentation, and the influence of previous measurements are controlled. Furthermore, there is evidence that the intervention occurred before the changes in the problem variable of thoughts of inadequacy.

An additional procedure at follow-up is to gather data through a questionnaire or interview; the clinical social worker gathers data at the same time the client sees the social worker for a scheduled interview. The data serve to assist the social worker in deciding whether to continue the termination of intervention or reintroduce intervention. The data also provide evidence

table 22	Computing S, Sc, and Z for Baseline and Follow-up in Figure 39				
Score (x)	x − M	(x − M)²	x_i	x − x_i	(x − x_i)²
9	5.77	33.29	10	−1	1
10	6.77	45.83	9	1	1
9	5.77	33.29	9	0	0
9	5.77	33.29	9	0	0
9	5.77	33.29	9	0	0
9	5.77	33.29	9	0	0
9	5.77	33.29	1	8	64
1	−2.23	4.97	0	1	1
0	−3.23	10.43	0	0	0
0	−3.23	10.43	1	−1	1
1	−2.23	4.97	0	1	1
0	−3.23	10.43	0	0	0
0	−3.23	10.43	0	0	0
0	−3.23	10.43	1	−1	1
1	−2.23	4.97	0	1	1
0	−3.23	10.43	0	0	0
0	−3.23	10.43	0	0	0
0	−3.23	10.43	1	−1	1
1	−2.23	4.97	0	1	1
0	−3.23	10.43	0	0	0
0	−3.23	10.43	−	−	−
68 = Σx		|369.75| = SS(x)	|73| = D²		
M = Σx/n		= 68/21	= 3.23		
C = 1 − D²/(2SS(x))		= 1 − 73/2(369.75)	= .90		
Sc = $\sqrt{(n-2)/(n+1)(n-1)}$ = $\sqrt{(21-2)/(21+1)(21-1)}$ = .20					
Z = C/Sc		= .90/.20	= 4.50		

NOTE: Because Z > 1.64, there are significant changes.

regarding the control of historical and matura-tional factors as well as multiple treatment inter-ference. At the last regularly scheduled meeting, the social worker might ask questions to help him or her uncover whether any other factors could be responsible for the persistence of re-sults and to discern new client needs (Appendix 5). As the responses in Appendix 5 indicate, the client received no help from other sources or persons, increased numbers of thoughts of inad-equacy did not recur, he did not change his daily living habits or living circumstances, neither he nor his family members were sick, no other ma-jor problems occurred, the client felt more en-ergetic and outgoing, and he was dating women more frequently. Probably no factors of history, maturation, or other forms of intervention were responsible for the consistent positive changes; hence there is partial evidence for a causal re-lationship between the cognitive intervention and the changes in the problem variable. The evidence suggests that the social worker should terminate services for the client because the cli-ent accomplished clinical objectives and no new problems emerged. On the other hand, the clin-ical social worker might arrange for one more follow-up interview one to two months later if he or she is not completely convinced that the results will continue to persist.

ADVANTAGES AND DISADVANTAGES OF OBTAINING FOLLOW-UP DATA

In considering the pros and cons of gathering follow-up data, it is helpful to separate follow-up into planned and unplanned follow-up, and into termination of a single objective as opposed to termination of all work with the client.

Condition 1: Planned Follow-up with Termination of Intervention for a Single Objective

In planned follow-up, the client is aware of and cooperates in data collection after withdrawal of the intervention. After terminating interven-tion for an objective, the clinical social worker continues to work with the client to attain other objectives using other interventions. Follow-up data in this circumstance have several advantag-es. For one, the social worker can easily obtain systematic measurements on the problem vari-able because the client continues to have contact with the social worker. For example, the client may have reported the number of times he or she shoplifted daily at baseline and at intervention, during which time the client reported no shop-lifting. The social worker may terminate inter-vention for reducing shoplifting and might use another intervention for increasing positive rela-tionships with the client's friends, a second clini-cal objective. The practitioner can obtain system-atic measurements (a log of daily self-reports on the number of times the client shoplifts daily). However, so that the information gathered will be treated as follow-up data, the social worker must provide a different intervention to attain the second objective. Otherwise, the data would reflect an extension of the intervention-the same intervention would be operative.

Other advantages of follow-up data are that the response rate for follow-up would be virtually 100 percent, and the costs would be minimal, reflecting only the social worker's time needed to gather and process the data. Furthermore, ac-countability would be high. The clinical social worker could use the follow-up data to detect any movement from goal attainment. The iden-tification of undesirable trends or complete re-lapse would enable the social worker to decide whether to reinstitute the intervention or to seek consultation or make referrals.

One of the disadvantages for gathering planned follow-up data when terminating intervention for an objective is that the social worker may not be able to easily withdraw the intervention while he or she still has contact with the client. The client may discuss the intervention with the social worker and may continue to focus on that intervention or other interventions for the same problem. For example, although the social worker withdraws an intervention based on cognitive theory for dealing with shoplifting, the client continues to discuss ways of dealing with shoplifting, in effect, extending the inter-vention into follow-up.

Furthermore, if the client is involved in data collection, for example, produces a log of the number of times he shoplifted daily, the client may pursue data collection less rigorously after he knows he and the practitioner have accomplished the objective and that he and the clinical social worker are focusing on other objectives. Another disadvantage is that costs could be excessive if there is an extensive amount of data collection requiring a great deal of the social worker's time.

Condition 2: Planned Follow-up with Termination of Client

Planned follow-up with termination of the client occurs when the clinician and client agree to monitor the client's progress on multiple objectives for which clinical objectives have been met. This condition has all the advantages of planned follow-up with the termination of an intervention for a single objective. In addition, the clinical social worker can obtain additional follow-up information, using a questionnaire, telephone interview schedule, or face-to-face interview schedule for two purposes. One is to assess whether new problems will arise for the client; the second is to obtain data to determine if the social worker can reduce internal validity threats and increase inferences about causal relationships between the intervention and changes in the problem variable. One disadvantage of this type of follow-up is that the response rate would be lower than in condition 1 because the social worker would have less frequent contact with the client. Furthermore, the costs for obtaining data and the chance for errors in data collection would be greater than in condition 1.

Condition 3: Unplanned Follow-up with Termination of Intervention for a Single Objective

In this condition, the social worker does not plan the gathering of follow-up data with the client. However, because the clinical social worker still has access to the client because intervention is occurring for other problems, he or she can obtain data about the client's potential relapse and about new problems with all of the advantages and disadvantages of condition 1. The chief problem is that if the social worker does not plan measurement in follow-up with the client, or considers such measurement only as an afterthought, the data collection might not be standardized across the baseline, intervention, and follow-up phases of the basic model

of single-case design. With unstandardized data, the social worker could not legitimately compare intervention with follow-up and baseline with follow-up.

Condition 4: Unplanned Follow-up with Termination of Client

In this condition, the clinical social worker terminates work with the client when clinical objectives for multiple problems have been attained but the client will not provide follow-up measurements of the problems after intervention has concluded. When there are no follow-up measurements of the problem, the clinician has not satisfied the requirements of the basic model of single-case design. The resulting baseline-intervention design does not permit analysis of the client's progress following withdrawal of the intervention. This condition is the most costly, has the lowest response rate, and is the least useful for making systematic comparisons across phases and generating the levels of knowledge the basic model of single-case design can produce.

Hence, the relative advantages and disadvantages for obtaining follow-up information depend on whether the social worker plans or does not plan the follow-up with the client and whether the clinician terminates intervention for a single or multiple objectives for the client. The most favorable conditions for gathering follow-up data are when the social worker plans the process with the client and systematically implements data gathering procedures for baseline, intervention, and follow-up. Moreover, follow-up is more likely to be cost-effective when the data collection involves the client's time in recording data and when the type of data obtained are not too extensive. Planned follow-up with client termination is more likely to produce unambiguous data that the practitioner can interpret easily when making comparisons among baseline, intervention, and follow-up. When data collection is unplanned, the client is more likely to use recall in describing events that transpired; therefore, retrospective falsification or distortion of the data can occur with client self-reports. Data not obtained from client self-reports are potentially less subject to measurement error but are more costly to gather.

INFORMATION DURING FOLLOW-UP

The clinical social worker can obtain three types of information during follow-up: (1) time-series on the problem variable measured at baseline and at intervention, (2) qualitative and quantitative information about new problems and factors that might influence the problem variable, and (3) qualitative and quantitative information about the client's perceptions of the clinical social worker and the intervention. The social worker obtains time-series measurements of the problem variable so that he or she can compare intervention with follow-up and baseline with follow-up. He or she follows the same procedures for data collection that he or she followed for the baseline and intervention phases. Data collection should be guided by the measurement plan for gathering time-series data in baseline and intervention. The number of measurements during follow-up is contingent upon the clinical objectives developed by the social worker and the client. For example, if the clinician expects that the results (assuming he or she has attained positive results) should persist for three months, then the client provides measurements for a three-month interval following withdrawal of the intervention. The clinician and client can schedule a follow-up appointment during which the client provides the social worker with the data that he or she has collected or arrangements can be made for the client to forward this information to the social worker by mail, telephone, or fax.

Moreover, the social worker should collect time-series measurements at follow-up in a manner that is consistent with clinical objectives. If the clinical objective is to sustain the magnitude of the problem variable attained during intervention for an additional three weeks following withdrawal of the intervention, then the practitioner should collect follow-up data until there is horizontal stability in the data pattern of intervention and follow-up measurements, or the absence of accelerating or decelerating trends. The practitioner can show horizontal stability by calculating C, Sc, and Z for intervention and follow-up measurements when there are a minimum of eight observations-the number that is sufficient for detecting trends.

The clinical social worker compares time-series data at follow-up with time-series data at intervention to determine whether there is a shift from intervention to follow-up and whether the shift is desirable. Suppose that a two-week intervention for a client showed a relatively stable pattern of moderate anxiety: 11 fours and three fives on a scale of 0 = no anxiety to 10 = the highest degree of anxiety (Figure 40). At least three kinds of patterns at follow-up might occur. Line EF shows a similar pattern for a two-week follow-up as line AB at intervention, reflecting a consistency in results from intervention to follow-up. Line GH shows an elevated stable pattern of high anxiety during this interval, which is undesirable, whereas line CD shows a reduced pattern of low anxiety, which is desirable.

The clinical social worker also can compare time-series data at follow-up with baseline to show whether there have been desirable changes in the time-series of a problem variable since intervention. Figure 41 shows the same follow-up data as depicted in Figure 40 compared with data from a two-week baseline. Line AB shows high anxiety at baseline. At follow-up, line GH, which also represents high anxiety, depicts no change; lines EF and CD show change in a desirable direction: the reduction of anxiety; and line CD indicates the greatest amount of desirable change.

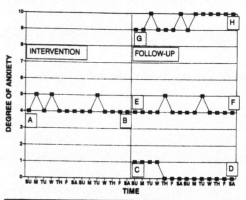

figure 40

Comparisons of Follow-up to Intervention on Self-Reported Daily Anxiety for Two-Week Intervals

NOTE: M = Monday, TU = Tuesday, W = Wednesday, TH = Thursday, F = Friday, SA = Saturday, SU = Sunday.

figure 41

*Comparisons of Follow-up to Baseline on
Self-Reported Daily Anxiety for Two Weeks*

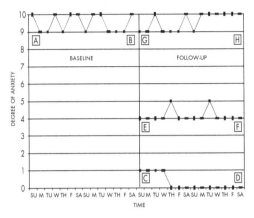

Using a follow-up questionnaire, the clinical social worker can obtain qualitative and quantitative information about new problems and factors influencing problem variables (see Vonk, Tripodi, & Epstein, 2006, for a more comprehensive discussion on collecting follow-up data). Appendix 5 is a generalized form that provides information on what has happened to the client after the clinical social worker has terminated contact with the client. The client's yes or no answers provide the quantitative data whereas his or her explanations about questions to which he or she answers yes provide the qualitative data. The question pertaining to the receipt of help from other sources or persons aims to obtain information on the extent to which other interventions might be responsible for the results. The client's response to the question regarding recurrences of the major problem should be consistent with the time-series data; the response to that question validates the data obtained from the measurement of the problem variable. If there are undesirable changes in the time-series data, the client should indicate that the major problem has recurred. On the other hand, there may be no undesirable changes reflected in the time-series data, but the client may still believe the problem has recurred. The qualitative data obtained in the client's explanation would clarify this belief. The client may have changed criteria for measurement, the client may have referred to another problem, or the measurement device may have been insufficiently sensitive to

detect the problem. Other problems should be obtainable by responses to the question, "Have any other major problems occurred?" Questions regarding daily habits, living circumstances, illnesses, and relationships are designed to elicit information about historical and maturational factors that might serve as stressors that could influence the problem variable. Furthermore, the question about unexpected positive or negative changes provides information about other influences of the intervention.

The social worker can present these general questions through face-to-face contact, by telephone interview, or by mailed questionnaire. Face-to-face contact or telephone interviews are preferred because they are likely to result in higher response rates and more valid information. Telephone interviewing is apt to be more efficient, saving the client travel or scheduled appointment costs.

The clinical social worker can make follow-up questionnaires more specific and personal for clients by designing questionnaires so they are geared to a client's specific circumstances. In constructing such questionnaires, the clinical social worker should aim to obtain unambiguous answers to clear, straightforward questions. For example, the follow-up questionnaire in Appendix 6 is intended to show aspects of the relationship between Tom, the client, and Jerry, Tom's brother. Tom, age 15, and Jerry, age 14, fought a great deal before intervention. Their white, middle-class parents, both of whom are employed as professional workers, singled out Tom as one who should receive help. The social worker's assessment was that Tom did initiate fights and that he was an appropriate target of intervention. Jerry appeared to respond positively or negatively depending on whether Tom behaved in a positive or negative fashion. The questions in Appendix 6 enable the social worker to assess the degree to which Tom and Jerry fight and whether any changes are apparent in their relationship. Furthermore, responses to these questions indicate the degree to which Tom believes the problem in his relationship is changing and is solvable. The social worker has phrased the questions to give Tom the opportunity to consider himself or his brother responsible for their fights and arguments. In addition, questions about the extent to which they like each other and their parents like them are asked. Moreover, specific questions ask about the nature of the relationship between Tom and Jerry, whether it has improved, and how it could be improved. Hence, the questions provide data about the clinical objective of reducing fights and arguments and include information that is pertinent to a reassessment of the problem.

Another kind of data the social worker can gather during follow-up is qualitative and quantitative information about the client's perceptions of the clinical social worker. The clinical social worker can use these data to analyze specific social work behaviors and attitudes that are important for effective implementation of the intervention; they can furnish clues regarding modifications the social worker might make with the client or for other clients who have yet to receive the intervention.

The social worker derives guidelines for forming follow-up questionnaires by considering questions and responses to dimensions that are relevant to implementation of an intervention and to the social worker's behaviors. Such dimensions include the social worker's sensitivity to client needs and the social worker's adherence to his or her obligations in the therapeutic relationship-keeping appointment times, reviewing progress for the client, explaining measurement procedures and client obligations, providing feedback to the client, specifying the problems on which the social worker and the client are working, clarifying clinical objectives for the client, providing sound advice for everyday practical problems, helping the client develop an understanding about his or her problems, and implementing the intervention. The follow-up questionnaire in Appendix 7 is designed to elicit information about these dimensions. It is geared to a client who is receiving a cognitive therapy intervention to help him or her reduce anxiety. The clinical objectives are to reduce anxiety and to prevent depression. For example, because the client becomes anxious in interpersonal relationships, the social worker focuses intervention on using role-plays about interpersonal conflicts

and on how to deal with those conflicts. In addition, the social worker discusses factors leading to anxiety and how the client might prevent anxiety-provoking situations. The clinical social worker also uses single-case design methodology to produce graphs of time-series data during baseline, intervention, and follow-up. The client makes daily self-ratings of anxiety on a 10-point anxiety scale ranging from 1 = no anxiety to 10 = a great deal of anxiety.

Responses to the questions in Appendix 8 will indicate which social worker's behaviors are necessary for implementing the intervention and for helping the client to reduce anxiety. A general form for assessing client satisfaction from a client who is receiving mental health services is Attkisson's Client Satisfaction Questionnaire (Corcoran & Fischer, 2000b, pp. 174–176). Although it is geared to programs, clinical social workers could use it to refer to their services.

GUIDELINES FOR CONDUCTING FOLLOW-UP

The following guidelines will enable the clinical social worker to obtain data and make inferences so that he or she may make effective decisions about the services offered to clients. For illustrative purposes here, it is assumed that the social worker has realized intervention objectives compared with baseline data before follow-up.

Specify Clinical Objectives

The most common objective is to maintain consistent progress on the problem variable. For example, if a client has stopped smoking-a clinical objective during intervention-the social worker expects that the client will continue to not smoke after termination of the intervention. An objective that varies given the nature of the problem and the intervention specifics for a particular client concerns the length of time desired changes should continue. For example, the practitioner might expect that a client who learns to be assertive will continue to be assertive for an unspecified amount of time, whereas a follow-up clinical objective might be that a father and his son will continue a positive relationship for at least six months and possibly longer.

The social worker should conceive the expected length of time for which observed changes during interventions persist in follow-up in terms of minimum and maximum expectations. A minimum expectation might be two weeks; a maximum expectation can be indefinite. The minimum expectation informs the social worker when to set up a follow-up appointment and for how long to obtain measurements during follow-up. It is simply impractical to follow up every client for a maximum (indefinite) period. The clinical social worker sets his or her objective regarding the minimum expectation for follow-up on the basis of clinical judgment about the individual client, the nature of the problem, and the degree to which the agency is mandated to provide follow-up information. For example, a felon who has served his or her time and is placed on parole has a follow-up period that is mandatory-perhaps one year or more.

Specify Data Collection Strategy

The clinical social worker collects two types of data by questionnaire or interview: (1) time-series and (2) follow-up information. The time-series data are the same measurements on the problem variable that the practitioner took at baseline and at intervention. The minimum time expectation for persistence of change at follow-up indicates the period during which the social worker should gather follow-up data on the problem variable. As part of the strategy for data collection, the social worker plans for the measurement (whether by the client or the social worker); for the frequency of measurement (for example, daily); and for the time of measurement (for example, by the client before bedtime). The client completes the follow-up questionnaire (mailed questionnaire) or the social worker administers the questionnaire by telephone or in a face-to-face interview at the specified minimum time expectation for follow-up.

Plan Follow-up Data Collection with Client

Before terminating intervention, the clinical social worker plans with the client an appointment (by phone or in a face-to-face interview) or a time to mail in data (such as the questionnaire or time-series data). The appointment time is based on the clinical objectives for follow-up. If the client is to provide daily self-report data on a log or record, the social worker must emphasize to the client consistency in the data collection process. Moreover, the practitioner should stress that follow-up time is an additional check on the client's progress and an opportunity for the client to continue with intervention, if needed.

Develop Follow-up Questionnaire

The social worker constructs the questionnaire so that the client can provide relatively simple quantitative and qualitative information. The data should be specific to the client's problem and to factors other than intervention that may assist in easing or exacerbating the problem. In addition, the questionnaire should elicit information that will identify for the social worker possible problems, hence enabling him or her to be helpful and responsive to the client.

Collect Data

The clinical social worker can assist the client who provides self-reported data by reminding the client, in a positive manner, to collect the data. For example, the practitioner may thank the client in a brief telephone exchange or through a brief note for taking the time to provide data. The social worker gathers data at follow-up and graphs the time-series data along with the data from baseline and intervention. He or she may extract data from follow-up as well as from intervention from the time-series and graph them for comparison.

Compare Phases in Graphs and Conduct Statistical Tests

The clinical social worker should compare the time-series at follow-up with the time-series at intervention to determine whether the data are consistent and to ascertain whether there are desirable positive changes. In addition, the practitioner should conduct statistical tests to verify the observations from the graphic patterns.

Evaluate Data and Decide Whether to Terminate Intervention or Continue Follow-up

The social worker evaluates data to locate other possible facilitators and barriers to the effectiveness of intervention, as well as to provide information about the client's perception of whether he or she has received help for the problem. In addition, the social worker gathers data about potential new problems and the client's willingness to participate in further intervention, if necessary.

The social worker also evaluates and analyzes the data with respect to the accomplishment of clinical objectives for the client. If relapse occurs (for example, return to baseline indicating a re-emergence of the problem), the social worker offers to reintroduce intervention to the client. New problems may have developed; thus, the social worker will offer the same or another intervention to the client. If the client continues to show progress, registering a low magnitude on the problem variable and no other problems, the clinical social worker may decide to terminate work with the client.

APPLYING THE GUIDELINES: THREE CLINICAL EXAMPLES

The following clinical examples—consistency in assertive behavior, relapse in coffee drinking, and further progress in the reduction of negative remarks—illustrate how the social worker may apply the guidelines for obtaining and analyzing follow-up information.

Consistency in Assertive Behavior

Specify Clinical Objectives. The client is a young woman enrolled in college liberal arts courses. She felt that she was unable to handle her interpersonal relationships effectively. In most encounters, she was submissive, doing things she did not want to do but feeling resentful. She rarely expressed her wants and desires and felt that "people were picking on me." She read about a counseling center on campus that dealt with problems such as difficulties in interpersonal relationships, academic difficulties, and speech anxieties. A major problem became evident in discussions with the clinical social worker: the client's lack of assertiveness in interpersonal encounters in the classroom, in the recreation hall, at meals, and so forth.

The clinical objective during intervention was to increase significantly the client's number of daily assertive behaviors over a two-week inter-

val. During week 1, the client fully discussed the meaning of assertive behaviors and the contexts in which she may exhibit those behaviors. The social worker taught the client that she should count these behaviors each night after dinner and daily for one week. Visual inspection of baseline data revealed that the client showed no assertive behaviors (Figure 42). The social worker introduced cognitive therapy intervention, including exercises on how to be assertive, role-play situations with the social worker, and discussions of how the client felt in a variety of interpersonal situations in college work and with her friends and family.

Assertive behaviors significantly increased from week 1 at baseline to week 3 during intervention (Figure 42). The social worker planned to terminate the intervention and to obtain follow-up information for two additional weeks. The clinical objectives for follow-up were for the client to show consistent, assertive behavior, demonstrate that assertive behavior at follow-up was significantly different from baseline, and provide information showing the absence of other problems.

Specify Data Collection Strategy. The client would provide the data by keeping a log of measurements of assertiveness, as well as mailing in the data at the end of each week in stamped envelopes addressed to the clinical social worker at

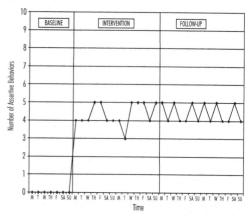

figure 42

Number of Daily Assertive Behaviors at Baseline, Intervention, and Follow-up

the counseling center. In addition, the social worker would mail a follow-up questionnaire to the client one week before an appointment scheduled in week 5 of follow-up. In the follow-up appointment, the social worker would ask the client to provide the desired information.

Plan Follow-up Data Collection with the Client. The practitioner instructed the client to obtain time-series measurements at follow-up in the same way she gathered them at baseline and intervention. Furthermore, the social worker told the client that she would receive a questionnaire in the mail one week before a scheduled appointment during week 5 after initial contact; the client would complete the questionnaire in a face-to-face interview with the social worker.

Develop Follow-up Questionnaire. The social worker developed the follow-up questionnaire (Appendix 9) to reflect information about the help the client received from the social worker, progress in expressing assertiveness, the location of other problems, and the extent to which other factors influenced the client's assertiveness.

Collect Data. The client gathered data on the time-series of assertive behaviors at follow-up; the follow-up data are shown in Figure 42. The responses to the questionnaire are in Appendix 9.

Compare Phases in Graphs and Conduct Statistical Tests. During eight days at follow-up, the client exhibited four assertive behaviors, and during six days, the client exhibited five assertive behaviors (Figure 42). This pattern is consistent with week 3 of intervention, which indicates persistence in the achievement of the clinical objectives for intervention and follow-up. Compared with baseline—seven days of no assertive behavior registered—the time-series data at follow-up are radically different in a desirable direction, indicating that the intervention has been effective.

The calculations of C, Sc, and Z for baseline and follow-up indicate significant differences between phases (Table 23). Furthermore, the calculations of C, Sc, and Z in Table 24 show no significant change from intervention to follow-up, verifying the graphic observations and indi-

cating similar patterns for intervention and follow-up. This is evidence that the social worker has achieved the clinical objective at follow-up.

Evaluate Data and Decide Whether to Terminate Intervention or Continue Follow-up. As indicated by the data in Appendix 9, the client reported that she had not failed to be assertive when appropriate, no other problems occurred during follow-up, the social worker helped her to understand when to be assertive, she discussed when she should be assertive in interpersonal situations, she has made progress in being assertive by overcoming her reluctance to be assertive, she has not received professional help from other persons, she does not believe she needs to continue seeing the social worker, other events have not influenced her assertive behaviors, and she obtained consistent measures of assertiveness. Therefore, the data indicate a strong relationship between the intervention and assertive behavior and the accomplishment of clinical objectives. The client changed her behavior in a positive manner and she has no other problems for which she needs help.

Furthermore, because the social worker has achieved the objectives and the client does not feel a need to continue to see the social worker, the practitioner should terminate the case. However, the social worker should tell the client that she can contact the social worker again should a relapse occur in assertiveness or if other problems should develop.

Relapse in Coffee Drinking

Specify clinical objectives. The client, a veteran of World War II, is an outpatient at a VA medical center. He has gallbladder and other intestinal problems, which are exacerbated by his excessive coffee drinking. The relationship between him and his spouse is positive and caring. He wants to reduce his coffee drinking, but he has become addicted since his days in the U.S. Navy, when he drank coffee continuously. He was referred to a clinical social worker who interviewed his wife and him, asking them to report the number of cups of coffee he consumed each day for one week. The clinical objective was to reduce the number of cups of coffee consumed

table 23	*Computing S, Sc, and Z for Baseline and Follow–up Data from Figure 42*				
Score (x)	x – M	$(x - M)^2$	x_i	$x - x_i$	$(x - x_i)^2$
0	–2.95	8.70	0	0	0
0	–2.95	8.70	0	0	0
0	–2.95	8.70	0	0	0
0	–2.95	8.70	0	0	0
0	–2.95	8.70	0	0	0
0	–2.95	8.70	0	0	0
0	–2.95	8.70	5	–5	25
5	2.05	4.20	4	1	1
4	1.05	1.10	5	–1	1
5	2.05	4.20	4	1	1
4	1.05	1.10	4	0	0
4	1.05	1.10	5	–1	1
5	2.05	4.20	4	1	1
4	1.05	1.10	5	–1	1
5	2.05	4.20	4	1	1
4	1.05	1.10	5	–1	1
5	2.05	4.20	4	1	1
4	1.05	1.10	4	0	0
4	1.05	1.10	5	–1	1
5	2.05	4.20	4	1	1
4	1.05	1.10	—	—	—

62 = Σx		194.901 = SS(x)	1361 = D^2	
M = $\Sigma x / n$	= 62/21		= 2.95	
C = $1 - D^2/(2SS(x))$	= 1 – 36/2(94.90)		= .81	
Sc = $\sqrt{(n - 2)/(n + 1)(n - 1)}$	= $\sqrt{(21 - 2)/(21 + 1)(21 - 1)}$		= .20	
Z = C/Sc	= .81/.20		= 4.05	

NOTE: Because Z > 1.64, there is a significant change in the time–series.

to no more than one or two cups per day; the social worker expected to attain this objective following a two-week intervention.

The clinical social worker met with the client twice a week after the first week of contact and used techniques from behavioral therapy, including the provision of rewards for drinking less coffee. The rewards were the client's small excursions with his wife to nearby cities and museums, an activity that he loved but in which he and his wife had not engaged for years. In addition, the social worker asked the client to substitute decaf-

feinated coffee for regular coffee. The clinical objective for follow-up was that he would continue to drink no more than one or two cups of coffee per day by week 5 of client contact.

The client consumed 15 cups of coffee per day during a one-week baseline, and during intervention, he drank one cup of coffee for seven out of 14 days and two cups on seven days (Figure 43). The social worker terminated intervention, and the client and his wife cooperated in collecting data on his coffee drinking. The social worker scheduled an appointment

table 24 *Computing S, Sc, and Z for Intervention and Follow–up Data from Figure 42*

Score (x)	x − M	(x − M)²	x_i	x − x_i	(x − x_i)²
4	−.39	.15	4	0	0
4	−.39	.15	4	0	0
4	−.39	.15	5	−1	1
5	.61	.37	5	0	0
5	.61	.37	4	1	1
4	−.39	.15	4	0	0
4	−.39	.15	4	0	0
4	−.39	.15	3	1	1
3	−1.39	1.93	5	−2	4
5	.61	.37	5	0	0
5	.61	.37	5	0	0
5	.61	.37	4	1	1
4	−.39	.15	5	−1	1
5	.61	.37	5	0	0
5	.61	.37	4	1	1
4	−.39	.15	5	−1	1
5	.61	.37	4	1	1
4	−.39	.15	4	0	0
4	−.39	.15	5	−1	1
5	.61	.37	4	1	1
4	−.39	.15	5	−1	1
5	.61	.37	4	1	1
4	−.39	.15	5	−1	1
5	.61	.37	4	1	1
4	−.39	.15	4	0	0
4	−.39	.15	5	−1	1
5	.61	.37	4	1	1
4	−.39	.15	–	–	–

123 = Σx	18.621 = SS(x)	1201 = D²
M = Σx/n	= 123/28	= 4.39
C = 1 − D²/(2SS(x))	= 1 − 20/2(8.62)	= −.16
Sc = $\sqrt{(n-2)/(n+1)(n-1)}$	= $\sqrt{(28-2)/(28+1)(28-1)}$ = .18	
Z = C/Sc	= −.16/.18	= −.88

NOTE: Because Z < 1.64, there is no change in the time–series.

for a telephone interview with the client after two weeks of follow-up. The social worker expected that coffee drinking would be consistent with that at intervention and that the interview would yield information indicating that conditions were favorable for the client's reduced coffee drinking.

Specify Data Collection Strategy. The client and his wife were to continue to monitor his daily coffee

figure 43

Number of Cups of Coffee Consumed at Baseline, Intervention, and Follow-up

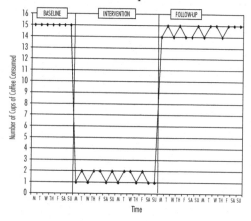

consumption, writing down each night at 10 p.m. the number of cups consumed during that day. They were to tally on a chart each cup consumed daily. The social worker would devise a follow-up questionnaire for a telephone interview and would mail the questionnaire to the client after one week of follow-up.

Plan Follow-up Data Collection with Client. The client was to report the data on coffee drinking to the clinical social worker by telephone each week. The social worker and the client scheduled an appointment for a follow-up telephone interview after two weeks of follow-up.

Develop Follow-up Questionnaire. The practitioner designed a follow-up questionnaire (Appendix 10) to provide information about the continued attainment of the clinical objective and to include information, in the event relapse occurred, on the conditions that might have led to relapse and how the social worker might be able to help.

Collect Data. The data on daily coffee consumption the client gathered and reported to the social worker are shown in the follow-up phase of Figure 43. Responses to the questionnaire are shown in Appendix 10.

Compare Phases in Graphs and Make Statistical Tests. The follow-up period was not consistent with intervention; rather, coffee consumption increased dramatically, indicating a relapse to the

original condition at baseline (Figure 43). Although during intervention, the client drank no more than two cups of coffee per day, follow-up showed consumption of 15 cups for eight days and 14 cups for six days. The follow-up period is similar to the baseline period, during which the client consumed 15 cups of coffee each day for seven days. Hence, the effectiveness of the intervention was not maintained during follow-up.

The calculations of C, Sc, and Z for baseline and follow-up data show no statistically significant differences (Table 25)—that is, coffee consumption before and after the intervention was virtually identical. Furthermore, there was a statistically significant shift in the time-series from intervention to follow-up (Table 26), further verifying that relapse occurred and that positive changes of reduced consumption were not maintained.

Evaluate Data and Decide whether to Terminate or Continue Follow-up. The client indicated that he has been drinking more than two cups of coffee per day because he has been upset (Appendix 10). An additional problem weighing heavily on the client is his wife's illness. He felt the social worker was able to help him by using the rewards of excursions with his wife. He drank more when his wife was tired and less available for making excursions. He has received no other professional help and he feels a need to continue to see the social worker to help him deal with his wife's illness and to control his coffee drinking. He also reported that he has had headaches and nausea and that he does not like decaffeinated coffee.

The data indicate that the rewards for drinking less coffee could no longer be effective when the client's wife was ill—that reinforcer is insufficient for behavioral therapy. The data also indicate that the client needs to understand and deal with his wife's illness, and that other therapeutic techniques such as listening, discussing the problem, and providing good advice might be necessary.

In addition, the client himself may need medical intervention. The clinical social worker arranges for a medical appointment for the client and makes an appointment to visit with the client and his wife. The social worker decides to obtain more information in the interview and

table 25 *Computing S, Sc, and Z for Baseline and Follow–up Data from Figure 43*

Score (x)	x − M	$(x - M)^2$	x_i	$x - x_i$	$(x - x_i)^2$
15	.29	.08	15	0	0
15	.29	.08	15	0	0
15	.29	.08	15	0	0
15	.29	.08	15	0	0
15	.29	.08	15	0	0
15	.29	.08	15	0	0
15	.29	.08	14	1	1
14	−.71	.50	15	−1	1
15	.29	.08	14	1	1
14	−.71	.50	15	−1	1
15	.29	.08	14	1	1
14	−.71	.50	14	0	0
14	−.71	.50	15	−1	1
15	.29	.08	14	1	1
14	−.71	.50	15	−1	1
15	.29	.08	15	0	0
15	.29	.08	14	1	1
14	−.71	.50	15	−1	1
15	.29	.08	15	0	0
15	.29	.08	15	0	0
15	.29	.08	—	—	—

309 = Σx		14.20 = SS(x)	110 = D^2		

$M = \Sigma x / n$ = 309/21 = 14.71

$C = 1 - D^2/(2SS(x))$ = 1 − 10/2(4.20) = −.19

$Sc = \sqrt{(n - 2)/(n + 1)(n - 1)} = \sqrt{(21 - 2)/(21 + 1)(21 - 1)}$ = .20

$Z = C/Sc$ = −.19/.20 = −.95

NOTE: Because Z < 1.64, there is no change in the time–series.

is considering using more than one therapeutic intervention. In particular, the practitioner believes it is necessary for the client to understand and cope with his wife's illness. If the social worker is to reintroduce behavioral therapy to reduce coffee consumption, he or she must modify the reward system because the client's wife does not appear strong enough to make excursions. However, the social worker first needs to obtain a better understanding of both the wife's and the client's illnesses to provide a more accurate context in which he or she delivers intervention.

Progress in Reduction of Negative Remarks

Specify Clinical Objectives. The client is a male adolescent, Jack, who lives in an upper middle-class area in a large Midwestern city. He lives with his father, a corporate executive, and his mother, a civil rights lawyer. Since his father took a new job, Jack has been verbally abusive to him and has begun acting up at school. The father in turn has responded in an even-tempered manner but has been preoccupied with his new job. Jack becomes irritable after he is verbally abusive to his father; the mother has tried to calm Jack down

Score (x)	x − M	$(x − M)^2$	x_i	$x − x_i$	$(x − x_i)^2$
1	−7.03	49.42	2	−1	1
2	−6.03	36.36	1	1	1
1	−7.03	49.42	2	−1	1
2	−6.03	36.36	2	0	0
2	−6.03	36.36	1	1	1
1	−7.03	49.42	2	−1	1
2	−6.03	36.36	1	1	1
1	−7.03	49.42	2	−1	1
2	−6.03	36.36	2	0	0
2	−6.03	36.36	1	1	1
1	−7.03	49.42	2	−1	1
2	−6.03	36.36	1	1	1
1	−7.03	49.42	1	0	0
1	−7.03	49.42	14	−13	169
14	5.97	35.64	15	−1	1
15	6.97	48.58	14	1	1
14	5.97	35.64	15	−1	1
15	6.97	48.58	14	1	1
14	5.97	35.64	14	0	0
14	5.97	35.64	15	−1	1
15	6.97	48.58	14	1	1
14	5.97	35.64	15	−1	1
15	6.97	48.58	15	0	0
15	6.97	48.58	14	1	1
14	5.97	35.64	15	−1	1
15	6.97	48.58	15	0	0
15	6.97	48.58	15	0	0
15	6.97	48.58	—	—	—

225 = Σx		11,202.94 = SS(x)	1188 = D^2		

M = Σx/n	= 225/28	= 8.03
C = 1 − D^2/(2SS(x))	= 1 − 188/2(1,202.94)	= .92
Sc = $\sqrt{(n − 2)/(n + 1)(n − 1)}$ = $\sqrt{(28 − 2)/(28 + 1)(28 − 1)}$		= .18
Z = C/Sc	= .92/.18	= 5.11

NOTE: Because Z > 1.64, there is a change in the time–series.

during incidents of verbal abuse, which usually occur at meals and in the evening before bedtime. The mother persuaded the family to seek family counseling at a family services agency. The family was involved in family therapy in which the major objective was that each family member would understand the needs of the others. The father spent little time at home; consequently, another goal was for him to become more involved in family life. A sub-objective was to reduce the number of negative comments Jack makes to his father by rewarding Jack with activities of his choice (such as watching a baseball game with his father).

During the first week after initial contact, the mother took a one-week baseline of Jack's negative remarks toward his father each day. The social worker decided to involve the family in a session once per week to achieve the major goals. To attain the sub-objective, the clinical social worker also met Jack alone for 30 minutes each week, discussing events that led up to negative remarks and Jack's reasons for making them as well as his feelings about them. In addition, the social worker described a system of rewards. The social worker expected the number of negative remarks would be significantly reduced by week 3 of intervention with the boy alone.

The number of negative remarks decreased dramatically from 14 to 15 at baseline to four to five during intervention (Figure 44). The social worker decided to terminate the individual work with Jack and to concentrate solely on the family members' being understanding and sensitive to each other's needs. The social worker terminated the intervention for reducing negative remarks. The objective for a two-week follow-up phase was that the number of negative remarks at 5 weeks would be consistent with the data for intervention at 3 weeks since initial client contact.

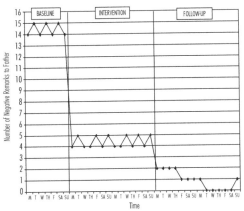

Number of Negative Remarks Made to Father at Baseline, Intervention, and Follow–up

Specify Data Collection Strategy. The mother would obtain data on the number of negative remarks; she would tabulate them each day, focusing on breakfast, dinner, and early evening hours when all the family was together. She would bring the data to the social worker during the regular family interviews each week. The social worker would give the follow-up questionnaire to the mother two weeks after termination of individual work with Jack. The mother would discuss the questionnaire with Jack. In the last family counseling session in the fifth week after initial contact with the client, the social worker would ask Jack to complete the responses.

Plan Follow-up Data Collection with Client. In addition to the scheduled activities, the social worker made sure the mother, the father, and Jack understood the meaning of negative remarks. Moreover, as a form of understanding the family equilibrium in discussions, the social worker used negative remarks as an assessment tool in family counseling.

Develop Follow-up Questionnaire. Because the family was to continue in family counseling, the follow-up questionnaire was relatively brief (Appendix 11). It focused on factors affecting Jack's negative comments and the progress he had made since termination of work with the clinical social worker on an individual basis.

Collect Data. Jack and his mother were cooperative in systematically collecting the time-series data and in considering the questions for the follow-up questionnaire. Jack completed the follow-up questionnaire and gave it to the social worker before a family counseling session in the 5th week after initial contact. The time-series data for follow-up are shown in Figure 44, and the responses to the questionnaire in Appendix 11.

Compare Phases in Graphs and Conduct Statistical Tests. At follow-up, there were four days with two negative comments, five days with one negative comment, and five days with no negative comments (Figure 44). This finding represents further desirable progress compared with intervention, when there were six days with five negative comments and eight days with four negative comments. Hence, the intervention (coupled with continued family counseling) appears to have been effective.

Statistical calculations indicate that the time-series at follow-up are significantly different from the time-series at intervention (Table 27), indicating continued progress. Also, there is a statistically significant difference in the time-series from baseline to follow-up in the desired direction of reducing negative comments (Table 28).

Evaluate Data and Decide whether to Terminate or Continue Follow-up. Jack indicated that he made a few negative comments but that he believed he had made progress (Appendix 11). No other problems had occurred. He said he understood what leads him to make negative comments to his father, and the social worker helped him in this regard by discussing interpersonal situations that would lead to those comments. Jack noted that his father spent more time with him in activities and this, as well as the social worker's intervention, helped him to reduce negative comments. Because the father spent more time with Jack as a reward for his reducing negative comments, the social worker could infer that the intervention was instrumental in helping Jack. Therefore, the questionnaire data verified the clinical sub-objective of reducing negative remarks.

Furthermore, the data indicate that the individual objective for Jack was maintained, with further progress indicated. Hence, the social worker decided to terminate the individual work for this particular objective. However, Jack will continue to see the social worker as a member of his family unit until the clinical objectives for the family have been attained.

TEACHING SUGGESTIONS

1. Engage students in a discussion of follow-up from both clinical and research perspectives. Ask students if, in their clinical practice, they routinely initiate follow-up contacts with their clients after intervention has terminated. Solicit their reasons for doing or not doing so. Discuss the advantages of follow-up from a clinical perspective. Using material presented in the chapter, illustrate the dis-

advantages of unplanned follow-up from the standpoint of practice evaluation.

2. Illustrate the type of discussion that would occur between the clinician and client to prepare the client for follow-up. Provide examples that include obstacles the client might raise and clinician responses to them. Break the class into four groups. Assign each group one of the follow-up conditions presented in the chapter. Drawing from their practice, ask each group of students to generate a sample dialogue between a clinician and client that is illustrative of the condition they have been assigned. Have each group select two students to role-play the scenario to the class. Following the role-plays for the two unplanned follow-up examples, ask the class to provide suggestions for initiating follow-up contact with the client to discuss the importance of follow-up and the possibility of implementing a follow-up measurement plan.

3. Distribute the hypothetical case example presented below to the class. Together with students, develop a follow-up plan that is based on the attainment of the short-term objectives described in the case. The plan should include the creation of questionnaires for assessing factors other than intervention that may be easing or exacerbating the identified problems and for determining the client's satisfaction with the social work services she received.

Case Example

The client is a young mother of two children who presents for services at a shelter for victims of domestic violence. The shelter provides temporary housing, mental health counseling, legal advocacy, and case management services. The short-term clinical objectives are for the client to obtain temporary assistance necessary for procuring housing; procure permanent housing; and appear in court for a temporary restraining order hearing. After achieving these objectives, the longer-term objectives are to address the negative effects of the emotional and physical abuse on the client and her children, and for the client to find employment. A case management plan is developed that details actions to be taken by the clinician and client. The client and social worker will apply for temporary assistance; the client will initiate contacts to identify housing

table 27 *Computing S, Sc, and Z for Intervention and Follow–up Data from Figure 44*

Score (x)	x – M	(x – M)²	x_i	x – x_i	(x – x_i)²
4	1.33	1.76	5	–1	1
5	2.33	5.42	4	1	1
4	1.33	1.76	4	0	0
4	1.33	1.76	5	–1	1
5	2.33	5.42	4	1	1
4	1.33	1.76	5	–1	1
5	2.33	5.42	4	1	1
4	1.33	1.76	4	0	0
4	1.33	1.76	5	–1	1
5	2.33	5.42	4	1	1
4	1.33	1.76	5	–1	1
5	2.33	5.42	4	1	1
4	1.33	1.76	5	–1	1
5	2.33	5.42	2	3	9
2	–.67	.44	2	0	0
2	–.67	.44	2	0	0
2	–.67	.44	2	0	0
2	–.67	.44	1	1	1
1	–1.67	2.78	1	0	0
1	–1.67	2.78	1	0	0
1	–1.67	2.78	1	0	0
1	–1.67	2.78	0	1	1
0	–2.67	7.12	0	0	0
0	–2.67	7.12	0	0	0
0	–2.67	7.12	0	0	0
0	–2.67	7.12	0	0	0
0	–2.67	7.12	1	–1	1
1	–1.67	2.78	—	—	—

75 = Σx		197.861 = SS(x)	123 = D²
M = Σx/n		= 75/28	= 2.67
C = 1 – D²/(2SS(x))		= 1 – 23/2(97.86)	= .88
Sc = $\sqrt{(n-2)/(n+1)(n-1)}$		= $\sqrt{(28-2)/(28+1)(28-1)}$ = .18	
Z = C/Sc		= .88/.18	= 4.88

NOTE: Because $Z > 1.64$, there is a statistically significant change in the time–series.

options; and the clinician will educate the client about what to expect in the upcoming hearing and accompany her to court on the date of the hearing. A baseline is constructed for the three variables of interest: temporary assistance, housing contacts, and court appearance. Values of zero are assigned to all three variables for a one-week interval prior to the client's arrival at the shelter—a time during which she was not engaged in any of these activities. After two weeks of case management services, all three clinical objectives are attained.

Score (x)	x − M	(x − M)^2	x$_i$	x − x$_i$	(x − x$_i$)^2
14	8.58	73.61	15	−1	1
15	9.58	91.77	14	1	1
14	8.58	73.61	15	−1	1
15	9.58	91.77	14	1	1
14	8.58	73.61	15	−1	1
15	9.58	91.77	14	1	1
14	8.58	73.61	2	12	144
2	−3.42	11.69	2	0	0
2	−3.42	11.69	2	0	0
2	−3.42	11.69	2	0	0
2	−3.42	11.69	1	1	1
1	−4.42	19.53	1	0	0
1	−4.42	19.53	1	0	0
1	−4.42	19.53	1	0	0
1	−4.42	19.53	0	1	1
0	−5.42	29.37	0	0	0
0	−5.42	29.37	0	0	0
0	−5.42	29.37	0	0	0
0	−5.42	29.37	0	0	0
0	−5.42	29.37	1	−1	1
1	−4.42	19.53	—	—	—

114 = Σx   1861.011 = SS(x)   1153 = D^2

$M = \Sigma x / n$ $= 114/21$ $= 5.42$

$C = 1 - D^2/(2SS(x))$ $= 1 - 153/2(861.01)$ $= .91$

$Sc = \sqrt{(n - 2)/(n + 1)(n - 1)} = \sqrt{(21 - 2)/(21 + 1)(21 - 1)} = .20$

$Z = C/Sc$ $= .91/.20$ $= 4.55$

NOTE: Because Z > 1.64, there is a statistically significant change in the time–series.

STUDENT EXERCISES

1. Describe the pros and cons of gathering follow-up data when follow-up is planned and unplanned for (1) a single objective, and (2) for multiple objectives (that is, all work with the case).

2. Using material presented in the chapter, describe the phase comparisons that a clinician would make using baseline, intervention, and follow-up data. For each comparison, discuss the potential findings that may result and the implications of each finding for treatment decision-making.

3. Using the published single-case design study selected for purposes of completing Exercise 1 in chapter 1, summarize data presented for the follow-up phase of the study. Describe analyses of follow-up data. Were phase comparisons made? If yes, what did the data reveal? Using the guidelines presented in Appendix 1, assess the strengths and limitations of the analyses used. What level(s) of knowledge can be inferred from reported findings?

CHAPTER 7

Design Variations

Three variations of the basic model of baseline, intervention, and follow-up are (1) multiple baseline design, (2) graduated intensity design, and (3) withdrawal-reversal design. Although potentially useful in clinical social work, the clinical social worker cannot use them in all cases, and they involve much more planning than does the basic model presented in previous chapters. Descriptions of these designs also appear in Blythe, Tripodi, and Briar (1994), Bloom, Fischer, and Orme (2006), Barlow and Hersen (1984), Vonk, Tripodi, and Epstein (2006), Jayaratne and Levy (1979), Kazi (1998), and Nugent, Sieppert, and Hudson (2001).

The major advantage of these designs is that they can control to some extent the internal validity threats of history, maturation, and multiple treatment interference that the basic single-case design model does not control. Recall that history refers to external events other than the intervention that might influence changes in successive measurements of the problem variable; maturation includes all those internal changes in the client, such as illness, that might influence the problem variable; and multiple treatment interference is the extent to which other interventions are responsible for observable changes (Cook & Campbell, 1979; Shadish, Cook, & Campbell, 2002). Hence, these designs can provide more evidence than the basic model regarding a causal link between intervention and changes in the problem variables. In addition, the multiple baseline design can provide some information regarding generalizability of the results.

The chief disadvantage of these designs is that they are complicated, requiring more procedures for their successful implementation and analysis. Furthermore, the resulting data must conform with the idealized data patterns required by the particular design variation. Hence, the designs require more time and effort by the clinical social worker. In general, they are more useful with simple interventions such as advice, didactic instruction, and reinforcement schedules. The designs are much more impractical for long-term psychodynamic and gestalt therapies that do not necessarily focus on particular symptoms or behaviors. In this chapter, each of the designs is defined and guidelines for their implementation are presented. Moreover, clinical examples including graphic and statistical analyses are provided so readers can gain a more comprehensive understanding of the procedures involved.

MULTIPLE BASELINE DESIGN

According to Rubin and Babbie (2001):

> Multiple-baseline designs also attempt to control for extraneous variables by having more than one baseline and intervention phase.... This is done by measuring different target behaviors in each baseline or by measuring the same target behavior in two different settings or across two different individuals. Although each baseline starts simultaneously, the intervention is introduced at a different point for each one. Thus, as the intervention is introduced for the first behavior, setting, or individual, the others are still in their baseline

phases. Likewise, when the intervention is introduced for the second behavior, setting, or individual, the third (if there are more than two) is still in its baseline phase.

The main logical principle here is that if some extraneous event, such as a significant improvement in the environment, coincides with the onset of intervention and causes the client's improved functioning, then that improvement will show up in the graph of each behavior, setting, or individual at the same time, even though some might still be in baseline. On the other hand, if the intervention is accountable for the improvement, then that improvement will occur on each graph at a different point that corresponds to the introduction of the intervention. (pp. 344–345)

This definition is elaborated in Figure 45, which contains idealized data patterns necessary for multiple baseline designs. The terms target behavior, individual, and setting in the preceding definition are synonymous with problem variable, client, and situation, respectively, in Figure 45.

The clinical social worker can simultaneously baseline two or more problem variables, clients, or situations in multiple baseline design.

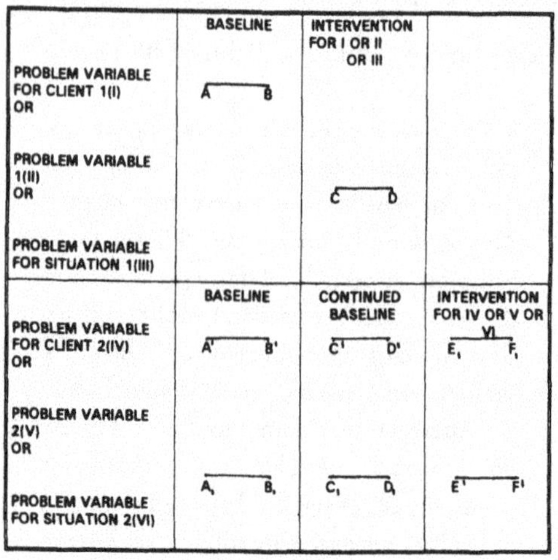

Although some authors (for example, Monette, Sullivan, & deJong, 1986) recommend that researchers use three or more baselines to increase the internal validity of these designs, it is simply impractical in many clinical situations. Therefore, the generalized multiple baseline model in Figure 45 depicts only two baselines.

In Figure 45, baselines are constructed simultaneously for a problem variable for two different clients, two different problem variables for the same client, or a problem variable in two different situations. Suppose that line AB represents the baseline for problem variable 1 (II); then either line A'B' or line A_1B_1 represents a comparative baseline for problem variable 2 (IV). For example, line AB might represent high consumption of alcohol and line A'B' might indicate high anxiety. The problem variables do not have to be measured in the same units or be of the same magnitude; hence, line A_1, B_1 might be the baseline used simultaneously with line AB, and it could refer, for example, to lack of assertiveness. Recall from chapter 4 that baselines should not show upward or downward trends—that is, they should be horizontally stable as depicted in the idealized version (a straight line in Figure 45).

After establishing baselines, the social worker applies an intervention to one client, problem variable, or situation, but continues to baseline the other client, problem variable, or situation. Hence, line CD shows a change from line AB at intervention, indicating an effective intervention. In contrast, the continued baseline shows no change from baseline—that is, lines A'B' and C'D' and lines A_1B_1 and C_1D_1 show similar patterns. Then, the social worker applies the intervention to the other client problem variable or situation whose baseline is continued. The ideal pattern would represent a significant change from C_1D_1 to E_1F_1 or from C'D' to E'F'.

To achieve a multiple baseline design, the clinical social worker must implement the procedures of simultaneous baselining, applying the intervention to one problem variable, client, or situation while continuing to baseline the other and then applying the intervention to the other

figure 45

Idealized Data Patterns for Multiple Baseline Designs

	BASELINE	INTERVENTION FOR I OR II OR III	
PROBLEM VARIABLE FOR CLIENT 1(I) OR	A——B		
PROBLEM VARIABLE 1(II) OR		C——D	
PROBLEM VARIABLE FOR SITUATION 1(III)			
	BASELINE	CONTINUED BASELINE	INTERVENTION FOR IV OR V OR VI
PROBLEM VARIABLE FOR CLIENT 2(IV) OR	A'——B'	C'——D'	E_1——F_1
PROBLEM VARIABLE 2(V) OR			
PROBLEM VARIABLE FOR SITUATION 2(VI)	A_1——B_1	C_1——D_1	E'——F'

problem variable, client, or situation. In addition, to obtain a multiple baseline design, he or she must ensure that the data patterns conform to the idealized patterns shown in Figure 45 (the time series do not have to be straight lines, but they should represent horizontal stability to the x-axis on the graph). The social worker can compute C, Sc, and Z to verify conformity to the idealized pattern. Therefore, there should be a trend in analyses comparing the data for lines AB and CD; there should be horizontal stability in analyses comparing lines A'B' and C'D' or lines A_1B_1 and C_1D_1; and there should be a trend in the time-series data for lines C'D' and E'F' or lines C_1D_1 and E_1F_1.

Guidelines for Implementing Multiple Baseline Designs

Multiple baseline designs are useful when the same intervention can be applied to two different problems or situations for the same client or to the same problem experienced by two different clients. When the problems, situations, or clients are independent, the use of this design can minimize the aforementioned internal validity threats and enable the practitioner to evaluate the effects of the intervention as it is applied to each problem, situation, or case. If the problems or situations for the same client are dependent (that is, if change in one produces change in the other), the clinician does not need to implement this design because intervention to address one problem or situation will produce change in the other. When the design is used to evaluate the same intervention with two different clients, the requirement of independence is met because the clients differ. This assumes that the two individuals are not known to each other and/or it is unlikely that the second client will indirectly receive the intervention through his or her interactions with the first. However, two additional requirements must be met for the clinician to use this design with more than one client. The first is that the clients must present for services at a similar point in time. The second is that delaying intervention for the second client while he or she is in the continued baseline phase would not be problematic (that is, it is feasible to do so based on the time interval between measurements and withholding intervention would not constitute

unethical practice). The general guidelines that follow can be used to implement multiple baseline designs.

Determine Whether There are Two Different Problems, Situations, or Clients. The clinician assesses if, for a given client, there are two or more problem variables (for example, anxiety and depression) or two or more situations for one problem variable (for example, lack of assertiveness (the problem variable) at home (situation 1) and school (situation 2), or if there are two or more clients with the same problem variable (for example, depression). If this condition is satisfied, the social worker determines if the problem variables or situations for the same client are independent of one other (for example, unrelated or uncorrelated). This determination is not necessary when there are two clients with the same problem; in this instance, independence is attained. When there are two different problem variables or situations for the same client, the problem variables or situations might be highly correlated. For example, the problem variables of anxiety and depression might be highly correlated for a particular client: when he or she is depressed, he or she is also anxious, and when he or she is not depressed, nor is he or she anxious. If the problem variables or situations are highly correlated, then the social worker will not obtain the idealized data pattern for a multiple baseline design because the variables not receiving intervention during the continued baseline (see Figure 45) will also change, not satisfying the requirement that lines A'B' and C'D' or lines A_1B_1 and C_1D_1 should be horizontally stable. When the clinician plans to use the same intervention for two clients, the aforementioned additional guidelines apply (that is, both should be engaged in treatment at a similar point in time and it should be feasible and ethical to delay intervention for the second client while intervention is being carried out with the first).

Construct Simultaneous Baselines. The social worker should specify and make systematic the procedures for measurement, in addition to constructing baselines following the guidelines in chapter 4. He or she might construct baselines by gathering data prospectively or retrospectively using archival data and available records or problem recall by the client and/or significant others. Both baselines should be horizontally stable. Furthermore, the scoring procedures and magnitudes for the graphs can be different, but it is recommended that the social worker use the same time interval between measurements and the same number of measurements for each baseline.

Specify the Clinical Objectives. The objectives for each of the problem variables, situations, or clients should be compatible. That is, the practitioner should expect changes after the same amount of intervention. The magnitude of changes may not be the same, but there should be evidence of a trend in the time series for both of the problem variables to verify adherence to the logic of the multiple baseline design.

Specify the intervention. The intervention should be equivalent for both problem variables, situations, or clients. The structure of interventions that are applied to two different situations or to two different problem variables for the same client should be similar, although the contents might differ. For example, an intervention might include discussion of the problem, focus on the problem, and rewards for solving the problem. When the intervention deals with tardiness in school, it is focused on the reasons for tardiness, rewards for being on time, and so on. Another problem variable of speech anxiety may not be the focus of treatment until the client goes to school on time. When focusing the intervention on speech anxiety, the clinical social worker follows the same structure as with lateness to school (that is, discusses the client's feelings about the problem, provides rewards for reducing the problem, and so forth), but the content varies. To the extent that the interventions are equivalent, the logic of multiple baseline design is applicable. If the interventions differ, the design is not a multiple baseline design; instead, it simply comprises two different, basic single-case designs. The simpler the interventions, the easier it is to argue for their similarity. Advice, didactic presentations, use of positive reinforcements, and focused group discussions are examples of interventions that can be similar, differing primarily in focus and contents.

Implement the Intervention for One Problem Variable, Client, or Situation. The practitioner implements the intervention until the expected change occurs in the problem variable. If no change occurs, the basic requirements for a multiple baseline design are not met.

Continue to baseline for the other problem variable, client, or situation. It is important to show that no changes occur during the continued baseline without intervention, yet, simultaneously, changes should occur in the idealized data pattern of the multiple baseline design when the practitioner provides intervention at the same time for the other problem variable. The occurrence of this pattern provides evidence that changes result from the intervention and not from historical or maturational factors.

Analyze the Graphic Patterns and Perform Statistical Analyses. The clinician should use graphic analysis and statistical testing to show that changes occur from baseline to intervention for I, II, or III (see Figure 45). In addition, he or she should analyze the differences between baseline and continued baseline to show there are no changes. If these patterns occur, then the clinical social worker can proceed to the next step in the multiple baseline design. Showing no changes between line AB (baseline) and line CD (intervention for I, II, or III) indicates there is no reason to shift the intervention to the other problem variable because it is ineffective with the first problem variable. On the other hand, changes may occur during intervention and during continued baseline (see Figure 45) for the following reasons:

- The intervention for one problem variable generalizes to the other problem variable.
- The problem variables are not independent, that is, they are highly correlated.
- The changes for both problem variables might result from historical or maturational factors or multiple treatment interference.

Withdraw the Intervention from Problem Variable 1 and Introduce It for Problem Variable 2. In Figure 45, it is apparent that the practitioner has withdrawn the intervention from I, II, or III and introduced it for IV, V, or VI. The interventions should be

DESIGN VARIATIONS

as similar as possible. If they are equivalent, the logic of the multiple baseline design is upheld.

Analyze the New Graphic Pattern and Perform Statistical Analyses. The social worker should make comparisons between the continued baseline and intervention for IV, V, or VI. That is, in Figure 45, the practitioner should compare line C'D' with line E'F' or line C_1D_1 with line E_1F_1. If there is a statistically significant change, then the criteria for a multiple baseline design have been met. Otherwise, the clinical social worker uses the same strategies for making decisions about the intervention as discussed in chapter 5 when comparing baselines and interventions.

The following are three examples of multiple baseline designs for clients, problem variables, and situations, complete with graphic presentations and statistical analyses. Two of the examples meet all of the criteria for a multiple baseline design; the other example results in two single-case designs. The guidelines for multiple baseline designs are applied in each example.

Multiple Baseline Design for One Client with Problem Variables of Productivity and Lateness

Determine whether there are two or more different problems, situations, or clients. A client's supervisor referred the client to an EAP. In an assessment, the social worker learns that the client has relationship difficulties with his girlfriend, low self-esteem, has been consistently late to work, and has been performing below productivity standards in his factory job. The clinical social worker's long-range goal is to increase the client's self-esteem and reduce his anxiety through cognitive therapy. Lateness to work and below-standard productivity are shorter term goals, both of which the social worker plans to treat through behavioral therapy; the goals can serve as the intervention objectives in a multiple baseline design that first focuses on lateness and subsequently on work productivity.

Construct Simultaneous Baselines. The social worker reconstructs both baselines. The client gives the clinical social worker permission to access his productivity and lateness records from his supervisor. Apparently, in a workweek that consists of five workdays, the client has been below productivity standards five days per week for the past five weeks, and he has been late to work every day for the past five weeks (Figure 46). Both baselines show that the client has major problems with productivity and lateness. In addition, both baselines are horizontally stable, showing no accelerating or decelerating trends.

Specify the Clinical Objectives. The clinical objectives are as follows:

- Reduce lateness to work to no more than one day per week by week 5 of intervention.
- Focus the intervention on increased productivity when the first objective has been achieved; the objective for productivity is that the number of days that the employee works below the standard productivity rate should be no more than one day per week.
- Although not immediately relevant for the multiple baseline design, anxiety should be reduced and self-esteem increased after three months of intervention.

figure 46

A Multiple Baseline Design for One Client with Problem Variables of Productivity and Lateness

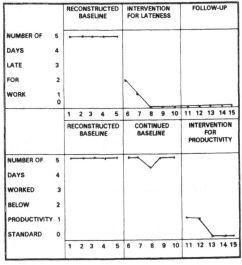

Specify the Intervention. The practitioner bases the intervention on the provision of one "reward unit" for each day the client is not late. Each reward unit is equivalent to one free meal at an inexpensive local restaurant, the client's preferred eatery. The restaurant is participating in the program for the next several months, a plan that the social worker devised. During the first intervention interview, the clinical social worker determined that a free meal would be the most powerful reinforcer for the client.

Implement the Intervention for One Problem Variable, Client, or Situation. The clinical social worker implements the intervention for lateness, the most immediate employee problem for the factory. The social worker explains the system to the client and indicates it will operate for the next five weeks. The social worker expects the client will reduce his lateness to no more than one time per week.

Continue to Baseline for the Other Problem Variable, Client, or Situation. The clinical social worker uses the lateness and productivity information provided by the client's supervisor each week. The practitioner plots the information on a graph (Figure 46).

Analyze the Graphic Patterns and Perform Statistical Analyses. Apparently, the clinical social worker has attained the objective of no more than one day of lateness per week (Figure 46). In the five weeks of intervention, the number of days late per week declined from two in week 6 to one in week 7 to three weeks of no days late. Table 29 verifies this shift: it shows a statistically significant shift between the reconstructed baseline and the intervention for lateness.

Simultaneously, the social worker observes no apparent changes between the reconstructed baseline and the continued baseline for productivity. The client performs below productivity standards every day for five weeks during the reconstructed baseline, and he is below standard every day except one during the five weeks of continued baseline with observations of 5, 5, 4, 5, and 5 for the number of days below productivity recorded on the graph. That there are no

table 29 *Computing S, Sc, and Z for Reconstructed Baseline and Intervention for Lateness Time Series in Figure 46*

Score (x)	x − M	$(x − M)^2$	x_i	$x − x_i$	$(x − x_i)^2$
5	2.20	4.84	5	0	0
5	2.20	4.84	5	0	0
5	2.20	4.84	5	0	0
5	2.20	4.84	5	0	0
5	2.20	4.84	2	3	9
2	−0.80	.64	1	1	1
1	−1.80	3.24	0	1	1
0	−2.80	7.84	0	0	0
0	−2.80	7.84	0	0	0
0	−2.80	7.84	−	−	−

28 = Σx	|51.60| = SS(x)	|11| = D^2

M = Σx/n	= 28/10	= 2.80
C = 1 − D^2/(2SS(x))	= 1 − 11/2(51.60)	= .89
Sc = $\sqrt{(n − 2)/(n + 1)(n − 1)}$	= $\sqrt{(10 − 2)/(10 + 1)(10 − 1)}$ = .28	
Z = C/Sc	= .89/.28	= 3.17

NOTE: Because Z > 1.64, there is a statistically significant change in the time-series.

DESIGN VARIATIONS

statistically significant differences between reconstructed and continued baselines is evident in Table 30.

Withdraw the intervention for problem variable 1 and introduce it for problem variable 2. The clinical social worker withdraws the intervention for lateness and introduces it for the problem of productivity. The social worker provides the same reinforcer of a free meal for each reward unit. For each day the client performs at or above the standard productivity level, he receives one reward unit. The clinical social worker explains to the client that the same system is operative but now is focused on productivity rather than lateness.

Analyze the New Graphic Pattern and Perform Statistical Analyses. As shown in Figure 46, the social worker observes 5, 5, 4, 5 and 5 days per week in which the client worked below productivity standards during the period of continued baseline. The client's productivity increased during interven-

tion: he worked below productivity standards only 1, 1, 0, 0, and 0 days per week. Furthermore, there is a statistically significant change in the time series from continued baseline to intervention for productivity (Table 31).

The overall graphic patterns and the statistical tests provide evidence that the criteria have been satisfied for the multiple baseline design for two different problem variables. Evidently, the intervention is generalizable across problem variables because in this instance, the intervention is effective for both productivity and lateness. In contrast, Figure 47 shows a data pattern that does not conform to the multiple baseline pattern. The intervention provides a shift from reconstructed baseline to intervention for lateness. However, the same pattern also occurs for productivity in which C'D' is significantly different from A'B'; this is identical to the pattern observed from AB to CD. Hence, associated with the intervention for lateness are shifts in the time series data for lateness and for productivity.

table 30 *Computing S, Sc, and Z for Reconstructed Baseline and Continued Baseline for Productivity Time-Series in Figure 46*

Score (x)	x − M	(x − M)²	xᵢ	x − xᵢ	(x − xᵢ)²
5	.1	.01	5	0	0
5	.1	.01	5	0	0
5	.1	.01	5	0	0
5	.1	.01	5	0	0
5	.1	.01	5	0	0
5	.1	.01	5	0	0
5	.1	.01	4	1	1
4	−.9	.81	5	−1	1
5	.1	.01	5	0	0
5	.1	.01	–	–	–

$49 = \Sigma x$		$1.901 = SS(x)$	$121 = D^2$		
$M = \Sigma x / n$		$= 49/10$	$= 4.90$		
$C = 1 - D^2/(2SS(x))$		$= 1 - 2/2(.90)$	$= -.11$		
$Sc = \sqrt{(n-2)/(n+1)(n-1)}$		$= \sqrt{(10-2)/(10+1)(10-1)} = .28$			
$Z = C/Sc$		$= -.11/.28$	$= -.39$		

NOTE: Because $Z < 1.64$, there are no statistically significant differences between the time-series at reconstructed baseline and continued baseline.

table 31 *Computing S, Sc, and Z for Continued Baseline and Intervention for Productivity Time-Series in Figure 46*

Score (x)	$x - M$	$(x - M)^2$	x_i	$x - x_i$	$(x - x_i)^2$
5	2.4	5.76	5	0	0
5	2.4	5.76	4	1	1
4	1.4	1.96	5	−1	1
5	2.4	5.76	5	0	0
5	2.4	5.76	1	4	16
1	−1.6	2.56	1	0	0
1	−1.6	2.56	0	1	1
0	−2.6	6.76	0	0	0
0	−2.6	6.76	0	0	0
0	−2.6	6.76	–	–	–

$26 = \Sigma x$		$150.401 = SS(x)$	$1191 = D^2$	
$M = \Sigma x/n$		$= 26/10$	$= 2.60$	
$C = 1 - D^2/(2SS(x))$		$= 1 - 19/2(50.40)$	$= .81$	
$Sc = \sqrt{(n-2)/(n+1)(n-1)}$		$= \sqrt{(10-2)/(10+1)(10-1)} = .28$		
$Z = C/Sc$		$= .81/.28$	$= 2.89$	

NOTE: Because $Z > 1.64$, there is a statistically significant shift in the time-series from continued baseline to intervention.

---

figure 47

Two Single-Subject Designs for One Client, for Lateness and for Productivity over Time

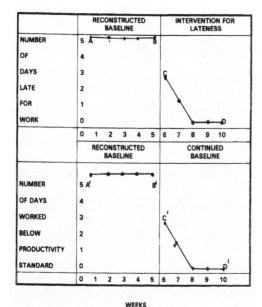

WEEKS

Multiple Baseline Design for Two Clients for the Problem Variable of Index of Sexual Satisfaction

This type of design can produce information about the generalizability of an intervention for more than one client. The same logic for the implementation of procedures and the analyses of data patterns is applicable. Because the design involves more than one client, it technically is not a single-case design. But it is included in this chapter because it is potentially useful when there are two or more clients with the same problem.

Determine Whether There are Two Different Problems, Situations, or Clients. The clinical social worker is involved in psychotherapy with two clients at a VA mental health clinic. Both clients are being treated for posttraumatic stress resulting from the Vietnam War. The basic intervention for both of them is psychodynamic therapy, including exploration of the past and the clients' feelings about the effects of the war on their environment; the social worker also develops cognitive strategies to deal with the clients' flashbacks of their war experiences. Both clients are married, and a relatively minor problem has been their dissatisfaction with sex. In addition to the ongoing therapy, the social worker decided to provide a program of sex therapy for both clients if the baseline assessments of sexual satisfaction indicated clinical problems.

Construct Simultaneous Baselines. The practitioner used Hudson's Index of Sexual Satisfaction (ISS) (Corcoran & Fischer, 1987, pp. 100–101) in Appendix 12 to measure sexual satisfaction. The ISS is useful because a score above 30 indicates a clinical problem; the lower the score, the greater the degree of sexual satisfaction.

The social worker makes observations every two days on the ISS because the practitioner believes that changes in the measure of sexual satisfaction might occur in two days but not in one day. The clinician observes that there are relatively stable horizontal baselines for both clients 1 and 2 (Figure 48). Although the magnitude of the problem is higher for client 2 (40 and above for eight measurements) than for client 1 (for which scores ranged from 35 to 37), both clients have scores that indicate clinical problems (the observations for both baselines do not have to be equivalent to meet the requirements of multiple baseline design).

Specify the Clinical Objectives. The clinical objectives are (1) to increase sexual satisfaction for client 2, after achieving it for client 1, and (2) to increase sexual satisfaction (significantly lower the average scores in the time series data at intervention) for client 1. The social worker should achieve these objectives by day 76 to day 90 after the initial baseline contact for client 1 and by day 150 to day 164 after the initial baseline contact for client 2. These objectives are those intended for the multiple baseline design.

Other objectives for both clients are longer-term objectives: to decrease the number of "flashbacks," to increase self-esteem, and to decrease anxiety.

Specify the Intervention. The clinician bases the intervention on a model of sex therapy, which

figure 48

A Multiple Baseline for Client 1 (A) and Client 2 (B) for the Problem Variable of Index of Sexual Satisfaction (ISS)

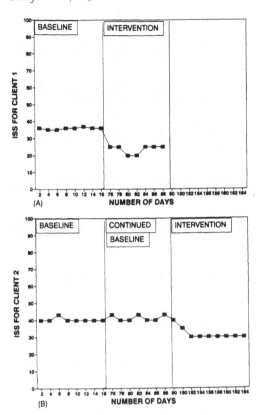

the therapist provides in an interview each week with each client and the clients' spouses; this interview is separate from an ongoing weekly interview with each client. The clinician and clients discuss problems, issues, and feelings involved in the clients' sex activities; the social worker offers suggestions for each couple to try in their homes; and the couples and the clinician discuss these sexual experiences in subsequent interviews. The focus is on teaching the clients and their spouses to be aware of and sensitive to each other's needs while overcoming their fears regarding sexual performance.

Implement the Intervention for One Problem Variable, Client, or Situation. The social worker implements the intervention of sex therapy for client 1 after the last observation in baseline. The clinician plans to continue until day 76 to day 90 since initial contact at baseline.

Continue to Baseline for the Other Problem Variable, Client, or Situation. The clinician continues the baseline for client 2 until day 90 from initial baseline contact.

Analyze the Graphic Patterns and Perform Statistical Analyses. A reduction in the sexual satisfaction scores for client 1 from baseline to intervention is evident from day 76 to day 90 since initial contact (Figure 48). The reduction is from a range of 35 to 37 at baseline to a range of 20 to 25 at intervention. All of the scores at intervention are below the cutting score of 30, which means a clinical problem no longer is evident (see Appendix 12). In contrast, the observations for baseline and continued baseline for client 2 are similar. At baseline, there are observations of 40, 40, 43, 40, 40, 40, 40, and 40; at continued baseline, the sexual satisfaction scores are slightly higher: 43, 40, 40, 43, 40, 40, 43, and 40.

The trends from baseline to intervention continued downward until the relatively stable pattern shown in intervention for client 1; the trend from baseline to continued baseline was neither upward nor downward, but relatively stable, consistent with the pattern shown for continued baseline for client 2.

Table 32 provides statistical calculations for client 1. There are changes beyond the .05 level of statistical significance between the time series at baseline and at intervention. Further supporting the data pattern for a multiple baseline design, Table 33 indicates that there is horizontal stability in the time series from baseline to continued baseline for client 2.

table 32	*Computing S, Sc, and Z for Baseline and Intervention, Client 1, in Figure 48*				
Score (x)	x − M	$(x - M)^2$	x_i	$x - x_i$	$(x - x_i)^2$
36	6.19	38.31	35	1	1
35	5.19	26.93	35	0	0
35	5.19	26.93	36	−1	1
36	6.19	38.31	36	0	0
36	6.19	38.31	37	−1	1
37	7.19	51.69	36	1	1
36	6.19	38.31	36	0	0
36	6.19	38.31	25	11	121
25	−4.81	23.13	25	0	0
25	−4.81	23.13	25	0	0
25	−4.81	23.13	20	5	25
20	−9.81	96.23	20	0	0
20	−9.81	96.23	25	−5	25
25	−4.81	23.13	25	0	0
25	−4.81	23.13	25	0	0
25	−4.81	23.13	–	–	–

477 = Σx		1628.341 = SS(x)	1175 = D^2		
M = Σx/n		= 477/16	= 29.81		
C = 1 − D^2/(2SS(x))		= 1 − 175/2(628.34)	= .86		
Sc = $\sqrt{(n-2)/(n+1)(n-1)}$		= $\sqrt{(16-2)/(16+1)(16-1)}$	= .23		
Z = C/Sc		= .86/.23	= 3.73		

NOTE: Because Z > 1.64, there is a statistically significant shift in the time-series from continued baseline to intervention.

DESIGN VARIATIONS

Score (x)	x − M	(x − M)²	x_i	x − x_i	(x − x_i)²
40	−.75	.56	40	0	0
40	−.75	.56	43	−3	9
43	2.25	5.06	40	3	9
40	−.75	.56	40	0	0
40	−.75	.56	40	0	0
40	−.75	.56	40	0	0
40	−.75	.56	40	0	0
40	−.75	.56	43	−3	9
43	2.25	5.06	40	3	9
40	−.75	.56	40	0	0
40	−.75	.56	43	−3	9
43	2.25	5.06	40	3	9
40	−.75	.56	40	0	0
40	−.75	.56	43	−3	9
43	2.25	5.06	40	3	9
40	−.75	.56	−	−	−

652 = Σx		126.961 = SS(x)	172 = D^2

M = Σx/n	= 652/16	= 40.75
C = 1 − D^2/(2SS(x))	= 1 − 72/2(26.96)	= −.33
Sc = $\sqrt{(n-2)/(n+1)(n-1)}$	= $\sqrt{(16-2)/(16+1)(16-1)}$	= .23
Z = C/Sc	= −.33/.23	= −1.43

table 33 *Computing S, Sc, and Z for Baseline and Continued Baseline, Client 2, in Figure 48*

NOTE: Because Z < 1.64, there are no statistically significant differences.

Withdraw the Intervention for Client 1 and Introduce It for Client 2. The social worker withdraws the intervention of sex therapy for client 1 and introduces it for client 2. Sex therapy for both clients is the same intervention given by the same therapist.

Analyze the New Graphic Pattern and Perform Statistical Analyses. The observations over time stop at day 90 and continue on day 150 (Figure 48). Again, as in day 16 to day 76, the social worker could have recorded the observations from day 92 to day 148, but did not do so for simplicity in presentation. Those observations showed a steady downward trend from continued baseline to intervention at 150 days. Furthermore, the magnitude of scores on sexual satisfaction (which means an increase in sexual satisfaction)

decreased from 40 to 43 at continued baseline to 35 for one observation and 30 for seven observations at intervention. This shift in the time series is statistically significant (Table 34). However, the clinician does not withdraw intervention because the score of 30 still indicates a problem in sexual satisfaction. Although there was a statistically significant change from continued baseline to intervention, indicating effectiveness of the intervention, the clinician can attain more progress until there is no clinical problem. That is, client 2 and his spouse appear to require more sex therapy intervention than did client 1 and his spouse. Nevertheless, their graphic analyses and the statistical analyses provide evidence that the multiple baseline criteria have been met and that sex therapy was effective for both clients.

Score (x)	x – M	$(x - M)^2$	x_i	$x - x_i$	$(x - x_i)^2$
43	7.13	50.83	40	3	9
40	4.13	17.05	40	0	0
40	4.13	17.05	43	–3	9
43	7.13	50.83	40	3	9
40	4.13	17.05	40	0	0
40	4.13	17.05	43	–3	9
43	7.13	50.83	40	3	9
40	4.13	17.05	35	5	25
35	–.87	.75	30	5	25
30	–5.87	34.45	30	0	0
30	–5.87	34.45	30	0	0
30	–5.87	34.45	30	0	0
30	–5.87	34.45	30	0	0
30	–5.87	34.45	30	0	0
30	–5.87	34.45	30	0	0
30	–5.87	34.45	–	–	–
$574 = \Sigma x$		$1479.641 = SS(x)$	$1951 = D^2$		

$M = \Sigma x/n$	$= 574/16$	$= 35.87$	
$C = 1 - D^2/(2SS(x))$	$= 1 - 95/2(479.64)$	$= .90$	
$Sc = \sqrt{(n-2)/(n+1)(n-1)}$	$= \sqrt{(16-2)/(16+1)(16-1)}$	$= .23$	
$Z = C/Sc$	$= .90/.23$	$= 3.91$	

NOTE: Because $Z > 1.64$, there are statistically significant differences between baseline and intervention.

Two Single-Case Designs for One Client for Lateness at Home and at School

This example shows the result of an attempt at a multiple baseline design for two situations for one client. The attempt fails, with two resulting single-case designs instead of the multiple baseline design. It does not meet the criteria of a multiple baseline design because the continued baseline for days late at home is significantly different from the reconstructed baseline (Figure 49).

Determine Whether There are Two or More Different Problems, Situations, or Clients. The client is an adolescent male whom the counseling staff at a public school has identified as a predelinquent; the staff has referred the adolescent to a behavioral therapy project for interventions aimed at re-ducing school tardiness and the days tardy at home. In addition, the project is designed to increase school attendance, increase grades, increase positive relations at home, and increase the client's self-esteem (Stuart, Jayaratne, & Tripodi, 1976).

Construct Simultaneous Baselines. The clinical social worker uses school records to show the number of days per week that the client was late for school. Based on an interview with the boy's mother, the clinical social worker reconstructs a baseline for five weeks before social work contact. Evidently, the client has a horizontally stable baseline of being late for school four out of five days per week and a horizontally stable baseline of being late arriving home three out of five days per week (Figure 49) (the two different

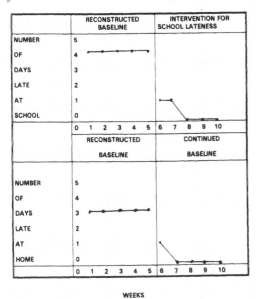

figure 49

Two Single-Subject Designs for One Client,
for Lateness to School and Arriving at Home

WEEKS

baselines do not have to have the same magnitude of observations to satisfy the criteria of a multiple baseline design).

Specify the Clinical Objectives. The short-term clinical objective is to significantly reduce the number of days per week late to school by week 5 of intervention (weeks 6 to 10); after achieving that objective, the clinical objective is to significantly reduce the number of days per week late arriving home.

Specify the Intervention. The intervention for achieving these objectives is behavioral therapy. The social worker rewards the boy for each week that he is not late more than one day. The social worker bases the reward on what is most meaningful for the boy: money to see movies on weekends.

Implement the Intervention for One Problem Variable, Client, or Situation. The clinician implements behavioral therapy to reduce the number of days late per week to school. The clinical social worker develops and explains the reward system and discusses with the boy reasons for being late to school and how he might resolve the problem.

The practitioner also involves the boy's family in the discussion, which occurs once per week.

Continue to Baseline for the Other Problem Variable, Client, or Situation. The boy's mother provides the clinical social worker with a report of the number of days the boy is late arriving home during school days. The report only covers weekdays to equalize the number of days for home lateness and school lateness.

Analyze the Graphic Patterns and Perform Statistical Analyses. There is a reduction in number of days late to school from four days per week at reconstructed baseline to one or zero days per week during the intervention (Figure 49). However, there is also a decrease from reconstructed baseline, from three days per week late arriving home to one or zero days per week during the continued baseline. Analyses verify these observations, showing statistically significant changes from reconstructed baseline to intervention for days per week late to school and for reconstructed baseline to continued baseline for days per week late arriving home (Tables 35 and 36).

Hence, the practitioner has attained the clinical objectives both for lateness to school and arriving home. However, because of the significant shift in the time-series from baseline to continued baseline for days late at home, it is unclear whether the intervention that was effective for school lateness generalized to home lateness, or whether the changes resulted from historical or maturational influences, or from an intervention the client received other than that provided by the clinician, for example, group therapy.

GRADUATED INTENSITY DESIGN

The graduated intensity design is similar to the basic single-case design. It involves baseline followed by an intervention; if the intervention phase is statistically different from baseline but not enough reduction in the problem variable has occurred, the intensity of the intervention is changed. If the time series with increased (or decreased) intervention is statistically significantly different from the time series at the first intervention stage, the resulting data pattern produces the graduated intensity design (Vonk,

table 35 *Computing S, Sc, and Z for Reconstructed Baseline and Intervention for School Lateness in Figure 49*

Score (x)	x − M	(x − M)²	x_i	x − x_i	(x − x_i)²
4	1.8	3.24	4	0	0
4	1.8	3.24	4	0	0
4	1.8	3.24	4	0	0
4	1.8	3.24	4	0	0
4	1.8	3.24	1	3	9
1	−1.2	1.44	1	0	0
1	−1.2	1.44	0	1	1
0	−2.2	4.84	0	0	0
0	−2.2	4.84	0	0	0
0	−2.2	4.84	–	–	–

22 = Σx	|33.60| = SS(x)	|10| = D²
M = Σx/n	= 22/10	= 2.20
C = 1 − D²/(2SS(x))	= 1 − 10/2(33.60)	= .85
Sc = $\sqrt{(n-2)/(n+1)(n-1)}$	= $\sqrt{(10-2)/(10+1)(10-1)}$ = .28	
Z = C/Sc	= .85/.28	= 3.07

NOTE: Because Z > 1.64, there are statistically significant differences in the time-series.

table 36 *Computing S, Sc, and Z for Reconstructed Baseline and Continued Baseline for Home Lateness in Figure 49*

Score (x)	x − M	(x − M)²	x_i	x − x_i	(x − x_i)²
3	1.40	1.96	3	0	0
3	1.40	1.96	3	0	0
3	1.40	1.96	3	0	0
3	1.40	1.96	3	0	0
3	1.40	1.96	1	2	4
1	−.60	.36	0	1	1
0	−1.60	2.56	0	0	0
0	−1.60	2.56	0	0	0
0	−1.60	2.56	0	0	0
0	−1.60	2.56	–	–	–

16 = Σx	|20.40| = SS(x)	|5| = D²
M = Σx/n	= 16/10	= 1.60
C = 1 − D²/(2SS(x))	= 1 − 5/2(20.40)	= .87
Sc = $\sqrt{(n-2)/(n+1)(n-1)}$	= $\sqrt{(10-2)/(10+1)(10-1)}$ = .28	
Z = C/Sc	= .87/.28	= 3.10

NOTE: Because Z > 1.64, there are statistically significant differences in the time-series.

DESIGN VARIATIONS

Tripodi, & Epstein, 2006). The ideal data pattern is depicted in Figure 50. There is a horizontally stable baseline followed by a change in magnitude during the first intervention, which, in turn, is followed by a change in magnitude during the phase in which the social worker has administered the changed intensity of the intervention.

Intensity can refer to the duration of each intervention contact, the number of contacts within a given period, the addition of new intervention components, the extent of the clinical social worker's involvement, or the degree of the client's participation. For example, a one-hour contact is more intense than contact for half an hour; two contacts per week is more intense than one contact per week; and cognitive therapy and behavioral techniques combined are more intense than cognitive therapy by itself. One can estimate the degree of involvement of the clinical social worker or the client by the amount of time either spends talking in a therapeutic session. A clinical social worker who by design talks five minutes in an hour-long session could increase his or her intensity by talking 30 minutes, for example.

The graduated intensity design can provide some control over the internal validity threats of history, maturation, and multiple treatment interference. The design is based on the supposition that intensity is related to effectiveness and on the notion that successive statistically

significant changes (from baseline to intervention and from intervention to a changed intensity of intervention) are more likely to indicate that the changes in magnitude of the problem variable result from the intervention and not extraneous factors (Carter, 1972; Jayaratne & Levy, 1979).

Furthermore, the graduated intensity design fits the practice of many clinical social workers. The social worker may achieve progress with an intervention without attaining the clinical objectives. For example, an alcoholic reduces the amount of his or her drinking, but still drinks; the adolescent reduces the number of days truant from school, but he or she still is truant; the young adult female increases her degree of assertiveness, but she continues to be unassertive in most situations. When the client has made such progress, the clinical social worker can make several possible decisions: continue the same intervention, change the intensity of the intervention, or substitute another intervention. Deciding to change the intensity involves a simple manipulation (for example, doubling the number of contacts per week). If no changes occur with the changed intensity, the graduated intensity design is not produced; rather, the basic baseline plus intervention phase is evident. Therefore, an unsuccessful graduated intensity design continues to represent two phases of the basic single-case design model.

The chief disadvantage of the graduated intensity design is that it requires the systematic collection of data over a relatively long time. To the extent that data collection is time-consuming and the data are difficult to collect, the design becomes impractical. However, if the client or the social worker can easily obtain data, the design is quite feasible and advantageous because it provides data directly relevant to the possible manipulations the clinical social worker makes in implementing the intervention. The other major disadvantage is that the ideal data pattern may not materialize; nevertheless, it is still important information for the clinical social worker to know whether changes in the problem variable occur with changes in the implementation of the intervention.

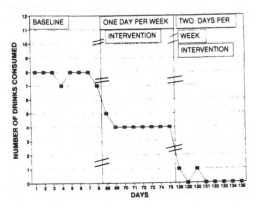

figure 50

Graduated Intensity Design

General Guidelines for Implementing the Graduated Intensity Design

Specify the Problem Variable. The clinical social worker should determine from an assessment of the client and his or her situation whether any problem variable needs change. The social worker should operationally define the variable and indicate how he or she will systematically measure it during baseline and intervention.

Obtain a Baseline. The practitioner should use procedures previously discussed (see chapter 4) and analyze the data pattern. The problem variable should be at a high enough magnitude to warrant intervention. A horizontally stable baseline or a baseline with increasing trends indicates that the problem is persistent, which further indicates the need for intervention.

Specify the Clinical Objectives. The clinician needs to specify how much change he or she desires and when he or she expects change to occur after introducing the intervention.

Specify the Intervention. The practitioner must specify the type of intervention and pay close attention to parameters of intensity, such as length of time for sessions, the number of contacts, client involvement, and so forth. The more specific the intervention is in relation to these parameters, the easier it is for the clinical social worker to change components of the intervention.

Introduce the Intervention. The social worker should introduce the intervention after obtaining the baseline. He or she should systematically implement the intervention, for example, with the same duration for each interview and the same number of contacts per week.

Compare the Intervention to Baseline. The clinical social worker should analyze the data graphically and statistically to determine whether there are significant changes in the desired direction. In addition, he or she should observe whether he or she has attained the clinical objectives. If the social worker has made progress but has not attained the clinical objectives, then he or she needs to proceed to the next step. If the practitioner has not made any progress or if he or she has already attained the clinical objectives,

then the design requirements of the graduated intensity design have not been met. The clinical social worker makes the decision that fits his or her clinical practice. For example, if the clinical social worker has achieved the objectives, then he or she may work on other objectives or make arrangements for termination and follow-up.

Change the Intervention Intensity. Changing the intensity could involve increasing or decreasing the parameters of intensity. Although the clinician bases increasing intensity on the assumption that the level of intensity is directly related to effectiveness, decreasing intensity is predicated on a different assumption: The level of intensity is inversely related to the degree of effectiveness—the more the intervention is reduced, the greater the degree of effectiveness. The clinical social worker bases his or her decision to increase or decrease intensity on judgment stemming from his or her clinical experience, on notions of the intervention applied, and on the assessment of the particular client.

Compare the Intervention with Changed Intensity to the Intervention Implemented after Baseline. The social worker needs to graphically and statistically analyze whether there are changes in the time series. In addition, the social worker must determine the extent to which he or she has realized clinical objectives. If there are statistically significant differences, then the social worker has fulfilled the criteria for the graduated intensity design. The realization of clinical objectives signifies that the clinical social worker can plan for termination and follow-up, assuming there are no other objectives to accomplish.

Example

Specify the Problem Variable. The client, an adult female, is an alcoholic. She is addicted to drinking Scotch, and she voluntarily sought help from a clinical social worker in private practice. From an assessment interview, the clinical social worker concludes that the client has problems with family as well as with other interpersonal relationships. Although the client, a professor of journalism, is successful at work and in community activities, she has a great deal of difficulty in pursuing and sustaining intimate relationships. The social worker views the alcoholism as a symptom of more deeply seated problems in the client's relationships with her family. The problem variable is that of the number of drinks of Scotch the client consumes daily. The client indicates that she has been consuming seven to eight glasses of Scotch daily for the past two months, and she is afraid that her work will soon deteriorate because of her excessive drinking.

Obtain a Baseline. A baseline of eight consecutive days indicates that the client drank eight drinks on six days and seven drinks on the other two days (Figure 50). The problem, as reported by the client to the clinical social worker, is severe; it is of high magnitude and it has been persistent. The baseline verifies the information the client reported in the initial assessment interview.

Specify the Clinical Objectives. The long-range clinical objectives are to increase the client's understanding of her drinking behavior and to discuss the extent to which the drinking is related to relationship problems with her family. The objective with respect to the drinking of alcohol is that the client stops drinking after two months (60 days) of intervention.

Specify the Intervention. The intervention is psychodynamic psychotherapy. Not wanting to reveal her problem to university associates, the client chooses not to enter into an Alcoholics Anonymous program. Both the client and the therapist believe that they need to unravel the client's problems with family relationships. Nevertheless, they also believe they should monitor the problem variable of alcohol consumption because it is a tangible symptom that might indicate overall progress; more importantly, if the client does not reduce her alcoholic consumption, her career could be in jeopardy. The intervention consists of exploration of family problems and relationships as well as discussion of thoughts, actions, and feelings involved when the need to drink Scotch is manifest. The social worker plans to use techniques of clarification, support, and interpretation to help the client gain perspective on why she needs to drink.

Introduce the Intervention. The intervention is of one-hour duration for one session per week. It commenced immediately after the baseline period of eight days ended.

Compare the Intervention to Baseline. In accordance with the clinical objectives, the practitioner compares the time series at intervention from day 68 to day 75 from initial contact with the client (two months after intervention began) with the baseline. Although not shown in Figure 50, the client recorded the number of drinks consumed daily and reported those numbers weekly to the clinical social worker. The number of drinks consumed did not depart from the baseline pattern until day 38 since initial client contact; then there was a gradual decline until the social worker obtained the pattern recorded in Figure 50. At baseline, the number of drinks consumed ranges from seven to eight, whereas at intervention, the client consumed four drinks daily for seven days and five drinks for one day. Hence, there was a reduction in the daily number of drinks consumed, but the social worker had not achieved the clinical objective of no drinking.

Computations of C, Sc, and Z to test for statistically significant differences in the problem variable from baseline to intervention one day per week are shown in Table 37. Because Z is greater than 1.64, there are differences beyond the .05 level of statistical significance.

Change the Intervention Intensity. Because the social worker did not achieve the clinical objectives, he or she believed more progress would be made by increasing the intensity of the intervention from one day to two days per week. Moreover, the practitioner changed the clinical objectives of no drinks per day after two months to no drinks per day after another two months, that is, at day 135 since initial client contact.

Compare the Intervention with Changed Intensity to the Intervention Implemented after Baseline. Figure 50 shows that during the intervention two days per week, the client had one drink daily for two days and no drinks daily for six days. Hence, the social worker did not achieve the clinical objective of no drinks daily. Although not shown in Figure 50, the trend was downward from four drinks at day 75 to one drink at day 128.

| **table 37** | *Computing S, Sc, and Z for Baseline to Intervention One Day Per Week in Figure 50* |

Score (x)	x – M	(x – M)²	x_i	x – x_i	(x – x_i)²
8	2.07	4.28	8	0	0
8	2.07	4.28	8	0	0
8	2.07	4.28	7	1	1
7	1.07	1.14	8	–1	1
8	2.07	4.28	8	0	0
8	2.07	4.28	8	0	0
8	2.07	4.28	7	1	1
7	1.07	1.14	5	2	4
5	–.93	.86	4	1	1
4	–1.93	3.72	4	0	0
4	–1.93	3.72	4	0	0
4	–1.93	3.72	4	0	0
4	–1.93	3.72	4	0	0
4	–1.93	3.72	4	0	0
4	–1.93	3.72	4	0	0
4	–1.93	3.72	–	–	–

| 95 = Σx | | 154.861 = SS(x) | 18 = D^2 | | |

$M = \Sigma x / n$ = 95/16 = 5.93

$C = 1 - D^2/(2SS(x))$ = 1 – 8/2(54.86) = .92

$Sc = \sqrt{(n - 2)/(n + 1)(n - 1)}$ = $\sqrt{(16 - 2)/(16 + 1)(16 - 1)}$ = .23

$Z = C/Sc$ = .92/.23 = 4.00

NOTE: Because $Z > 1.64$, there are statistically significant differences.

Table 38 provides statistical evidence that there were significant changes in the time-series from the one-day-per-week intervention to the two-days-per-week intervention. Thus, the social worker has met the basic requirements of a graduated intensity design with respect to procedures for manipulating intensity of the intervention and to the resulting data patterns. Moreover, Table 39 provides further evidence that the time series at intervention for two days per week is significantly different from the time series for the problem variable at baseline.

Therefore, the practitioner has met the short-term goals for the client. The clinical social worker decides to continue to monitor alcohol consumption but is now ready to specify more precise objectives with the client for establishing more positive relationships. During the process of psychotherapy, the social worker discovered that the client and her mother spent a great deal of hostile energy in competing for attention from the client's father and the client had been encouraged to seek new relationships, both with men and with women. This discovery illustrates that the client and the social worker may accomplish an objective during the course of therapy and subsequently pursue other objectives. Obviously, with problems such as alcoholism, the danger of relapse is present, particularly with this client, who may revert to drinking behavior if she does not achieve successful new relationships with a clearer understanding of the influence of her familial relationships on her contemporary ones.

table 38 *Computing S, Sc, and Z, Intervention One Day Per Week Compared with Intervention Two Days per Week in Figure 50*

Score (x)	x − M	$(x − M)^2$	x_i	$x − x_i$	$(x − x_i)^2$
5	2.82	7.95	4	1	1
4	1.82	3.31	4	0	0
4	1.82	3.31	4	0	0
4	1.82	3.31	4	0	0
4	1.82	3.31	4	0	0
4	1.82	3.31	4	0	0
4	1.82	3.31	4	0	0
4	1.82	3.31	1	3	9
1	−1.18	1.39	0	1	1
0	−2.18	4.75	1	−1	1
1	−1.18	1.39	0	1	1
0	−2.18	4.75	0	0	0
0	−2.18	4.75	0	0	0
0	−2.18	4.75	0	0	0
0	−2.18	4.75	0	0	0
0	−2.18	4.75	−	−	−

35 = Σx		162.401 = SS(x)	1131 = D^2	
$M = \Sigma x / n$	= 35/16		= 2.18	
$C = 1 − D^2/(2SS(x))$	= 1 − 13/2(62.40)		= .89	
$Sc = \sqrt{(n − 2)/(n + 1)(n − 1)}$	= $\sqrt{(16 − 2)/(16 + 1)(16 − 1)}$		= .23	
$Z = C/Sc$	= .89/.23		= 3.86	

NOTE: Because Z > 1.64, there are statistically significant differences.

WITHDRAWAL–REVERSAL DESIGN

The withdrawal–reversal design involves four stages; the first three stages are identical to the basic model of baseline, intervention, and follow-up, whereas the last stage calls for the reintroduction of the intervention. First, the social worker establishes a baseline of the problem variable to indicate there is a problem of sufficient magnitude to warrant intervention. Then he or she introduces the intervention; if the time series of the problem variable shows a significant decrease in the problem and the attainment of clinical objectives for addressing it, the social worker discontinues (withdraws) the intervention. During the follow-up stage, if there is a significant reversal to indicate that the problem is again of sufficient magnitude

to warrant intervention, the practitioner re-introduces the intervention. The clinician has fully met the requisites of the withdrawal-reversal design if the time series of the problem variable again show a significant decrease. This idealized pattern is observable in Figure 51: At baseline, there is a problem of noncompliance with a diet regimen; at intervention, the client increases compliance (that is, the problem is decreased); at follow-up or withdrawal of the intervention, the problem recurs; and at the re-introduction of the intervention, the problem again decreases.

The withdrawal–reversal design is an unplanned extension of the basic model of single-case design that involves reintroducing the original intervention when clinical objectives are attained

table 39 *Computing S, Sc, and Z, Baseline Compared with Intervention Two Days Per Week in Figure 50*

Score (x)	x − M	(x − M)²	x_i	x − x_i	(x − x_i)²
8	4	16	8	0	0
8	4	16	8	0	0
8	4	16	7	1	1
7	3	9	8	−1	1
8	4	16	8	0	0
8	4	16	8	0	0
8	4	16	7	1	1
7	3	9	1	6	36
1	−3	9	0	1	1
0	−4	16	1	−1	1
1	−3	9	0	1	1
0	−4	16	0	0	0
0	−4	16	0	0	0
0	−4	16	0	0	0
0	−4	16	0	0	0
0	−4	16	−	−	−

64 = Σx	|228| = SS(x)	|42| = D²	

$$M = \Sigma x/n \qquad = 64/16 \qquad = 4$$

$$C = 1 - D^2/(2SS(x)) \qquad = 1 - 42/2(228) \qquad = .90$$

$$Sc = \sqrt{(n-2)/(n+1)(n-1)} = \sqrt{(16-2)/(16+1)(16-1)} = .23$$

$$Z = C/Sc \qquad = .90/.23 \qquad = 3.91$$

NOTE: Because Z > 1.64, there are statistically significant differences.

during intervention but the effects of intervention are not sustained through follow-up. The clinical social worker would not withdraw the intervention if clinical objectives were not achieved; to do so would constitute unethical practice. If, on the other hand, the clinician has reason to believe that the original intervention was insufficient to sustain the desired level of change through follow-up, he or she can implement an alternate intervention. If the clinician does so, the design requirements of the withdrawal-reversal design would not be met. For a discussion of the resulting design and additional design variations for use in clinical practice, the reader should consult relevant texts on the subject. Recommended texts are presented at the end of this chapter.

The withdrawal–reversal design variation provides a degree of control over the internal validity threats of maturation, history, expectancy, and multiple treatment interference if during baseline, the clinician could attribute changes to the intervention and the internal validity threats. However, the increase in the problem during follow-up indicates that the decrease in the problem during intervention probably did not result from the internal validity threats, which are still operative at follow-up when the social worker withdrew the intervention. This inference is further substantiated with the reintroduction of the intervention when the problem again is reduced. In effect, the problem is present when the intervention is not and it is diminished when the intervention is present.

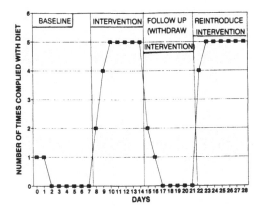

figure 51

An Idealized Data Pattern for a Withdrawal–Reversal Design

Hence, this design, which the practitioner only achieves using the procedures of introduction, withdrawal, and reintroduction of the intervention as well as the data pattern described, controls internal validity threats (Monette et al., 1986; Rubin & Babbie, 2001; Vonk, Tripodi, & Epstein, 2006).

The chief advantage of this design is that it can occur naturally in clinical social work practice. If all the data patterns from stage to stage do not occur, what remains is a basic design of baseline, intervention, and follow-up. In contrast, the major disadvantage is that it is difficult to reintroduce the exact intervention that was in effect before follow-up. The more complex the intervention, the more unlikely it is that the social worker will reintroduce the same intervention. It is necessary to have the same intervention to control for internal validity threats.

Guidelines for Implementing the Withdrawal–Reversal Design

This design is most practical when the intervention is relatively simple and involves routine, identifiable actions, for example, making a phone call or directly giving advice. In addition, the implementation of the withdrawal–reversal design is most feasible with short-term interventions. The following are general guidelines for implementing the withdrawal-reversal design.

Specify the Problem Variable. The practitioner should define the problem variable, indicating how he or she will measure it. The clinician must use the same measurement procedure throughout all of the stages of the design.

Obtain a Baseline. The social worker should obtain a baseline, analyze the data pattern, and determine whether there is a problem of sufficient magnitude to warrant intervention.

Specify the Clinical Objectives. The clinician should indicate the magnitude of change expected and when he or she expects the change to occur. If possible, the social worker should estimate how long the change should persist after withdrawal of the intervention as a result of termination.

Specify the Intervention. The clinical social worker needs to specify the intervention so that he or she can easily replicate it following withdrawal.

Introduce the Intervention. The social worker should introduce and systematically implement the intervention in accordance with the specified plan.

Compare the Intervention to Baseline. The practitioner needs to graphically analyze the data patterns and perform statistical tests. If he or she has met the clinical objectives, then the social worker proceeds to the next step.

Withdraw the Intervention. The clinician should continue to measure the problem variable and compare the withdrawal stage to the intervention stage. If there are statistically significant differences and the social worker has not met the clinical objectives, then he or she proceeds to the next step.

Reintroduce the Intervention. In this step, the clinician obtains measurements of the problem variable and compares the time series in this phase with that of the withdrawal phase. If there are statistically significant differences in the direction of reducing the problem, then the social worker has met the basic criteria for the withdrawal-reversal design. At this point, the clinical social worker has to decide whether to continue the intervention or to withdraw it again. To avoid the problem of reversal, the clinical social worker may decide to gradually reduce the intervention in small increments and continually monitor the problem variable to locate the possibility of another reversal.

Using the Withdrawal–Reversal Design

Specify the Problem Variable. The client is a male outpatient with diverticulitis. The hospital nutritionist recommended a plan for a diet regimen that would control the disease and possibly prevent the client's having to undergo surgery. However, the client had difficulty complying with the diet; the nutritionist referred him to the clinical social worker to discuss the psychosocial aspects of his disease, including the change of routine family patterns and the necessity to adhere to the regimen prescribed in the diet. Essentially, the client was to eat five times per day and he was to avoid fried foods, alcohol, coffee, uncooked vegetables, and spicy foods. The nutritionist prescribed a menu for the client. The problem variable is compliance with the diet—this means compliance with all five prescribed meals daily.

Obtain a Baseline. The social worker obtains a baseline for one week and instructs the client's wife to observe whether he complied with the requirements of each meal, because he remained at home using his home as a business office. The social worker tells the wife to offer the client the food, but not to nag him about eating desirable foods and to avoid eating and drinking nonprescribed foods and beverages. The baseline observed in Figure 51 indicates that after the first two days of complying with only one out of five meals, he did not comply with any meals for five straight days. Thus, apparently an intervention is warranted.

Specify the Clinical Objectives. The short-term clinical objective is to immediately help the client comply with the diet regimen. From the assessment interview, the social worker observes that the client does not realize the seriousness of his illness and the importance of adhering to his diet. Hence, the clinical social worker has the longer-range objective of helping him understand the nature of his illness and how he can adapt to it. The social worker believes that once the client

has achieved full compliance (five meals a day), he will continue to comply with the diet for an unlimited period.

Specify the Intervention. The intervention for the short-term goal is a phone call the clinical social worker makes to the client one time each day at noon. The phone call is brief; the social worker asks how the client is doing with his diet and stresses how important it is for him to comply with it.

Introduce the Intervention. The practitioner introduces the intervention the next day after completing the baseline. Furthermore, the social worker continues to make telephone calls every day of the week at exactly the same time.

Compare the Intervention to Baseline. The time-series at intervention contains five straight days of full compliance after the first two days of two and four times complied (Figure 51). This is a dramatic change from baseline to intervention, reflected in Table 40, which shows statistically significant changes from baseline to intervention.

Withdraw the Intervention. The clinical social worker ceases making telephone calls from day 15 to day 21. Instead of continuing to maintain the diet as the clinical social worker had predicted, the client reverts to the baseline pattern with no compliance from day 17 to day 21 (see Figure 51). Statistical analysis reveals significant differences from intervention to intervention withdrawal (Table 41).

The clinical social worker speaks with the client on day 21. The social worker learns that the client believes that sticking to the diet is unimportant because the social worker stopped calling him. The social worker explains to him that it is very important, indicating why the client should continue on his diet. She resumes the telephone intervention on day 22.

Reintroduce the Intervention. The social worker reintroduces the intervention and maintains it for the next seven days. The client again fully complies with the diet regimen; in fact, he was in full compliance for six out of the seven days (Figure 51). Again, there was a dramatic increase from

table 40	*Computing S, Sc, and Z Comparing Baseline with Intervention in Figure 51*					
Score (x)	x − M	$(x - M)^2$	x_i	$x - x_i$	$(x - x_i)^2$
1	−1.35	1.82	1	0	0
1	−1.35	1.82	0	1	1
0	−2.35	5.52	0	0	0
0	−2.35	5.52	0	0	0
0	−2.35	5.52	0	0	0
0	−2.35	5.52	0	0	0
0	−2.35	5.52	2	−2	4
2	−.35	.12	4	−2	4
4	1.65	2.72	5	−1	1
5	2.65	7.02	5	0	0
5	2.65	7.02	5	0	0
5	2.65	7.02	5	0	0
5	2.65	7.02	5	0	0
5	2.65	7.02	–	–	–

33 = Σx		169.181 = SS(x)		110 = D^2	
M = Σx/n		= 33/14		= 2.35	
C = 1 − D^2/(2SS(x))		= 1 − 10/2(69.18)		= .92	
Sc = $\sqrt{(n - 2)/(n + 1)(n - 1)}$		= $\sqrt{(14 - 2)/(14 + 1)(14 - 1)}$		= .24	
Z = C/Sc		= .92/.24		= 3.83	

NOTE: Because Z > 1.64, there are statistically significant differences between baseline and intervention.

follow-up to the reintroduction of the intervention. The statistical analysis verifies this increase, indicating a significant shift in the time series (Table 42).

OTHER VARIATIONS

Readers who wish to learn about other variations should consult the following references: Barlow and Hersen (1984), whose book is the most authoritative text on variations of single-case designs. The examples are from behavioral psychology and the interventions are of short-term duration. It is difficult to read, but is most comprehensive in the variety of designs presented. Also, the Bloom and colleagues (2006) book presents a number of variations on single-case design. Its focus is on the evaluation of practice in social work; it includes many technical procedures and statistical analysis strategies. In addition, the text by Blythe and colleagues (1994) contains many designs and research procedures

that social workers in human services agencies can use. It also includes a number of statistical techniques for analyzing the results of research.

Those books include a number of references that should enable students to gain a detailed knowledge of single-case designs. It is hoped that the basic concepts presented in this book will serve as a useful introduction for clinicians to consider the applicability of single-case designs to their practice.

TEACHING SUGGESIONS

Develop a hypothetical case that includes examples of the internal validity threats of history, maturation, and multiple treatment interference. Present data from a study that uses the basic model of single-case design to evaluate work with this case. Discuss the limitations of this design for controlling these internal validity threats. Using examples from the chapter, illustrate the

table 41 *Computing S, Sc, and Z Comparing Intervention with Intervention Withdrawal in Figure 51*

Score (x)	$x - M$	$(x - M)^2$	x_i	$x - x_i$	$(x - x_i)^2$
2	−.42	.17	4	−2	4
4	1.58	2.49	5	−1	1
5	2.58	6.65	5	0	0
5	2.58	6.65	5	0	0
5	2.58	6.65	5	0	0
5	2.58	6.65	5	0	0
5	2.58	6.65	2	3	9
2	−.42	.17	1	1	1
1	−1.42	2.01	0	1	1
0	−2.42	5.85	0	0	0
0	−2.42	5.85	0	0	0
0	−2.42	5.85	0	0	0
0	−2.42	5.85	0	0	0
0	−2.42	5.85	−	−	−

$34 = \Sigma x$		$167.341 = SS(x)$	$1161 = D^2$		

$M = \Sigma x / n$ $\quad = 34/14$ $\quad = 2.42$

$C = 1 - D^2/(2SS(x))$ $\quad = 1 - 16/2(67.34)$ $\quad = .88$

$Sc = \sqrt{(n - 2)/(n + 1)(n - 1)} = \sqrt{(14 - 2)/(14 + 1)(14 - 1)} = .24$

$Z = C/Sc$ $\quad = .88/.24$ $\quad = 3.66$

NOTE: Because $Z > 1.64$, there are statistically significant differences between the time-series at intervention and intervention withdrawal.

ways in which the multiple baseline, graduated intensity, and withdrawal-reversal designs can minimize these internal validity threats.

Review the time-series analyses a clinician would use to evaluate data within and across phases of each of the designs presented in the chapter. Discuss the implications of findings that reveal horizontal stability in measurements and findings that reveal evidence of a trend.

STUDENT EXERCISES

1. Using the hypothetical data presented in each of the examples below, identify the design used in each example and provide a rationale for your selection. Graph and analyze the observed patterns within and across phases. Discuss the results of your findings in terms of their clinical and statistical significance.

- Example 1. The hypothetical problem in this case, A, is measured daily on a five-point scale where higher ratings indicate greater problem magnitude. The client self-monitors A for a one-week interval. Baseline measurements of A are as follows: 5, 4, 5, 5, 4, 5, 5. The clinical objective is to reduce A to a magnitude of three over a two-week interval. Intervention measurements of A are as follows: 5, 4, 5, 4, 4, 5, 4, 4, 4, 4, 4, 4, 4, 4. An additional week of intervention is provided during which the client is instructed to complete daily homework assignments in addition to the previously agreed-upon intervention activities. Intervention measurements of A in week 3 are as follows: 4, 4, 3, 3, 3, 3, 3.
- Example 2. The hypothetical problem in this case, B, is adversely affecting the client's functioning at home and at work.

table 42 *Computing S, Sc, and Z, Comparing Intervention Withdrawal with Reintroduction of Intervention in Figure 51*

Score (x)	x – M	(x – M)²	x_i	x – x_i	(x – x_i)²
2	–.64	.40	1	1	1
1	–1.64	2.68	0	1	1
0	–2.64	6.96	0	0	0
0	–2.64	6.96	0	0	0
0	–2.64	6.96	0	0	0
0	–2.64	6.96	0	0	0
0	–2.64	6.96	4	–4	16
4	1.36	1.84	5	–1	1
5	2.36	5.56	5	0	0
5	2.36	5.56	5	0	0
5	2.36	5.56	5	0	0
5	2.36	5.56	5	0	0
5	2.36	5.56	5	0	0
5	2.36	5.56	–	–	–

37 = Σx		173.081 = SS(x)	1191 = D^2		
M = Σx/n		= 37/14	= 2.64		
C = 1 – D^2/(2SS(x))		= 1 – 19/2(73.08)	= .87		
Sc = $\sqrt{(n-2)/(n+1)(n-1)}$		= $\sqrt{(14-2)/(14+1)(14-1)}$ = .24			
Z = C/Sc		= .87/.24	= 3.62		

NOTE: Because Z > 1.64, there are statistically significant differences between the intervention withdrawal and reintroduction of intervention.

The client self-monitors the daily frequency of B in each of these situations using a 10-point scale in which higher ratings indicate greater frequency. Baseline measurements of B at home and work are as follows: 8, 7, 8, 7, 8, 7, 8 (home); 5, 4, 5, 4, 5, 4, 5 (work). The clinical objective is to reduce the frequency of B at home to three by the third week of intervention. When this objective is achieved, the clinical objective is to reduce the frequency of B at work to three over the same interval. Intervention measurements of B at home are as follows: 7, 6, 7, 7, 6, 6, 6, 5, 5, 6, 5, 5, 4, 4, 4, 4, 3, 3, 3, 3, 3. Continued baseline measurements of B at work are as follows: 5, 4, 5, 4, 5, 4, 5, 4, 4, 5, 4, 5, 4, 5, 4, 5, 4, 5, 4, 5, 4. The clinician withdraws the intervention for B at home and introduces it for B at work. Follow-up measurements of B at home are as follows: 3, 3, 3, 3, 3, 3, 3, 3, 3, 3, 3, 3, 3, 3, 3, 3, 3, 3, 3, 3, 3. Intervention measurements of B at work are as follows: 4, 4, 3, 4, 4, 4, 4, 4, 4, 3, 3, 4, 3, 3, 3, 3, 3, 3, 3, 3, 3.

- Example 3. The hypothetical problem in this case, C, is measured daily using a 10-point scale in which higher ratings indicate greater problem severity. The client self-monitors C for a one-week interval. Baseline measurements of C are as follows: 9, 8, 10, 9, 8, 10, 9. The clinical objective is to reduce C to a magnitude of seven over a two-week interval. Intervention measurements of C are as follows: 9, 8, 8, 9, 8, 8, 8, 7, 8, 7, 7, 7, 7, 7. The clinical objective for the follow-up phase is to maintain C at a magnitude of seven for a two-week interval. Follow-up measurements of C are as follows: 7, 7, 8, 7, 8, 8, 8, 9, 9, 8, 9, 10, 9, 10. The clinician reintroduces the intervention for an additional two-week interval. The following intervention measurements of C are obtained: 9, 8, 8, 9, 8, 8, 8, 7, 8, 7, 7, 7, 7, 7.

2. Using the hypothetical data presented below, assess whether the requirements for using a multiple baseline design have been met. Provide a rationale for your conclusion. Graph the measurements and present findings from your analyses of the data. Discuss the clinical course of action that is implicated by the data and the options that are available to the clinician for evaluating their subsequent work with this case.

   • Clients 1 and 2 present for services to address problem A. Simultaneous baselines are constructed to measure the daily frequency of A over a one-week interval. The following baseline measurements of A are obtained: 8, 7, 8, 7, 8, 7, 8 (client 1); 9, 8, 9, 8, 9, 9, 9 (client 2). The clinician implements an intervention to reduce A with client 1 to a frequency of four over a two-week interval; during this interval, baseline measurements of A are collected from client 2. The following intervention measurements of A are obtained during intervention for client 1: 8, 8, 7, 7, 6, 6, 5, 5, 5, 4, 4, 4, 4, 4. The following measurements are obtained for client 2 during the extended baseline: 9, 9, 8, 8, 8, 7, 7, 7, 7, 6, 6, 5, 5, 5.

3. Discuss the advantages and disadvantages of using multiple baseline, graduated intensity, and withdrawal–reversal designs. Provide case examples to illustrate the ideal circumstances under which a clinician might use each of these designs to evaluate their practice.

Appendixes

Guidelines for Evaluating Single-Case Design Studies

INTRODUCTION

1. Is there a brief description of the case and the agreed-upon targets for intervention?
2. Is sufficient information provided regarding why the intervention selected is ideally suited to the problem to be addressed with this case? Do the authors summarize available evidence of intervention efficacy? If the approach proposed has not undergone efficacy testing, is this explicitly stated and a rationale provided for examining the clinical utility of the approach with the target problem? With the case?
3. Does the introduction conclude with a clear statement of research questions and/or hypotheses?

METHOD

Case

1. Is sufficient information provided regarding the case (e.g., demographic characteristics and features of the case that are relevant to work with the problem described)?
2. Is the unit of analysis (individual, couple, family, or group) specified?
3. Is there a description of the intervention setting, the scope of services provided in the setting, and the types, length, and duration of typical client contacts?

Case Variables and Their Measurement

1. Are the targets for intervention specified?
2. Are problem indicators for operationally defining each target described?
3. Has sufficient detail been provided regarding the measurement and data collection plan (for example, who will collect the data, the time interval between measures, how measurements will be taken, and how repeated measures of problem indicators will be documented)? Are factors that influenced the design of the measurement plan addressed with respect to relevance, feasibility, reliability, validity, and nonreactivity?
4. Are procedures for ensuring that repeated measures were collected reliably and validly described?

Design

1. Do the authors specify the single-case design used in the study (for example, baseline, intervention, follow-up; multiple baseline, graduated intensity, withdrawal–reversal) and provide a rationale for their selection? Is the choice of design described in terms of the levels(s) of knowledge sought, feasibility concerns relevant to implementing the design in practice, and the extent to which the design and procedures used minimize internal validity threats of history, maturation, initial measurement effects, instrumentation, statistical regression, multiple treatment interference, expectancy effects, interactions, and other unknown factors?
2. Are phases of the design well specified (for example, is information provided regarding the length of each phase and the factors that informed the timeframes chosen)?

Intervention

1. Are clinical intervention objectives specified? Do the authors state these objectives, anticipated timeframes for their completion, and how long observed changes are expected to endure? Are the timeframes tied to the relevant intervention literature?
2. Is the intervention well specified? Is sufficient information provided regarding the contents of intervention, the intervenor(s), and the location, frequency, and duration of intervention?

3. Are procedures for ensuring that the intervention was implemented as intended and reliably described?

ANALYSIS

1. Are procedures for evaluating the time-series data presented? Is information provided regarding phase comparisons and procedures for evaluating the time-series data? If statistical analyses were performed, is information for confirming that assumptions of the statistics used have been met? Are statistics and their corresponding probability values reported?
2. Are analyses appropriate for addressing study hypotheses and generating the level(s) of knowledge sought?

Results

1. Are findings from evaluation procedures summarized?
2. Are findings discussed relative to their statistical and clinical significance?
3. Do graphs depicting repeated measurements accompany descriptive information regarding data collected over the course of the study?
4. Are the graphs sufficiently detailed? Do the graphs summarize progress described in the narrative, clearly delineate baseline, intervention, and follow-up phases, include labels for the time-series shown if data for multiple client variables are displayed together, and indicate values corresponding to clinical objectives for intervention and follow-up phases? Is progress or deterioration that occurred in the case evident from looking at the graphs?

Discussion

1. Do the authors state whether hypotheses were supported and address alternative explanations (threats to internal validity) that may account for study findings?
2. Is the discussion limited to conclusions that can be made from the data?
3. Are the implications of findings for clinical social work practice and practice-based research discussed?
4. Are findings discussed relative to previous single-case design studies in similar agency settings and with similar cases? If the study reports findings from the application of a novel intervention approach that has not previously been evaluated, is the study replicable? Is it feasible to carry out the study in similar settings and with similar cases? Would a replication of the study generate knowledge for practice regarding the utility of the intervention?

Index of Self-Esteem (ISE)

INDEX OF SELF-ESTEEM (ISE)

Name: _____ Today's Date: _____

Context: _____

This questionnaire is designed to measure how you see yourself. It is not a test, so there are no right or wrong answers. Please answer each item as carefully and as accurately as you can by placing a number beside each one as follows.

  1 = None of the time
  2 = Very rarely
  3 = A little of the time
  4 = Some of the time
  5 = A good part of the time
  6 = Most of the time
  7 = All of the time

1. ____ I feel that people would not like me if they really knew me well.
2. ____ I feel that others get along much better than I do.
3. ____ I feel that I am a beautiful person.
4. ____ When I am with others I feel they are glad I am with them.
5. ____ I feel that people really like to talk with me.
6. ____ I feel that I am a very competent person.
7. ____ I think I make a good impression on others.
8. ____ I feel that I need more self-confidence.
9. ____ When I am with strangers I am very nervous.
10. ____ I think that I am a dull person.
11. ____ I feel ugly.
12. ____ I feel that others have more fun than I do.
13. ____ I feel that I bore people.
14. ____ I think my friends find me interesting.
15. ____ I think I have a good sense of humor.
16. ____ I feel very self-conscious when I am with strangers.
17. ____ I feel that if I could be more like other people I would have it made.
18. ____ I feel that people have a good time when they are with me.
19. ____ I feel like a wallflower when I go out.
20. ____ I feel I get pushed around more than others.
21. ____ I think I am a rather nice person.
22. ____ I feel that people really like me very much.
23. ____ I feel that I am a likeable person.
24. ____ I am afraid I will appear foolish to others.
25. ____ My friends think very highly of me.

3. 4. 5. 6. 7. 14. 15. 18. 21. 22. 23. 25.

APPENDIX 3

Michigan Alcoholism Screening Test (MAST)

Please circle either Yes or No for each item as it applies to you.

Yes No (2) 1. Do you feel you are normal drinkers?
Yes No (2) 2. Have you ever awakened the morning after some drinking the night before and found that you could not remember a part of the evening before?
Yes No (1) 3. Does your wife (or do your parents) ever worry or complain about your drinking?
Yes No (2) 4. Can you stop drinking without a struggle after one or two drinks?
Yes No (1) 5. Do you ever feel bad about your drinking?
Yes No (2) 6. Do friends or relatives think you are a normal drinker?
Yes No (0) 7. Do you ever try to limit your drinking to certain times of the day or to certain places?
Yes No (2) 8. Are you always able to stop drinking when you want to?
Yes No (5) 9. Have you ever attended a meeting of Alcoholics Anonymous (AA)?
Yes No (1) 10. Have you gotten into fights when drinking?
Yes No (2) 11. Has drinking ever created problems with you and your wife?
Yes No (2) 12. Has your wife (or other family member) ever gone to anyone for help about your drinking?
Yes No (2) 13. Have you ever lost friends or girlfriends/boyfriends because of drinking?
Yes No (2) 14. Have you ever gotten into trouble at work because of drinking?
Yes No (2) 15. Have you ever lost a job because of drinking?
Yes No (2) 16. Have you ever neglected your obligations, your family, or your work for two or more days in a row because you were drinking?
Yes No (1) 17. Do you ever drink before noon?
Yes No (2) 18. Have you ever been told you have liver trouble? Cirrhosis?
Yes No (5) 19. Have you ever had delirium tremens (DTs), severe shaking, heard voices, or seen things that weren't there after heavy drinking?
Yes No (5) 20. Have you ever gone to anyone for help about your drinking?
Yes No (5) 21. Have you ever been in a hospital because of drinking?
Yes No (2) 22. Have you ever been a patient in a psychiatric hospital or on a psychiatric ward of a general hospital where drinking was part of the problem?
Yes No (2) 23. Have you ever been seen at a psychiatric or mental health clinic, or gone to a doctor, social worker, or clergyman for help with [an] emotional problem in which drinking had played a part?
Yes No (2) 24. Have you ever been arrested, even for a few hours, because of drunk behavior?
Yes No (2) 25. Have you ever been arrested for drunk driving after drinking?

Source: Selzer, M.L. (1971). The Michigan Alcoholism Screening Test: The quest for a new diagnostic instrument. *American Journal of Pyschiatry, 127*, 89–94. Copyright 1994, the American Psychiatric Association. Reprinted by permission.

Client Questionnaire to Monitor Clinical Social Worker's Implementation of Posthospital Planning

1. Were insurance and discharge forms filled out by the social worker?

    Yes ___ No ___ Don't know ___

2. Did the social worker discuss medication with you?

    Yes ___ No ___ Don't know ___

  With your family?

    Yes ___ No ___ Don't know ___

3. Did the social worker discuss what your living arrangements with your family will be after you leave the hospital?

    Yes ___ No ___ Don't know ___

4. Did the social worker discuss different community living arrangements for you?

    Yes ___ No ___ Don't know ___

5. Did the social worker talk with your family?

    Yes ___ No ___ Don't know ___

6. Did the social worker refer you to another social worker in the community?

    Yes ___ No ___ Don't know ___

7. Did the social worker discuss employment with you?

    Yes ___ No ___ Don't know ___

8. Did the social worker discuss education with you?

    Yes ___ No ___ Don't know ___

9. Did the social worker make an appointment to see you after you leave the hospital?

    Yes ___ No ___ Don't know ___

Follow-Up Questionnaire

Have you received help from other resources or persons?
 Yes __ No ✓
  If yes, please explain _____
Have you had any recurrences of the major problem for which you received help?
 Yes __ No ✓
  If yes, please explain _____
Have you changed any of your daily habits?
 Yes __ No ✓
  If yes, please explain _____
Have there been any changes in your living circumstances?
 Yes __ No ✓
  If yes, please explain _____
Have you been ill?
 Yes __ No ✓
  If yes, please explain _____
Have any of your family members been sick?
 Yes __ No ✓
  If yes, please explain _____
Have there been any changes in your personal relationships with family and friends?
 Yes ✓ No __
  If yes please explain *I am dating women more often.*_____
Have any other major problems occurred?
 Yes __ No ✓
  If yes, please explain _____
Have there been any unexpected positive or negative changes resulting from the services you received from the social worker?
 Yes ✓ No __
  If yes, please explain *I have felt more energetic.*_____

Follow-Up Questionnaire for Tom and His Relationship to Jerry

Does Jerry try to pick fights with you?
　　Yes ___ No ___
　　　　If yes, indicate how often he does this:
　　　　Once a week ___ Two to three times per week ___
　　　　Four to five times per week ___
　　　　Six to seven times per week ___
Do you try to pick fights with Jerry?
　　Yes ___ No ___
　　　　If yes, indicate how often you do this:
　　　　Once a week ___ Two to three times per week ___
　　　　Four to five times per week ___
　　　　Six to seven times per week ___
Have you argued with Jerry in the past week?
　　Yes ___ No ___
　　　　If yes, indicate about how many arguments you had:
　　　　One ___ Two to five ___ Six to eight ___
　　　　Nine or more ___
To what extent do you believe you are responsible for the arguments and fights with Jerry?
　　Not at all responsible ___ Somewhat responsible ___
　　Completely responsible ___
To what extent do you believe Jerry is responsible for arguments and fights with you?
　　Not at all responsible ___ Somewhat responsible ___
　　Completely responsible ___
Do you believe your father:
　　Likes you and Jerry about the same ___ Favors you ___
　　Favors Jerry ___
Do you believe your mother:
　　Likes you and Jerry about the same ___ Favors you ___
　　Favors Jerry ___
Do you like or dislike Jerry?
　　Dislike ___ Like ___ Neither like nor dislike ___
Does Jerry like or dislike you?
　　Dislike ___ Like ___ Neither like nor dislike ___
In the past week, have Jerry and you gone places together to have a good time (such as the movies, a baseball game, a tennis match, sailing)?
　　Yes ___ No ___
　　　　If yes, indicate how many times ___
Please describe the nature of your relationship with Jerry _____
Has your relationship with Jerry changed since you have had contacts with the social worker?
　　Yes ___ No ___
　　　　If yes, please explain _____
How could the relationship between you and Jerry be improved? _____

Follow-Up Questionnaire About the Intervention and the Clinical Social Worker

To what extent has the social worker been sensitive to your needs as expressed in interviews?

    Very sensitive ___ Moderately sensitive ___

    Neither sensitive nor insensitive ___

    Moderately insensitive ___ Very insensitive ___

Did the social worker meet with you on time for your appointments?

    All of the time ___ Most of the time ___

    Some of the time ___ Not at all ___

Did the social worker review progress with you?

    Yes ___ No ___

        If yes, how often?

        Every session ___ Every other session ___

        Every third session ___

        At least every fourth session ___

Did the social worker provide you with graphic information about your progress?

    Yes ___ No ___

Did the social worker explain how to make self-ratings of anxiety?

    Yes ___ No ___

Did the social worker explain how to use the standardized instrument for measuring depression?

    Yes ___ No ___

Did the social worker help you identify the problem(s) you worked on?

    Yes ___ No ___

        If yes, please describe the problem(s) _____

Did the social worker provide you with good advice that you could use on everyday practical problems?

    Yes ___ No ___

Did the social worker help you to understand when and why you become anxious?

    Yes ___ No ___

Did the social worker use role playing of interpersonal situations in your sessions?

    Yes ___ No ___

Were you comfortable discussing your personal problems with the social worker?

    Yes ___ No ___

        If no, what could the social worker have done to make you more comfortable?

_____

Did the social worker give you homework assignments after each session?

    Yes ___ No ___

        If yes, to what extent were these assignments helpful?

        Very helpful ___ Helpful ___

        Moderately helpful ___ Not at all helpful ___

Was the social worker helpful to you?

    Yes ___ No ___

        Please describe _____

Client Satisfaction Questionnaire (CSQ-8)

CSQ-8 English

CLIENT SATISFACTION QUESTIONNAIRE

CSQ-8

Please help us improve our program by answering some questions about the services you have received. We are interested in your honest opinions, whether they are positive or negative. *Please answer all of the questions.* We also welcome your comments and suggestions. Thank you very much. We appreciate your help.

CIRCLE YOUR ANSWERS

1. How would you rate the quality of service you received?

4 *Excellent*	3 *Good*	2 *Fair*	1 *Poor*

2. Did you get the kind of service you wanted?

1 *No, definitely not*	2 *No, not really*	3 *Yes, generally*	4 *Yes, definitely*

3. To what extent has our program met your needs?

4 *Almost all of my needs have been met*	3 *Most of my needs have been met*	2 *Only a few of my needs have been met*	1 *None of my needs have been met*

4. If a friend were in need of similar help, would you recommend our program to him or her?

1 *No, definitely not*	2 *No, I don't think so*	3 *Yes, I think so*	4 *Yes, definitely*

5. How satisfied are you with the amount of help you received?

1 *Quite dissatisfied*	2 *Indifferent or mildly dissatisfied*	3 *Mostly satisfied*	4 *Very satisfied*

6. Have the services you received helped you to deal more effectively with your problems?

4 *Yes, they helped a great deal*	3 *Yes, they helped somewhat*	2 *No, they really didn't help*	1 *No, they seemed to make things worse*

7. In an overall, general sense, how satisfied are you with the service you received?

4 *Very satisfied*	3 *Mostly satisfied*	2 *Indifferent or mildly dissatisfied*	1 *Quite dissatisfied*

8. If you were to seek help again, would you come back to our program?

1 *No, definitely not*	2 *No, I don't think so*	3 *Yes, I think so*	4 *Yes, definitely*

Follow-Up Questionnaire for Client: Assertive Behaviors

Have you failed to be assertive in interpersonal situations in which you should have been assertive?

    Yes ___ No ✓

        If yes, please explain _____

Have other problems occurred for you since you finished your work with the social worker?

    Yes ___ No ✓

        If yes, please explain _____

Do you understand why you should be assertive in certain situations?

    Yes ✓ No ___

        If yes, did you acquire this understanding in your work with the social worker?

            Yes ✓ No ___

        If no, how should the social worker have helped you acquire this understanding? ___
_____

Did you discuss with the social worker interpersonal situations in which you should be assertive?

    Yes ✓ No ___

        If no, should you have discussed these situations with the social worker?

            Yes ___ No ___

Have you made progress in being assertive since your first contact with the social worker?

    Yes ✓ No ___

        If yes, please explain *I have understood my reluctance to be assertive, and I have overcome my hesitation to be assertive by practicing with the social worker.*

Have you received professional help from other persons since you finished your work with the social worker?

    Yes ___ No ✓

        If yes, please explain _____

Have you felt a need to continue to work with the social worker on assertiveness or on other problems?

    Yes ___ No ✓

        If yes, please explain _____

Have any events occurred recently that facilitated your assertiveness?

    Yes ___ No ✓

        If yes, please explain _____

Have any events occurred recently that prevented you from being assertive?

    Yes ___ No ✓

        If yes, please explain _____

Have you reported the daily number of times you were assertive in a consistent manner?

    Yes ✓ No ___

        If no, please explain _____

Did the social worker help you to become more assertive?

    Yes ✓ No ___

        If no, how could the social worker have helped? _____

Follow-Up Questionnaire for Client: Excessive Coffee Consumption

Have you been drinking more than two cups of coffee per day?
Yes ✓ No __
If yes, please explain *I've been upset.*

Have other problems occurred for you since you finished your work with the social worker?
Yes ✓ No __
If yes, please explain *My wife was diagnosed as having cancer, and she's very tired during the day.*

Do you understand why you should not drink more than two cups of coffee per day?
Yes ✓ No __
If no, should the social worker try to help you understand?
Yes __ No __

Have you made progress in drinking less coffee since your first contact with the social worker?
Yes ✓ No __
Please explain *At first there was progress when I was able to go on excursions with my wife. But then I drank a lot more after I learned about her illness.*

Have you received professional help from other persons since you finished your work with the social worker?
Yes __ No ✓
If yes, please explain _____

Have you felt a need to continue to work with the social worker on reducing your coffee consumption or on other problems?
Yes ✓ No __
If yes, please explain *I need to control my coffee drinking when I get upset.*

Have any events occurred recently that facilitated your reduction in coffee consumption?
Yes __ No ✓
If yes, please explain _____

Have any events occurred recently that prevented you from reducing your coffee consumption?
Yes ✓ No __
If yes, please explain *My wife is ill, diagnosed as having cancer.*

Have you reported the daily number of cups of coffee consumed in a consistent manner?
Yes ✓ No __
If no, please explain _____

Have you been able to substitute decaf for regular coffee?
Yes __ No ✓
If no, please explain *It doesn't taste as good as regular coffee.*

Have you had frequent stomachaches in the past two weeks?
Yes ✓ No __

Have you had any other illness in the past two weeks?
Yes ✓ No __
If yes, please explain *I've had headaches and feelings of nausea.*

Did the social worker help you to drink fewer cups of coffee?
Yes ✓ No __
If no, how could the social worker have helped?
She helped by having my wife and I go on excursions, but I wasn't prepared for illness. I need to be able to deal with my wife's illness as well as control my coffee drinking.

Follow-Up Questionnaire for Jack: Reduction of Negative Remarks to His Father

Have you made unwarranted negative remarks to your father?

Yes ✓ No __

If yes, please explain *I have made a few negative comments, but they were not as negative as before.*

Have other problems occurred for you since you finished your individual work with the social worker?

Yes __ No ✓

If yes, please explain _____

Do you understand what leads you to make negative remarks to your father?

Yes ✓ No __

If yes, did you acquire this understanding in your work with the social worker?

Yes ✓ No __

If no, how should the social worker have helped you acquire this understanding? __ _____

Did you discuss with the social worker interpersonal situations in which you should reduce your negative remarks to your father?

Yes ✓ No __

If no, should you have discussed these situations with the social worker? _____

Have you made progress in reducing unwarranted negative remarks to your father since your first contact with the social worker?

Yes ✓ No __

Please explain. *I've decreased the number of negative remarks to my father.*

Have any events occurred recently that facilitated a reduction in unwarranted negative remarks to your father?

Yes ✓ No __

If yes, please explain *My father has spent more time with me in recreational activities.*

Have any events occurred recently that prevented you from reducing unwarranted negative remarks to your father?

Yes __ No ✓

If yes, please explain _____

Did the social worker help you to reduce the daily number of negative remarks to your father?

Yes ✓ No __

If no, how could the social worker have helped? _____

Index of Sexual Satisfaction (ISS)

⊞ **INDEX OF SEXUAL SATISFACTION (ISS)**

Name: _____ Today's Date: _____

This questionnaire designed to measure the degree of satisfaction you have in the sexual relationship with your partner. It is not a test, so there are no right or wrong answers. Answer each item as carefully and as accurately as you can by placing a number beside each one as follows.

1 = None of the time
2 = Very rarely
3 = A little of the time
4 = Some of the time
5 = A good part of the time
6 = Most of the time
7 = All of the time

---

1. ____ I feel that my partner enjoys our sex life.
2. ____ Our sex life is very exciting.
3. ____ Sex is fun for my partner and me.
4. ____ Sex with my partner has become a chore for me.
5. ____ I feel that our sex is dirty and disgusting.
6. ____ Our sex life is monotonous.
7. ____ When we have sex it is too rushed and hurriedly completed.
8. ____ I feel that my sex life is lacking in quality.
9. ____ My partner is sexually very exciting.
10. ____ I enjoy the sex techniques that my partner likes or uses.
11. ____ I feel that my partner wants too much sex from me.
12. ____ I think that out sex is wonderful.
13. ____ My partner dwells on sex too much.
14. ____ I try to avoid sexual contact with my partner.
15. ____ My partner is too rough or brutal when we have sex.
16. ____ My partner is a wonderful sex mate.
17. ____ I feel that sex is a normal function of our relationship.
18. ____ My partner does not want sex when I do.
19. ____ I feel that our sex life really adds a lot to our relationship.
20. ____ My partner seems to avoid sexual contact with me.
21. ____ It is easy for me to get sexually excited by my partner.
22. ____ I feel that my partner is sexually pleased with me.
23. ____ My partner is very sensitive to my sexual needs and desires.
24. ____ My partner does not satisfy me sexually.
25. ____ I feel that my sex life is boring.

1, 2, 3, 9, 10, 12, 16, 17, 19, 21, 22, 23.

References

American Psychiatric Association. (2000). *Diagnostic and statistical manual of mental disorders* (4th ed.-text rev.). Washington, DC: Author.

Ashford, J. B., LeCroy, C. W., & Lortie, K. L. (1997). *Human behavior in the social environment: A multidimensional perspective.* Pacific Grove, CA: Brooks/Cole.

Balgopal, P. R. (2000). *Social work practice with immigrants and refugees.* New York: Columbia University Press.

Barlow, D. H., & Hersen, M. (1984). *Single case experimental design: Strategies for studying behavior change* (2nd ed.). Tarrytown, NY: Pergamon Press.

Beck, A. T., Ward, C. H., Mendelson, M., Mock, J., & Erbaugh, J. (1961). An inventory for measuring depression. *Archives of General Psychiatry, 4,* 53–63.

Berlin, S. B., & Marsh, J. C. (1993). *Informing practice decisions.* New York: Macmillan.

Bloom, M., Fischer, J., & Orme, J. G. (2006). *Evaluating practice: Guidelines for the accountable professional* (5th ed.). New York: Allyn & Bacon.

Blumberg, C. J. (1984). Comments on "A simplified time-series analysis for evaluating treatment interventions." *Journal of Applied Behavior Analysis, 17,* 539–542.

Blythe, B. J., & Briar, S. (1985). Developing empirically based models of practice. *Social Work, 30,* 483–488.

Blythe, B. J., & Tripodi, T. (1989). *Measurement in direct practice.* Newbury Park, CA: Sage Publications.

Blythe, B. J., Tripodi, T., & Briar, S. (1994). *Direct practice research in human service agencies.* New York: Columbia University Press.

Briar, S. (1992). The practitioner-scientist: Ten years later. In A. J. Grasso & I. Epstein (Eds.), *Research utilization in the social services: Innovations for practice and administration* (pp. 37–49). Binghamton, NY: Haworth Press.

Buchwald, D., Manson, S. M., Brenneman, D. L., Dingles, N. G., Keane, E. M., Beals, J., & Kinzie, J. D.. (1995). Screening for depression among newly arrived Vietnamese refugees in primary care settings. *Western Journal of Medicine, 163,* 341–345.

Burns, D. D., & deJong, M. D. (1980). *The feeling good handbook.* New York: Penguin Books.

Campbell, D., & Stanley, J. (1963). *Experimental and quasi-experimental designs for research.* Chicago: Rand McNally.

Carter, R. (1972). *Designs and data patterns in intensive experimentation* (Course Monographs: Research in Interpersonal Influence). Ann Arbor: University of Michigan, School of Social Work.

Congress, E. P. (1998). *Social work values and ethics.* Chicago: Nelson-Hall.

Conners, C. K., Sitarenios, G., Parker, J. D. A., & Epstein, J. N. (1998). The Revised Connors' Parent Rating Scale (CPRS-R): Factor structure, reliability, and criterion validity. *Journal of Abnormal Child Psychology, 26,* 257–268.

Cook, T. D., & Campbell, D. T. (1979). *Quasiexperimentation: Design and analysis issues for field settings.* Chicago: Rand McNally.

Corcoran, K., & Fischer, J. (1987). *The clinical measurement package: A field manual.* Chicago: Dorsey Press.

Corcoran, K., & Fischer, J. (2000a). *Measures for clinical practice: Vol. 1. Couples, families, and children* (3rd ed.). New York: Free Press.

Corcoran, K., & Fischer, J. (2000b). *Measures for clinical practice: Vol. 2. Adults* (3rd ed). New York: Free Press.

Cormier, W. H., & Cormier, L. S. (1999). *Interviewing strategies for helpers* (3rd ed.). Pacific Grove, CA: Brooks/Cole.

Cox, C. E., & Ephross, P. H. (1998). *Ethnicity and social work practice.* New York: Oxford University Press.

Crosbie, J. (1989). The inappropriateness of the C statistic for assessing stability or treatment effects with single-subject data. *Behavioral Assessment, 11*, 315–325.

De Anda, D. (1984). Bicultural socialization: Factors affecting the minority experience. *Social Work, 29*, 172–181.

Deyo, R. A., Diehl, A. K., Hazuda, H., & Stern, M. P. (1985). A simple language-based acculturation scale for Mexican Americans: Validation and application to health care research. *American Journal of Public Health, 75*, 51–55.

Dore, M. M. (1990). Functional theory: Its history and influence on contemporary social work practice. *Social Service Review, 64*, 358–374.

Epstein, I., & Tripodi, T. (1977). *Research techniques for program planning, monitoring, and evaluation.* New York: Columbia University Press.

Fischer, J. (1973). Is casework effective? A review. *Social Work, 18*, 5–20.

Fischer, J. (1976). *The effectiveness of social casework.* Springfield, IL: Charles C Thomas.

Fischer, J. (1993). Empirically-based practice: The end of ideology? *Journal of Social Service Research, 18*, 19–64.

Fowers, B. J., & Olson, D. H. (1993). ENRICH marital satisfaction scale: A brief research and clinical tool. *Journal of Family Psychology, 7*, 176–185.

Fowler, F. J. (1988). *Survey research methods* (rev. ed.). Newbury Park, CA: Sage Publications.

Franklin, R. D., Allison, D. B., & Gorman, B. S. (1997). *Design and analysis of single-case research.* Mahwah, NJ: Lawrence Erlbaum.

Gellis, Z., & Reid, W. J. (2004). Strengthening evidence-based practice. *Brief Treatment and Crisis Intervention, 4*, 155–165.

Germain, C. B. (1974). Casework and science: A study in the sociology of knowledge (Doctoral dissertation, Columbia University, 1974). *Dissertation Abstracts International, 34*, 6749.

Gonzalez, J. T. (1990). Factors relating to frequency of breast self-examination among low-income Mexican American women. *Cancer Nursing, 13*, 134–142.

Grinnell, R. M. (2001). *Social work research and evaluation: Quantitative and qualitative approaches* (6th ed.). Itasca, IL: F. E. Peacock.

Hansen, N. D. (2002). Teaching cultural sensitivity in psychological assessment: A modular approach used in a distance education program. *Journal of Personality Assessment, 79*, 200–206.

Hayes, S. C. (1992). Single-case experimental design and empirical clinical practice. In A.E. Kazdin (Ed.), *Methodological issues and strategies in clinical research* (pp. 491–522). Washington, DC: American Psychological Association.

Hepworth, D. H., Rooney, R. H., & Larsen, J. (1997) *Direct social work practice: Theory and skills* (5th ed.). Pacific Grove, CA: Brooks/Cole.

Hersen, M., & Barlow, D. H. (1976). *Single-case experimental designs.* Tarrytown, NY: Pergamon Press.

Hollis, F. (1964). *Casework: A psychosocial therapy.* New York: Random House.

Howard, M., & Jensen, J. (1999). Clinical practice guidelines: Should social work develop them? *Research on Social Work Practice, 9*, 283–301.

Hudson, W. W., & Thyer, B. A. (1987). Research measures and indices in direct practice. In A. Minahan (Ed.-in-Chief), *Encyclopedia of social work* (18th ed., pp. 487–498). Silver Spring, MD: National Association of Social Workers.

Ivanoff, A., Blythe, B. J., & Tripodi, T. (1994). *Involuntary clients in social work practice: A research-based approach.* New York: Aldine de Gruyter.

Jayaratne, S. (1977). Single-subject and group designs in treatment evaluation. *Social Work Research & Abstracts, 13*, 35–42.

Jayaratne, S., & Levy, R. L. (1979). *Empirical clinical practice.* New York: Columbia University Press.

Jones, W. P. (2003). Single-case time series with Bayesian analysis: A practitioner's guide. *Measurement and Evaluation in Counseling and Development, 36*, 28–39.

Joseph, M. V. (1985). A model for ethical decision-making in clinical practice. In C.B. Germain (Ed.), *Advances in clinical practice* (pp. 207–217). Silver Spring, MD: National Association of Social Workers.

Kazdin, A. E. (Ed.). (1992). *Methodological issues and strategies in clinical research.* Washington, DC: American Psychological Association.

Kazi, M. A. F. (1998). *Single-case evaluation by social workers.* Brookfield, VT: Ashgate.

Kellner, R. (1987). A symptom questionnaire. *Journal of Clinical Psychiatry, 48*, 268–274.

Kerlinger, F. N. (1985). *Foundations of behavioral research* (3rd ed.). New York: Holt, Rinehart and Winston.

Kinzie, J. D., Manson, S. M., Vinh, D. T., Tolan, N. T., Anh, B., & Pho, T. N. (1982). Development and validation of a Vietnamese-language depression rating scale. *American Journal of Psychiatry, 139*, 1276–1281.

Knapp, S. J. (2006). Assessment. In S. Knapp & L. VandeCreek (Eds.). *Practical ethics for psychologists: A positive approach* (pp. 175–190). Washington, DC: American Psychological Association.

Kopp, J. (1989). Self-observation: An empowerment strategy in assessment. *Social Casework, 70*, 276–284.

Land, H., & Hudson, S. (1997). Methodological considerations in surveying Latina AIDS caregivers: Issues in sampling and measurement. *Social Work Research, 21*, 233–246.

Lee, J. A. B. (2001). *The empowerment approach to social work practice*. New York: Columbia University Press.

Lee, J. W., Jones, P. S., Menyama, Y., & Zhang, X. E. (2002). Cultural differences in response to a Likert scale. *Research in Nursing and Health, 25*, 295–306.

Lin, E. H., Ihle, L. J., & Tazuma, L. (1985). Depression among Vietnamese refugees in a primary care clinic. *American Journal of Medicine, 78*, 41–44.

Lin, N. (1989). Measuring depressive symptomatology in China. *Journal of Nervous and Mental Disease, 177*, 121-131.

Lowenberg, F., & Dolgoff, R. (1996). *Ethical decisions for social work practice* (5th ed.). Itasca, IL: F.E. Peacock.

Marino, R., Green, R. G., & Young, E. (1998). Beyond the scientist–practitioner model's failure to thrive: Social workers' participation in agency-based research activities. *Social Work Research, 22*, 188–192.

Mason, T. C. (2005). Cross-cultural instrument translation: Assessment, translation, and statistical applications. *American Annals of the Deaf, 150*, 67–72.

Mattaini, M. A. (1996). The abuse and neglect of single-case designs. *Research on Social Work Practice, 6*, 83–90.

McCubbin, H. I., & Thompson, A. I. (1987). *Family assessment inventories for research and practice*. Madison: University of Wisconsin Press.

McGoldrick, M., Giordano, J., & Garcia-Preto, N. (2005). *Ethnicity and family therapy* (3rd ed). New York: Guilford.

Melis, A. I., Lipson, J. G., & Paul, S. M. (1992). Ethnicity and health among five Middle Eastern immigrant groups. *Nursing Research, 41*, 98–103.

Meyer, C. H. (1993). *Assessment in social work practice*. New York: Columbia University Press.

Meyer, H., Borgatta, E., & Jones, C. W. (1965). *Girls at vocational high: An experiment in social work intervention*. New York: Russell Sage Foundation.

Minahan, A. (Ed-in-Chief). (1987). *Encyclopedia of social work* (18th ed.). Silver Spring, MD: National Association of Social Workers.

Monette, D. R., Sullivan, T. J., & deJong, C. R. (1986). *Applied social research: Tool for the human services*. New York: Holt, Rinehart and Winston.

Mullen, E. J., & Dumpson, J. R. (1972). *Evaluation of social intervention*. London: Jossey-Bass.

National Association of Social Workers, (2000). *Code of ethics of the National Association of Social Workers*. Washington, DC: Author.

Nugent, W. R., Sieppert, J. D., & Hudson, W. (2001). *Practice evaluation for the 21st century*. Belmont, CA: Brooks/Cole.

Nurius, P. S., & Gibson, J. (1990). Clinical observation, inference, reasoning, and judgment in social work: An update. *Social Work Research & Abstracts, 26*, 18–25.

Nurius, P. S., Wedenoja, M., & Tripodi, T. (1987). Prescriptions, proscriptions, and generalizations in social work practice literature. *Social Casework, 68*, 589–596.

Olson, M. J. (2003). Counselor understanding of Native American spiritual loss. *Counseling and Values, 47*, 109–117.

Padilla, A. M. (2001). Issues in culturally appropriate assessment. In L. A. Suzuki, J. G., Ponterotto, & P. J. Meller (Eds.), *Handbook of multicultural assessment: Clinical, psychological, and educational applications*. San Francisco: Jossey-Bass.

Reamer, F. G. (1999). *Social work values and ethics*. New York: Columbia University Press.

Reamer, F. G. (2004). *The social work ethics audit: A risk management tool*. Washington, DC: NASW Press.

Reid, W. J. (1994). The empirical practice movement. *Social Service Review, 68*, 165–184.

Richmond, M. E. (1917). *Social diagnosis*. New York: Russell Sage Foundation.

Rosen, A., & Proctor, E. (Eds.). (2003). *Developing practice guidelines for social work interventions: Issues, methods, and research agenda*. New York: Columbia University Press.

Rubin, A., & Babbie, E. (2001). *Research methods for social work* (4th ed). Belmont, CA: Brooks/Cole.

Shadish, W. R., Cook, T. D., & Campbell, D. T. (2002). *Experimental and quasi-experimental designs for generalized causal inference*. Boston: Houghton-Mifflin.

Siegel, D. (1984). Defining empirically based practice. *Social Work, 29*, 325–331.

Stephenson, M. (2000). Development and validation of the Stephenson Multigroup Acculturation Scale (SMAS). *Psychological Assessment, 12*, 77–88.

Stuart, R. B., Jayaratne, S., & Tripodi, T. (1976). Changing adolescent deviant behavior through reprogramming the behaviour of parents and teachers: An experimental evaluation. *Canadian Journal of Behavioral Science, 8*, 132–144.

Sue, S., & Zane, N. (1987). The role of culture and cultural techniques in psychotherapy. *American Psychologist, 42*, 37–45.

Thyer, B. A. (1991). Guidelines for evaluating outcome studies on social work practice. *Research on Social Work Practice, 1*, 76–91.

Thyer, B. A. (1996). Forty years of progress toward empirical clinical practice? *Social Work Research, 16*, 77–81.

Thyer, B. A. (2004). What is evidence-based practice? *Brief Treatment and Crisis Intervention, 4*, 167–176.

REFERENCES

Thyer, B. A., & Thyer, K. B. (1992). Single-system research designs in social work practice: A bibliography from 1965 to 1990. *Research on Social Work Practice, 2*, 99–116.

Tripodi, T. (1983). *Evaluative research for social workers.* Englewood Cliffs, NJ: Prentice Hall.

Tryon, W. W. (1982). A simplified time-series analysis for evaluating treatment interventions. *Journal of Applied Behavior Analysis, 15, 423-429.*

Tyron, W. W. (1984). A simplified time-series analysis for evaluating treatment interventions: A rejoinder to Blumberg. *Journal of Applied Behavior Analysis, 17,* 543–544.

Vonk, M. E., Tripodi, T., & Epstein, I. (2006). *Research techniques in clinical social work* (2nd ed.). New York: Columbia University Press.

Warnecke, R. B., Johnson, T. P., Chávez, N., Sudman, S., O'Rourke, D. P., Lacey, L., & Horm, J. (1997). Improving question wording in surveys of culturally diverse populations. *Annals of Epidemiology, 7,* 334–342.

Witkin, S. L. (1991). Empirical clinical practice: A critical analysis. *Social Work, 36,* 158–163.

Witkin, S. L. (1996). If empirical practice is the answer, then what is the question? *Social Work Research, 20,* 69–75.

Wood, K. M. (1978). Casework effectiveness: A new look at the research evidence. *Social Work, 23,* 437–459.

Woods, M. E., & Hollis, F. (2000). *Casework: A psychosocial therapy* (5th ed.). Boston: McGraw-Hill.

Zane, N., Hatanka, H., Park, S. P., & Akutsu, P. (1994). Ethnic-specific mental health services: Evaluation of the parallel approach for Asian-American clients. *Journal of Community Psychology, 22,* 68–81.

Index

Questionnaires
follow-up, 133–135
as type of measure, 55–56, 68–71

Rapid assessment instruments (RAIs), 56
Rating scales, 55, 61–64, 62
Ratio measurement scales, 45
Reamer, F.G., 35, 39, 41
Records
client access to, 39
confidentiality of, 38–39
Referrals (standard of practice), 1
Relational dimension, 25
Relevance, of variable, 48
Reliability, of variable, 9, 48–50
Research
approaches, 2
experimental research studies, 11–12
group research, 13
practice research, 13
Resources
cultural, 33
identifying, 26
Response systems, 62
Richmond, Mary, 11

Self-anchored rating scales, 14, 54–55, 60–61
Self-control management skills, 26
Self-esteem index, 175
Self-Rating Anxiety Scale, 50
Single-case design. *See also* Single-case design study
guidelines
advantages of, 12–14
disadvantages of, 15–16
explanation of term, 2
historical context, 10–12
information for the profession using, 14
levels of knowledge, 9, 13
methodology, 6–9
phases, 6 (*See also* Baseline; Follow-up;
Intervention)
relationship with clinical practice, 10
Single-case design study guidelines, 16–19, 175–176
discussion, 19
introduction, 17
method, 17–19
analysis, 18–19
case, 17
case variables and measurement, 17–18
design, 18
intervention, 18
results, 19
Social cognition and regulation skills, 26
Social Diagnosis (Richmond), 11
Social diversity, 36
Social work group classifications, 23
Somatic dimension, 24–25
Specialized practice skills and intervention (standard of
practice), 1
Standardized instruments, 56–60

Standards of practice, 1–2
Statistical significance, calculating, 115–117
Stephenson Multigroup Acculturation Scale (SMAS),
58
Stimulus systems, 62
Strengths, identifying, 26
Sue, S., 34
Supervision and consultation (standard of practice), 1
Symptom Questionnaire, 56
Systematic observations, 64–71
counting devices and, 64–65
principles, 65–68

Task groups, 23
Technology (standard of practice), 1
Test-retest reliability, 49
Time-series data, 16, 79–87
clinical judgment in selection of time intervals,
80
comparing phases of, 135
definition, 79
at follow-up, 130
horizontal stability and, 80–83
measurement plan development, 84–85
measurement plan implementation, 85–87
Treatment
evaluation, 6
evidence of effectiveness of, 12
implementation decisions, 5–6
specifying objectives of, 62
Treatment groups, 23
Treatment objectives, 4
Tripodi, T., 88, 103

Unplanned follow-up, 126, 130–131

Validity, of variable, 9, 50–51
Variables
cultural relevance, 52–54
describing relationships between defined, 29
existence, magnitude, duration, frequency of,
28
feasibility, 51–52
relationship of, to assessment/evaluation, 45–47
relevance, 48
reliability, 48–50
types of, 45
validity, 9, 50–51
Vietnamese Depression Scale (VDS), 59–60
Vonk, M.E., 4

Wedenoja, M., 101
Withdrawal-reversal design, 165–169
advantage of, 167
implementation guidelines, 167–168
stages of, 165
using, 168–169
Working hypotheses, 21

Zane, N., 34

About the Authors

Jennifer Di Noia, **PhD**, **LCSW**, is associate research scientist at Columbia University School of Social Work, New York City. She has been teaching a course on clinical practice evaluation to graduate social work students for the past 10 years and has published numerous intervention outcome studies.

Tony Tripodi, **DSW**, **ACSW**, was dean and is professor emeritus, Ohio State University College of Social Work, and was the visiting Moses Professor at Hunter College School of Social Work (2006–07). He has published extensively on program evaluation, research methodology, and research utilization.